XML

Addison-Wesley Nitty Gritty

PROGRAMMING SERIES

XML

Magnus Stein Ingo Dellwig

ADDISON-WESLEY

An imprint of Pearson Education

Boston • San Francisco • New York • Toronto • Montreal • London • Munich
Paris • Madrid • Cape Town • Sydney • Tokyo • Singapore • Mexico City

PEARSON EDUCATION LIMITED

Head Office
Edinburgh Gate, Harlow, Essex CM20 2JE
Tel: +44 (0)1279 623623 Fax: +44 (0)1279 431059

London Office
128 Long Acre, London WC2E 9AN
Tel: +44 (0)20 7447 2000 Fax: +44 (0)20 7240 5771
Websites:
www.it-minds.com www.aw.com/cseng

First published in Great Britain 2002

First published in 2001 as *XML Nitty-Gritty* by Addison-Wesley Verlag, Germany.

Library of Congress Cataloguing Publication Data
Applied for.

British Library Cataloguing in Publication Data
A CIP catalogue record for this book can be obtained from the British Library.

ISBN 0-201-75874-1

10 9 8 7 6 5 4 3 2 1

Translated and typeset by Berlitz GlobalNET (UK) Ltd. of Luton, Bedfordshire.
Printed and bound in Great Britain by Biddles Ltd. of Guildford and King's Lynn.

The publishers' policy is to use paper manufactured from sustainable forests.

Contents

Preface

Dear Reader,

The very fact that you are looking at this book proves that you are interested in a language with a future, since the possibilities for XML are downright enormous. We will do all we can to provide you with a quick, concise introduction to the subject. If you already have some prior knowledge about HTML, you will be better able to put it into practice with the aid of this book. If not, you will also find here an HTML crash course and the corresponding reference with the most important tags.

Read more about the following technologies: DTD, SGML, CSS, XSL, XSLT, XLINKS and XHTML. You will get to know the underlying interrelationships. Unfortunately, it would be beyond the scope of this book for us to go into detail about each of these topics, but, when you have read the book, you will know at which point you should hook into XML in order to achieve your goals.

At this point, we would like to thank those people who have been especially helpful to us in writing this book. The first person to mention is Christina Gibbs who, as editor, showed great patience when the deadline for the manuscript had to be pushed back for unavoidable reasons. Thanks to her organizational talent, we were still able to meet the publication date.

We would also like to thank the secretary to the director of SPECTROsoftware GmbH, Hildegund Dellwig, who constantly shielded us from any other problems, so that we were able to concentrate on our writing in peace.

We hope you will enjoy reading this book and quickly learn what you need to know.

Magnus Stein and Ingo Dellwig

About the authors

This book has been written by two computer scientists who belong to the team of authors (SPECTROauthors) at SPECTROsoftware GmbH in Werne. We briefly introduce them below:

Magnus Stein

... is a state-certified IT Assistant, currently studying computer science at Dortmund technical college. He developed an early interest in computer hardware and programming. In writing this book, Stein is making his debut as an author.

Ingo Dellwig

... has been working with computers since 1986. He is CEO of SPECTROsoftware GmbH, which he founded as a private company while he was still studying computer science. In addition to databanks, the company offers Internet launches and training courses in this area. Over the last three years, Dellwig has written ten books about the Internet and programming.

Part I

Start up!

SGML, HTML and XML on the Internet

XML stands for `Extensible Markup Language` and is actually a simplified form of `Standard Generalized Markup Language`, or SGML for short. SGML is an international documentation standard defining the markup languages used in the creation of documents. SGML is known as a `metalanguage`. The advantage of markups defined in a metalanguage is the uniform document structure they provide. They are easy to learn and independent of your operating system. The best known markup language in SGML format is `HTML`. HTML defines the appearance of a text document on the web. But the standards defining both SGML and HTML are too inflexible for the web. So in 1996 work started on producing a form better suited to the Internet. The aim was to extend HTML and make it simpler than SGML.

Contrary to the opinion that XML is a markup language like HTML, XML is a metalanguage just like SGML. A markup language is a page description language, but XML is much more flexible than that. Not only can XML format text, it can also structure the content.

XML will not take over from HTML, at least not right away. This is partly because XML as a whole is still in the development stage, as you will see at several points in the book, and partly because XML is still reliant on HTML.

1.1 Crash course in HTML

XML works in a similar fasion to HTML. The two languages are therefore quite often used in combination. For this reason we should take a brief but detailed look at HTML.

The HTML concept is quite easy to grasp. It simply involves writing text and using things called tags to define the apperanace of elements within the documents. You can also incorporate pictures, tables and multimedia elements. We should look at this in a bit more detail.

START UP!

1.1.1 Creating HTML pages

First open your editor and create a new text file. We want the computer to interpret this file later as a page of HTML, so we have to identify it as such in two ways. The first thing is that the text has to start with `<HTML>` and close with `</HTML>`.

You are probably wondering what those angled brackets are all about, so you may like to know that you have just learnt your first tag. In most cases there is a starting tag and a closing tag. A closing tag only differs from a starting tag by containing a forward slash. All of the text between the starting tag `<HTML>` and the closing tag `</HTML>` is interpreted as HTML language. Now enter the following:

```
<HTML>
</HTML>
```

You can now save this file on to your hard disk. The filename is the second means of identification, namely that all HTML file names must end in `.HTM` or `.HTML`. Since some operating systems are unable to accept four characters after the point, it would be better to use `.HTM`. Now save the file as `index.htm` in a new folder (such as `c:\xml`).

You may be wondering why we suggested `index` as the file name. Quite simple: If there are several HTML files in a sub-folder, the browser will always select a file with the name `index.htm` before any other. If you then wanted to call this up, you would be unable to see much because there is no content. The browser is only able to identify that it is working with an HTML file.

1.1.2 Head and body

In order to breathe some life into the page it would be a good idea to input some text. But before you start you need to be aware of something else: Think of HTML pages as being in two parts. The first part is called the head and is identified by the tag `<HEAD>`. The head occupies an area, so it has to have a closing tag too, in this case `</HEAD>`. The things you include in the head of an HTML page will not be visible on the page itself afterwards, though they make their presence known in other ways. For instance you should choose a title for your homepage. In most browsers it will be quoted in the title bar alongside the name of the browser itself. The title is identified by the tag `<TITLE>`.

The page itself is still blank and would stay that way because the title does not appear on the page. Since every head must have a body, we should add the tag `<BODY>`. Everything you enter in the body usually appears on the actual page. So now you can add to your text.

```
<HTML>
<HEAD>
<TITLE>TEST</TITLE>
</HEAD>
<BODY>
Test: Successful
</BODY>
</HTML>
```

And finally you would like to see some results. So save this text in index.htm again and then start your browser. The standard now lays down that the upper part of a browser shall include a text box called "URL:", "Address:" or "GoTo:". In this text box you can input the page that you want to review. Your new HTML file is on your hard disk and you can open it by typing in `file:///c:/xml/index.htm`. If you chose a different folder or drive when you saved the file, just change the command line as necessary. Now press Return or Enter and you will get the display shown in Figure 1.1.

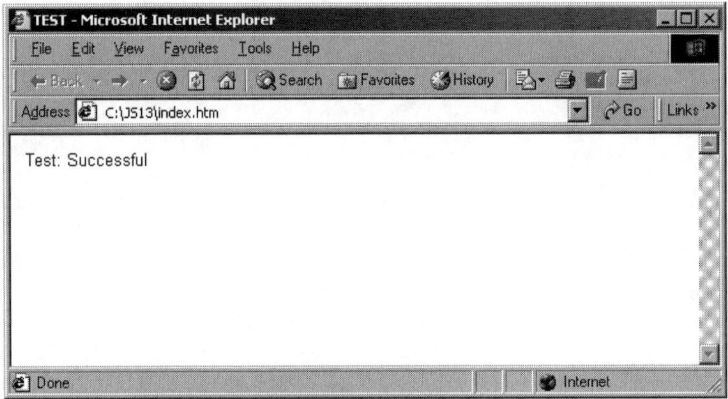

Figure 1.1 ***The page heading and text are displayed just as expected***

You may find that the file is not displayed because the input "file://..." was not interpreted correctly. If this happens then open your browser and select Open from the File menu and then find and open the file you have just created. You have now created and displayed your first HTML page.

2 Requirements

If you want to program in XML, you will need a few things to back you up. For one thing you have to create your source text and for another you should be able to view the results of your source text with the aid of a browser.

2.1 Text editor

All you need to create your source text is a basic text editor. Every operating system has one. In Windows this is the usual Editor or Notepad whilst Macs use Simple Text or BBEdit. Linux and Unix provide you with joe and vi among others. But remember the main thing is that the editor can save your source text as a standard text file, because you are not allowed to save any extra control commands in the file.

2.2 Browser

You need to be a bit more choosy about your browser, because not all of them support every aspect of XML.

2.2.1 Microsoft Internet Explorer

Microsoft has been working on support for XML ever since Internet Explorer 4. At that time XML was still at the planning stage. Since then support has reached the stage where Internet Explorer can treat XML documents exactly like HTML documents. Similarly Internet Explorer supports the display of CSS and XSL stylesheets. In the absence of a stylesheet, Internet Explorer displays the document tree.

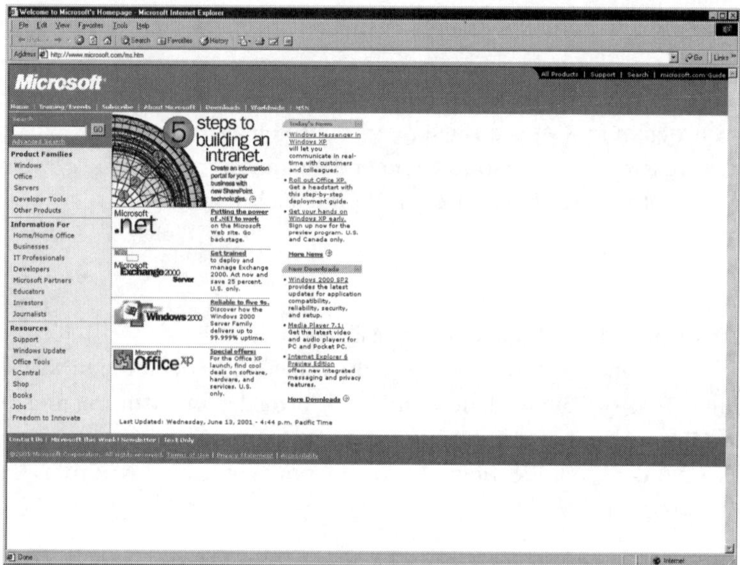

Figure 2.1 ***Internet Explorer 5.5***

2.2.2 *Netscape*

Netscape 6 supports XML but not quite so well as Internet Explorer. Though it is XML compliant and supports CSS stylesheets better than Internet Explorer, sadly it does not support XSL. Hopefully this feature will be available before long.

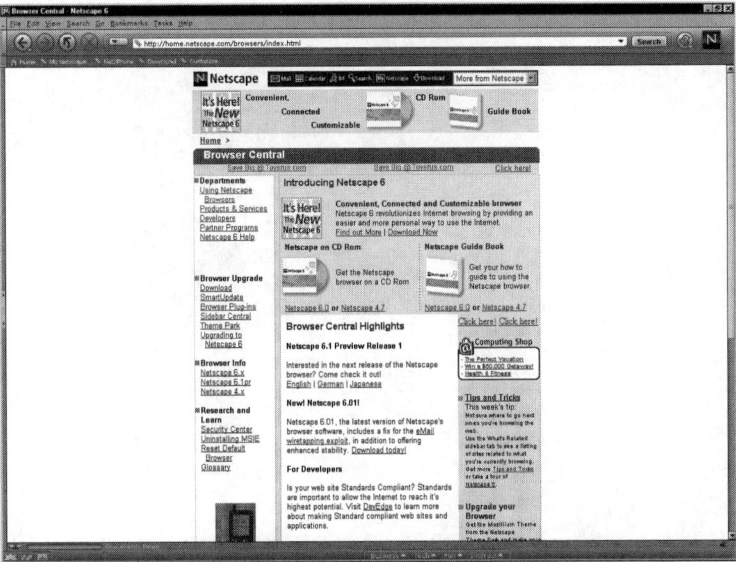

Figure 2.2 ***Netscape 6***

2.2.3 Opera

With regard to XML, development of the Opera 5 browser has reached exactly the same stage as Netscape 6. It supports XML files and XML with CSS style sheets, but not XSL stylesheets.

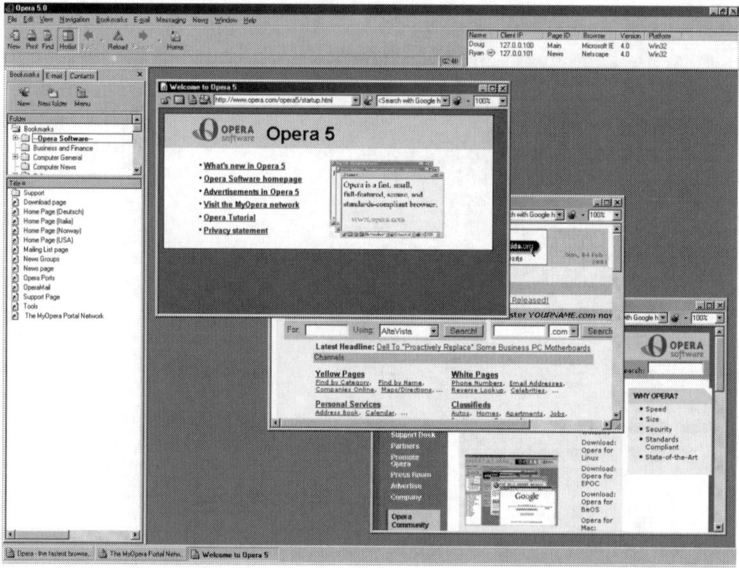

Figure 2.3 *Opera 5*

2.2.4 Sun HotJava

In the case of the Sun browser the outlook for XML support is very poor since it is unable to recognize XML documents. HotJava is therefore quite unsuitable for your purposes.

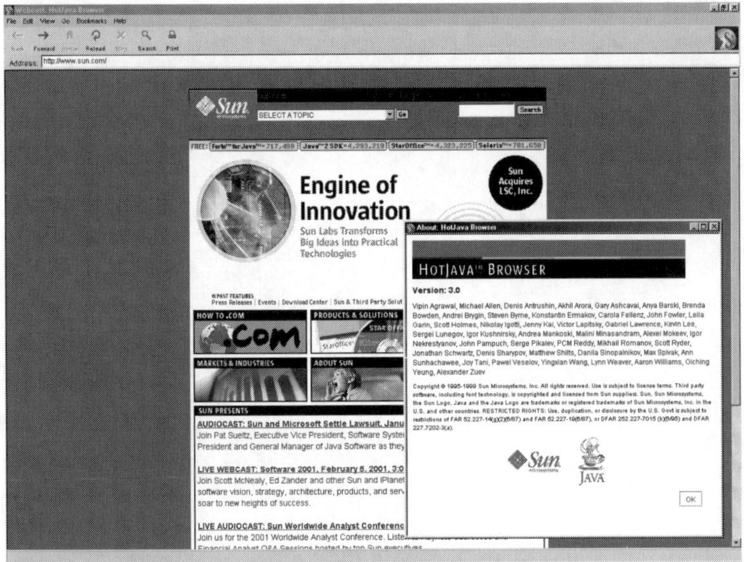

Figure 2.4 ***Sun HotJava 3.0***

2.3 Other XML editors

Clearly an ordinary editor is adequate for programming in XML, but it is just as clear that there are a number of tools intended to make the task a bit easier. Only you can decide whether you want to use such a tool and if so which.

2.3.1 Microsoft XML Notepad

XML Notepad from Microsoft is not particularly feature-laden, but its clear tree structure makes it easy to work with because it takes hardly any time to get used to. Microsoft XML Notepad is quite safe to use on smallish projects, but provides only limited help with large projects.

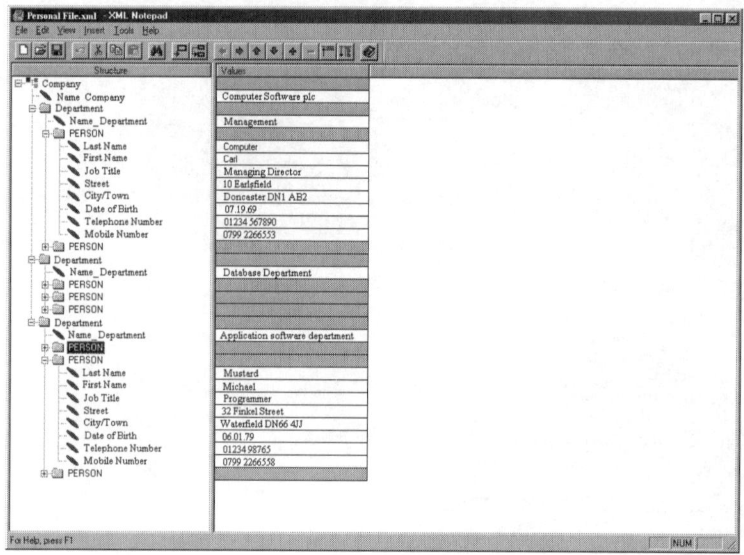

Figure 2.5 ***Microsoft XML Notepad***

2.3.2 *Stilo WebWriter*

WebWriter from Stilo is aimed at experienced XML programmers who already know all about tags. This program also makes it an easy matter to produce and edit stylesheets. It also deserves a special mention for its ability to link in with a database.

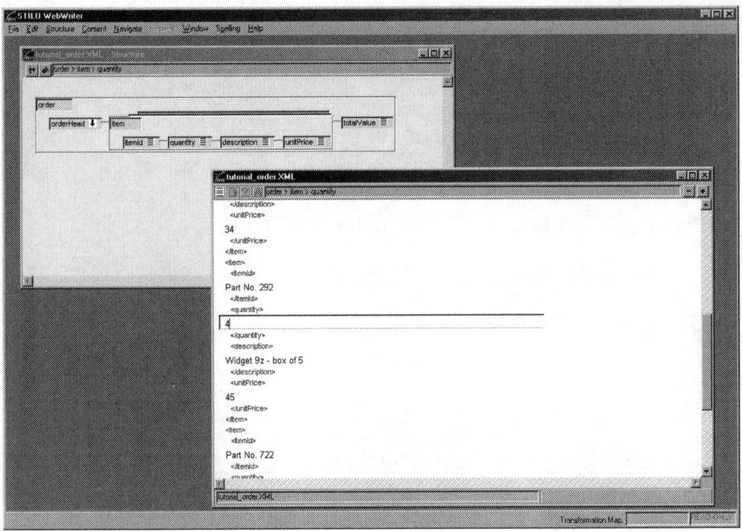

Figure 2.6 ***Stilo WebWriter***

2.3.3 *Softquad XMetal*

XMetal provides an excellent way of handling XML files. Its interface is clear and intuitive. It has very useful element and attribute windows to make programming easy. CSS stylesheets are also easy to create and edit.

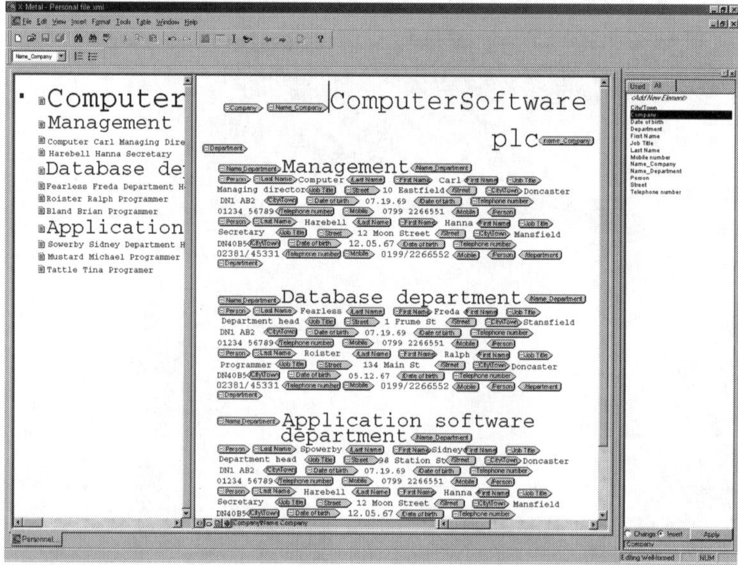

Figure 2.7 ***Softquad XMetal***

2.3.4 *Altova XML Spy*

XML Spy from Altova supports every relevant XML file format. It also provides the best overview for anyone wanting to work with XML. Apart from XMLwriter it is the only one of the five XML editors that also supports XSL. All in all an excellent development environment that lightens the load for developers.

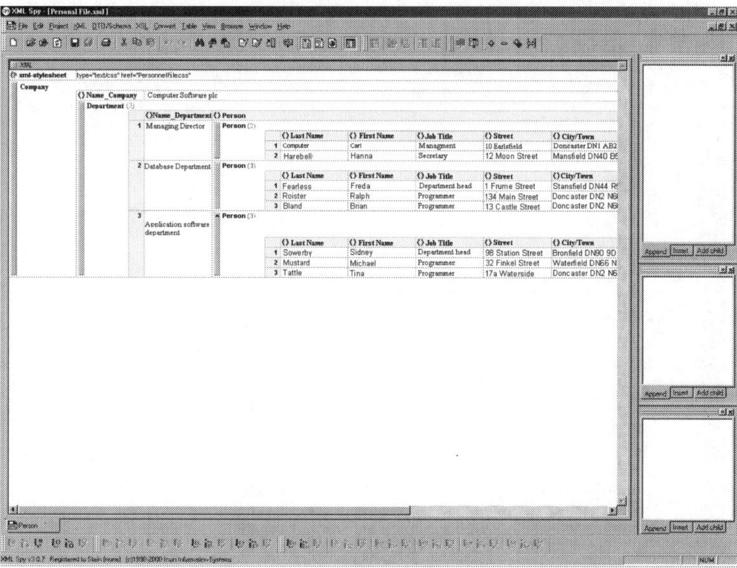

Figure 2.8 ***Altova XML Spy***

2.3.5 Wattle Software XMLwriter 1.21

As already mentioned, XMLwriter also supports XSL, but from the point of view of user-friendliness it cannot compare with the other editors. The only view it provides apart from the source code is the same kind of tree structure that you also get with Internet Explorer from Microsoft.

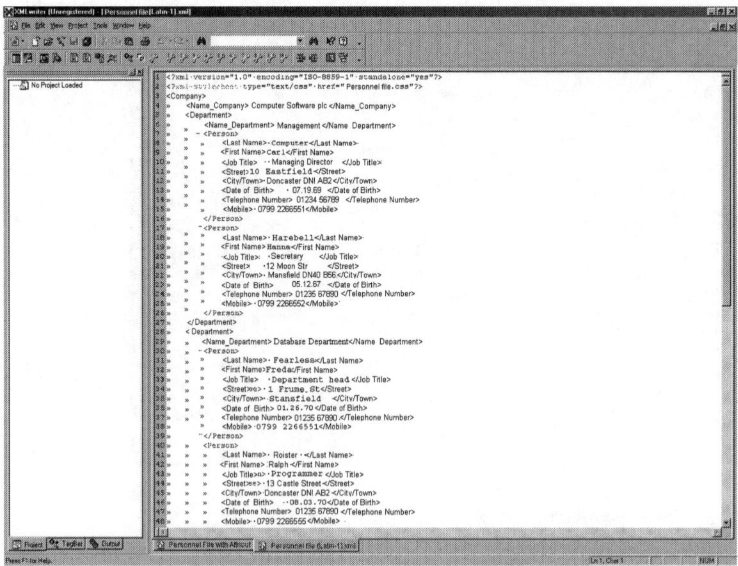

Figure 2.9 ***Wattle Software XMLwriter 1.21***

The essentials of XML

This chapter will show you how to create simple XML documents with the aid of elements that have a particular significance within documents of this kind. You will also be shown how to use stylesheets and write your first short XML documents. You will then be able to view these with the aid of a web browser.

3.1 Hello World!

It is traditional for the first program in a new programming language to send the words `Hello World!` to the screen. So let's use this as our first example.

Launch you editor and enter the following line:

```
<?xml version="1.0" standalone="yes"?>
<!-- XML data starts here -->
<A00>
Hello World!
</A00>
```

We should look at the individual lines in a bit more detail.

The first line is the XML declaration. `<?xml version="1.0" standalone="yes"?>`. The declaration tells you that this is an XML document. It is always located at the beginning of an XML file. In this instance it contains the information that on the one hand the document should comply with Version 1.0 of the XML standard, and on the other hand the attribute `standalone="yes"` indicates that all the data required for display is already in the file and there is no need to import anything from other files.

The next line is a comment intended to make the source text easier to understand. In XML comments always begin and end with `<!--` and `-->`. The browser ignores everything between the angled brackets. Comments must not appear before the XML declaration or within an XML element tag.

The next three lines together form the element A00.

```
<A00>
Hello World!
</A00>
```

An XML element consists of a starting tag and a closing tag, in this instance <A00> and </A00>. These enclose the contents of element A00.

So far, though, you have not defined the element A00. Unlike HTML, XML is not reliant on predefined tags. XML lets you create your own tags and give them the meaning that you have planned for the element concerned. You could have given the element quite a different name, such as <P>, and it would still carry out the same task because of the meaning assigned to it. In the case of tags <P> and </P>, a web browser that understands only HTML would assign them the meaning Paragraph. The computer simply follows the predefined rules, and in the case of tag <A00> or tag <P> it makes no difference whether the computer displays a blank line before the next element. A tag receives its meaning from style sheets.

Let's take a look at the result next. To be able to view your document, you need to save the source text to your hard disk. First you should create a folder on your hard disk, where you can save this and any future XML files that you create. Now give your document a name of your choice (such as HelloWorld.xml), making sure that the extension .xml is included in the name.

Tip Please also note that the source text has to be saved in text format. If you save a document in Word format, for instance, additional control characters are saved as well. These make an XML file unusable.

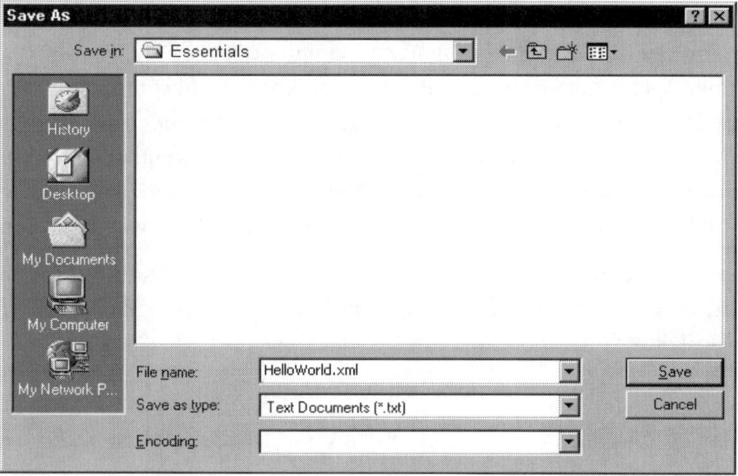

Figure 3.1 ***XML files must be saved in text format***

Now that you have created your first XML file, you naturally wish to view the result. To do this we need an XML-compliant web browser, such as Internet Explorer 5.0. The result differs from one browser to another.

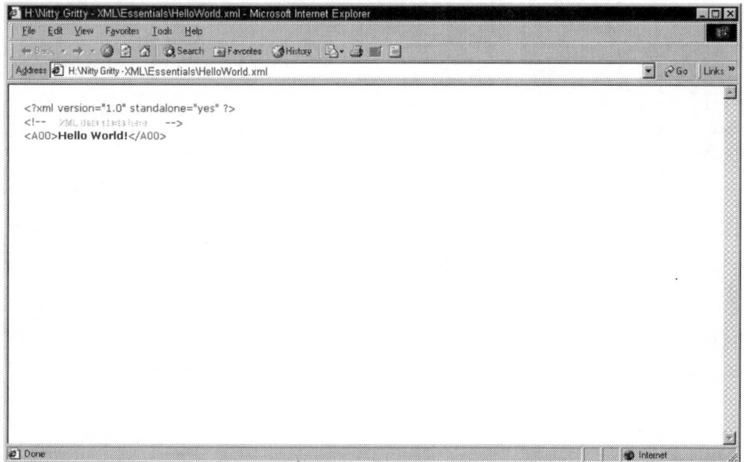

Figure 3.2 ***Output from the XML document***

If your output looks like Figure 3.2, you have done everything properly. As already mentioned, the browser has no idea what to do with the `A00` element and the resulting output is not particularly attractive. You can change this situation by using stylesheets.

3.2 Stylesheets

As mentioned above, in XML you can assign your own definition to all the tags you need. This means that no browser can know in advance which tags you are using and which rules apply to such tags. We therefore need a method of informing the browser when and how it must handle the contents of elements. At the present time this method uses Cascading Stylesheets (CSS), which have been supported ever since the first generation of XML- compliant web browsers.

The `Hello World!` example contains only one tag, so we need only define this one. To do this, launch your editor again, create a new file called `hello-world.css` and enter the following line:

```
A00 {font-size: 48pt; font-weight: bold;}
```

Use the file extension `.css` when saving cascading stylesheets. Please make sure that you save this file in text format only, too.

This listing is a very simple stylesheet which defines that the contents of element `A00` will be displayed in font size 48 bold.

Having created the XML document and CSS stylesheet you must now link the two files together, in other words you must instruct the browser to apply the stylesheet to the document. Please extend your XML document as follows:

```
<?xml version="1.0" standalone="yes"?>
<?xml-stylesheet type="text/css" href="helloworld.css"?>
<!-- XML data starts here -->
<A00>
Hello World!
</A00>
```

The new instruction `<?xml-stylesheet ?>` uses the `type` attribute to specify the stylesheet language you intend using and the `href` attribute to specify the URL that indicates where the stylesheet is stored. In this instance the instruction has specified that a stylesheet is to be applied to the document. The stylesheet is called `helloworld.css` and is written in the CSS stylesheet language.

You should now view your XML document again. That looks better, doesn't it?

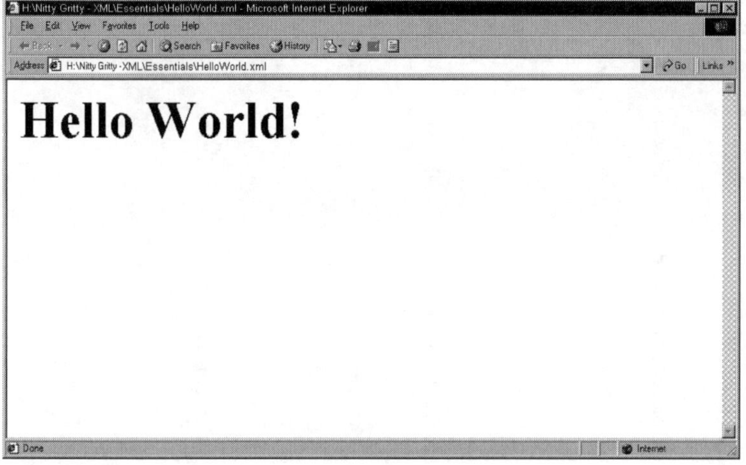

Figure 3.3 ***Output from the XML document when using a stylesheet***

3.3 Personnel file

Now for a slightly more extensive example which will widen and deepen your experience of handling XML elements. The first step is to analyze the existing data and convert it to XML.

Assume you are going to create a personnel file for a small software company called "ComputerSoftware plc" owned by Carl Computer. What data is available? The employees provide a lot of data: Last names, first names, dates of birth, addresses, telephone numbers, mobile numbers, etc. However, data about their department and job title in the company is also relevant.

The table below contains some fictitious data along these lines. Any resemblance to real persons is entirely coincidental and unintentional. ☺

Roister	Fearless	Harebell	Computer	***Last name***
Ralph	Freda	Hanna	Carl	***First name***
134 Main Street	1 Frume Street	12 Moon Street	10 Eastfield	***Street***
Doncaster DN2 N66	Stansfield DN44 R55	Mansfield DN40 B56	Doncaster DN1 AB2	***City/town***
03.08.70	01.26.70	05.12.67	07.19.69	***Date of birth***
01234 57912	01236 78901	01235 67890	01234 56789	***Telephone number***
0199/2266555	0799 2266553	0799 2266552	0799 2266551	***Mobile number***
Database department	Database department	Management	Management	***Department***
Programmer	Department Head	Secretary	Managing Director	***Job title***

Table 3.1 ***Data in the personnel file***

Last name	Tattle	Mustard	Sowerby	Bland
First name	Tina	Michael	Sidney	Brian
Street	17a Waterside	32 Finkel Street	98 Station Street	13 Castle Street
City/town	Doncaster DN3 4JJ	Waterfield DN66 N77	Bronfield DN90 9DN	Doncaster DN3 4BC
Date of birth	09.01.79	06.17.77	10.30.74	12.23.75
Telephone number	01234 98765	01238 91011	01237 46810	01234 13579
Mobile number	0799 2266558	0799 2266557	0799 2266554	0799 2266556
Department	Application software department	Application software department	Application software department	Database department
Job title	Programmer	Programmer	Department Head	Programmer

As you can see, we have soon managed to get a fair amount of data together and in fact each column defines an XML element. We therefore need to use elements for Last name, First name, Street, City/town, Date of birth, Telephone number, Mobile number, Department and Job title.

3.3.1 Conversion to XML

XML elements can contain text or even other XML elements. These child elements can also contain both text and other child elements, but at the present time this practice is not encouraged.

Before you can convert your data to XML you have to consider what it will contain, in other words which element is going to be the child of another element. For example is an employee a child within a department or does a department have several children (employees)? The answer is not at all obvious. An employee can also leave one department and move to another. It is quite common to find that there is more than one way to organize your data in XML.

We may decide that several employees belong to one department because on this occasion we are interested in the membership of each department. Let's handle it that way.

3.3.2 Declaration and root element

As previously mentioned, an XML document is recognized by its declaration. This declaration is always located at the beginning of an XML file.

```
<?xml version="1.0" standalone="yes"?>
```

Every valid XML document must have a root element. A root element is distinguished by the fact that it covers all the other elements in an XML file. This means that all the other elements are child elements of the root element. So in this case it would be best to use Company as the root element and all the other elements are then to be found between the starting tag `<Company>` and the closing tag `</Company>`.

So far your document looks like this:

```
<?xml version="1.0" standalone="yes"?>
<Company>
</Company>
```

Since your XML document is about a particular company you should now add the name of the company to the document. The way to do this is to create an element that will contain the company name from now on. As you would expect, there are several ways of defining the element and you have a completely free hand, but if you just use <Name> as the element definition you will quickly get in a mess. In this small example alone there are three opportunities for defining an element as Name. It would therefore be better to use a less ambiguous definition such as <Name_Company>.

```
<?xml version="1.0" standalone="yes"?>
<Company>
  <Name_Company>
    ComputerSoftware plc
  </Name_Company>
</Company>
```

The example above uses indentation for each individual element. This was done to show you that the element <Name_Company> is the child element of the root element <Company>. We also want to encourage you to use good programming style so that you manage to maintain a better overview, particularly in the case of a lengthy document.

```
<?xml version="1.0" standalone="yes"?><Company>
<Name_Company>ComputerSoftware plc</Name_Company></Company>
```

If you place all the elements on one line, perhaps to save space, then XML allows this. It simply makes it more difficult to read the source text.

```
<?xml version="1.0" standalone="yes"?><Company><
Name_Company>ComputerSoftware plc</Name_Company></
Company>
```

In fact a mixture of the two extremes is generally used provided readability does not suffer, for instance if an element takes up a whole line.

3.3.3 The Department element

Mr. Computer's company has three departments. You can include them in your XML document as follows:

```
<?xml version="1.0" standalone="yes"?>
<Company>
<Name_Company>ComputerSoftware plc</Name_Company>
  <Department>
    <Name_Department>Management</Name_Department>
  </Department>
  <Department>
    <Name_Department>Database department </Name_Department>
  </Department>
  <Department>
    <Name_Department>
```

```
      Application software department
    </Name_Department>
  </Department>
</Company>
```

3.3.4 The Person element

The rest of the data now consists of child elements of the `<Person>` element and in this case there is no further need to use nesting.

```
<Person>
<Last_Name>Computer</Last_Name>
<First_Name>Carl</First_Name>
<Job_Title>Managing Director</Job_Title>
<Street>10 Eastfield</Street>
<City_Town>Doncaster DN1 AB2</City_Town>
<Date_of_Birth>07.19.69</Date_of_Birth>
<Telephone_Number>01234 56789</Telephone_Number>
<Mobile_Number>0799 2266551</Mobile_Number>
</Person>
```

3.3.5 The XML personnel file in full

So far you have only examined parts of the personnel file. Now it's time to bring all the parts together.

```
<?xml version="1.0" standalone="yes"?>
<Company>
  <Name_Company>ComputerSoftware plc</Name_Company>
  <Department>
    <Name_Department>Management</Name_Department>
    <Person>
      <Last_Name>Computer</Last_Name>
      <First_Name>Carl</First_Name>
      <Job_Title>Managing Director</Job_Title>
      <Street>10 Eastfield</Street>
      <City_Town>Doncaster DN1 AB2</City_Town>
      <Date_of_Birth>07.19.69</Date_of_Birth>
      <Telephone_Number>01234 56789</Telephone_Number>
      <Mobile_Number>0799 2266551</Mobile_Number>
    </Person>
    <Person>
      <Last_Name>Harebell</Last_Name>
```

```
    <First_Name>Hanna</First_Name>
    <Job_Title>Secretary</Job_Title>
    <Street>12 Moon Street</Street>
    <City_Town> Mansfield DN40 B56</City_Town>
    <Date_of_Birth>05.12.67</Date_of_Birth>
    <Telephone_Number>01235 67890</Telephone_Number>
    <Mobile_Number>0799 2266552</Mobile_Number>
  </Person>
</Department>
<Department>
  <Name_Department>Database department</Name_Department>
  <Person>
    <Last_Name>Fearless</Last_Name>
    <First_Name>Freda</First_Name>
    <Job_Title>Department Head</Job_Title>
    <Street>1 Frume Street</Street>
    <City_Town>Stansfield DN44 R55</City_Town>
    <Date_of_Birth>01.26.70</Date_of_Birth>
    <Telephone_Number>01236 78901</Telephone_Number>
    <Mobile_Number>0799 2266553</Mobile_Number>
  </Person>
  <Person>
    <Last_Name>Roister</Last_Name>
    <First_Name>Ralph</First_Name>
    <Job_Title>Programmer</Job_Title>
    <Street>134 Main Street</Street>
    <City_Town>Doncaster DN2 N66</City_Town>
    <Date_of_Birth>03.08.70</Date_of_Birth>
    <Telephone_Number>01234 57912</Telephone_Number>
    <Mobile_Number>0799 2266555</Mobile_Number>
  </Person>
  <Person>
    <Last_Name>Bland</Last_Name>
    <First_Name>Brian</First_Name>
    <Job_Title>Programmer</Job_Title>
    <Street>13 Castle Street</Street>
    <City_Town>Doncaster DN3 4BC</City_Town>
    <Date_of_Birth>12.23.75</Date_of_Birth>
    <Telephone_Number>01234 13579</Telephone_Number>
    <Mobile_Number>0799 2266556</Mobile_Number>
  </Person>
</Department>
```

```
  <Department>
    <Name_Department>
      Application software department
    </Name_Department>
    <Person>
      <Last_Name>Sowerby</Last_Name>
      <First_Name>Sidney</First_Name>
      <Job_Title>Department Head</Job_Title>
      <Street>98 Station Street</Street>
      <City_Town>Bronfield DN90 9DN</City_Town>
      <Date_of_Birth>10.30.74</Date_of_Birth>
      <Telephone_Number>01237 46810</Telephone_Number>
      <Mobile_Number>0799 2266554</Mobile_Number>
    </Person>
    <Person>
      <Last_Name>Mustard</Last_Name>
      <First_Name>Michael</First_Name>
      <Job_Title>Programmer</Job_Title>
      <Street>32 Finkel Street</Street>
      <City_Town>Waterfield DN66 N77</City_Town>
      <Date_of_Birth>06.17.77</Date_of_Birth>
      <Telephone_Number>01238 91011</Telephone_Number>
      <Mobile_Number>0799 2266557</Mobile_Number>
    </Person>
    <Person>
      <Last_Name>Tattle</Last_Name>
      <First_Name>Tina</First_Name>
      <Job_Title>Programmer</Job_Title>
      <Street>17a Waterside</Street>
      <City_Town>Doncaster DN3 4JJ</City_Town>
      <Date_of_Birth>09.01.79</Date_of_Birth>
      <Telephone_Number>01234 98765</Telephone_Number>
      <Mobile_Number>0799 2266558</Mobile_Number>
    </Person>
  </Department>
</Company>
```

Hopefully you feel the source text is quite comprehensive. Displaying data in this form at least has the advantage of being self-explanatory. Incidentally we have also remained true to the tenth objective of the XML draft: The brevity of XML markup is scarcely significant.

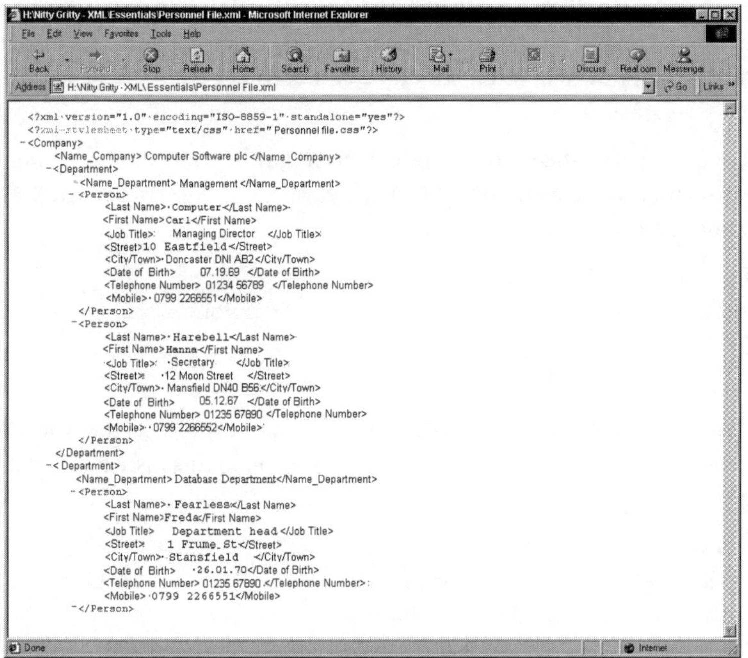

Figure 3.4 ***Output from the personnel file***

3.3.6 *The personnel file stylesheet*

As in the "Hello World!" example you now need to create a stylesheet for the personnel file. But unlike the previous example, when `<A00>` was the only XML element that you could define, on this occasion you can create a definition for each of the thirteen elements. However, you only need concern yourself with three because a CSS stylesheet for one element passes on its characteristics to all its child elements. Only a separate instruction can cancel this.

Launch your editor yet again and create a stylesheet using the following lines. The suggested name for this stylesheet is personnelfile.css.

```
Name_Company {font-size: 36pt; display: block; text-align:
right; font-weight: bold}
Name_Department {font-size: 24pt; display: block; font-
weight: bold}
Person {font-size: 12pt; display: block}
```

You have already met the attributes `font-size: 48pt` and `font-weight: bold`. For now just use font size 36. When you use `display: block` an element is displayed as a block element, which means that the element sidesteps the main contents without following the same course as the rest of the document. The element Name_Company will be displayed right-justified by using the attribute text-align: right. You can only use attribute text-align: to display block elements right-justified, left-justified or centered (right, left, center).

Having created your stylesheet you then have to link it to your XML document. Do this by inserting the instruction <?xml-stylesheet?> between the XML declaration and the root element:

```
<?xml version="1.0" standalone="yes"?>
<?xml-stylesheet type="text/css" href="personnelfile.css"?>
<Company>
...
```

This instruction assumes that the stylesheet is in the same folder as the XML document. However, you can enter a full path specification in this instruction if necessary. Here is an example:

```
<?xml version="1.0" standalone="yes"?>
<?xml-stylesheet type="text/css" href="H:\Nitty Gritty -
XML\Essentials\personnelfile.css"?>
<Company>
...
```

Your XML document should now look something like this.

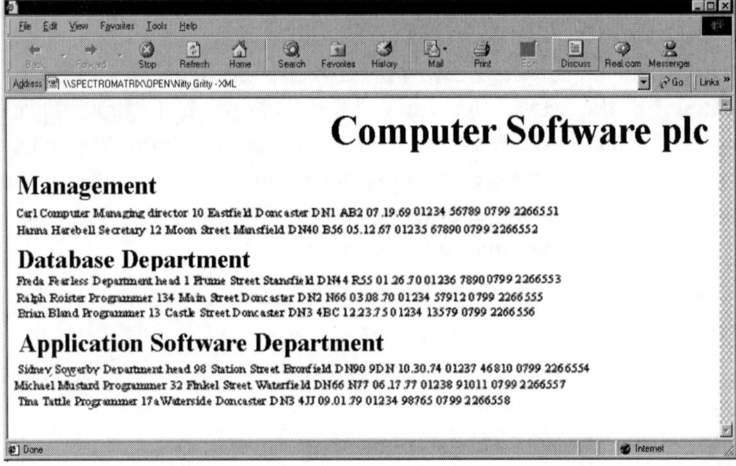

Figure 3.5 ***Output from the personnel file when using a stylesheet***

3.3.7 Attributes

So far you have been storing all data in individual elements, but that it not your only option. XML elements are like HTML tags in that they too can have attributes. These consist of a name, which can appear only once in every element, and a value, which is enclosed in quotation marks. Together they form a name-value pair (Name="Value"). You have already used attributes in the XML declaration:

```
<?xml version="1.0" standalone="yes"?>
```

This has two attributes. One is the attribute `version` with the value `1.0` and the other is the attribute `standalone` with the value `yes`. You can also apply this attribute syntax to the XML elements in your personnel file. Instead of setting up the company name as a child element of the `Company` element as on previous occasions

```
<Company>
  <Name_Company> ComputerSoftware plc</Name_Company>
</Company>
```

you can insert the name into the `Company` element as an attribute.

```
<Company Name="ComputerSoftware plc">
</Company>
```

You could include all child elements as attributes in the root element if there is no need for the attribute names within an element to be unique. So, for example, you should not define the `Company` element like this:

```
<Company Name="ComputerSoftware plc"
Department="Management"
Department="Database department"
Department="Application software department">
</Company>
```

Another reason for avoiding this way of dividing things up is that the element `Department` has several child elements and these cannot be used as attributes. Due to the close link between an element and its attribute, however, you can use `Name` to represent the name of the attribute without in this case running the risk of getting names confused, as was the case with elements. You can therefore code the departments something like this:

```
<Department Name="Management">
</Department>
<Department Name="Database department">
</Department>
<Department Name="Application software department">
</Department>
```

The element Person has many possible attributes:

```
<Person City_Town="Doncaster DN1 AB2"
Date_of_Birth="07.19.69" First_Name="Carl"
Job_Title="Managing Director" Last_Name="Computer"
Mobile_Number="0799 2266551" Street="10 Eastfield"
Telephone_Number="01234 56789"></Person>
```

3.3.8 Empty tags

If an element consists only of attributes without contents, you can use empty tags as short cuts. These are treated in exactly the same way as tags which are not empty. They differ from ordinary elements in consisting of just one tag, namely a starting tag. This tag ends with /> instead of just >. For example, the element Person then looks like this:

```
<Person City_Town="Doncaster DN1 AB2"
Date_of_Birth="07.19.69" First_Name="Carl"
Job_Title="Managing Director" Last_Name="Computer"
Mobile_Number="0799 2266551" Street="10 Eastfield"
Telephone_Number="01234 56789"></Person>
```

3.3.9 The XML personnel file with attributes

Here is the whole of the personnel file using the new attribute style:

```
<?xml version="1.0" standalone="yes"?>
<Company Name="ComputerSoftware plc">
  <Department Name="Management">
    <Person CityTown="Doncaster DN1 AB2"
DateOfBirth="07.19.69" FirstName="Carl"
JobTitle="Managing Director" LastName="Computer"
MobileNumber="0799 2266551" Street="10 Eastfield"
TelephoneNumber="01234 56789"/>
    <Person CityTown="Mansfield" DN40 B56"
DateOfBirth="05.12.67" FirstName="Hanna"
JobTitle="Secretary" LastName="Harebell"
MobileNumber"0799 2266552" Street="12 Moon Street"
TelephoneNumber="01235 67890"/>
  </Department>
  <Department Name="Database department">
    <Person CityTown="Stanfield DN44 R55"
DateOfBirth="01.26.70" FirstName="Frida"
JobTitle="Department Head" LastName="Fearless"
MobileNumber="0799 2266553" Street="1 Frume Street"
```

```
TelephoneNumber="01236 78901"/>
    <Person CityTown="Doncaster DN2 N66"
DateOfBirth="08.03.70" FirstName="Ralph"
JobTitle="Programmer" LastName="Roister"
MobileNumber="0799 2266555" Street="134 Main Street"
TelephoneNumber="01234 57912"/>
    <Person CityTown="Doncaster DN3 4BC"
DateOfBirth="23.12.75" FirstName="Brian"
JobTitle="Programmer" LastName="Bland"
MobileNumber="0799 266556" Street="13 Castle Street"
TelephoneNumber="01234 13579"/>
  </Department>
  <Department Name="Application software department">
    <Person CityTown="Bronfield DN90 9DN"
DateOfBirth="10.30.74" FirstName="Sidney"
JobTitle="Department Head" LastName="Sowerby"
MobileNumber="0799 2266554" Street="98 Station Street"
TelephoneNumber="01237 46810"/>
    <Person CityTown="Waterfield DN66 N77"
DateOfBirth="17.06.77 FirstName="Michael"
JobTitle="Programmer" LastName="Mustard"
MobileNumber="0799 2266557" Street="32 Finkel Street"
TelephoneNumber="01238 91011"/>
    <Person CityTown="Doncaster DN3 4JJ"
DateOfBirth="01.09.79" FirstName="Tina"
JobTitle="Programmer" LastName="Tattle"
MobileNumber="0799 266558" Street="17a Waterside"
TelephoneNumber="01234 98765"/>
  </Department>
</Company>
```

As you can appreciate, the options of representing all data as elements or all data as attributes are two absolute extremes and in practice a middle course between these options is much more likely. The method you subsequently choose and the extent to which you mix both methods will depend on your personal choice and the requirements of your document.

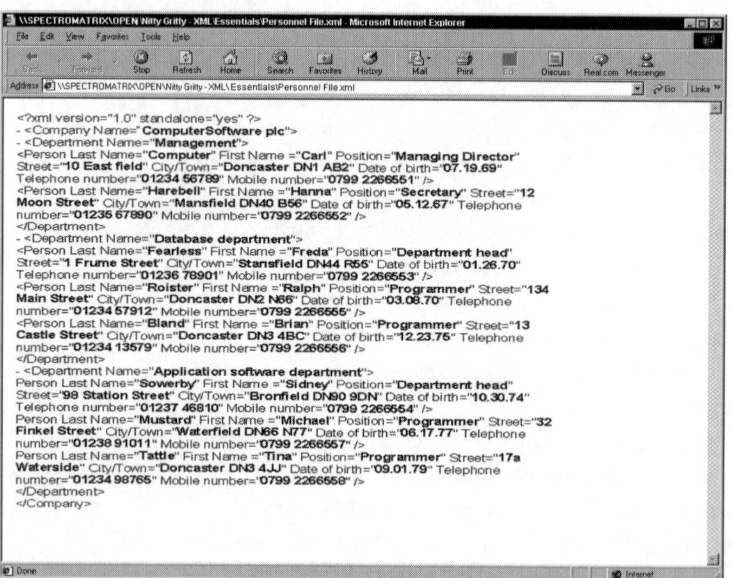

```
<?xml version="1.0" standalone="yes" ?>
- <Company Name="ComputerSoftware plc">
- <Department Name="Management">
<Person Last Name="Computer" First Name ="Carl" Position="Managing Director"
Street="10 East field" City/Town="Doncaster DN1 AB2" Date of birth="07.19.69"
Telephone number="01234 56789" Mobile number="0799 2266551" />
<Person Last Name="Harebell" First Name ="Hanna" Position="Secretary" Street="12
Moon Street" City/Town="Mansfield DN40 B56" Date of birth="05.12.67" Telephone
number="01235 67890" Mobile number="0799 2266552" />
</Department>
- <Department Name="Database department">
<Person Last Name="Fearless" First Name ="Freda" Position="Department head"
Street="1 Frume Street" City/Town="Stansfield DN44 R55" Date of birth="01.26.70"
Telephone number="01236 78901" Mobile number="0799 2266553" />
<Person Last Name="Roister" First Name ="Ralph" Position="Programmer" Street="134
Main Street" City/Town="Doncaster DN2 N66" Date of birth="03.08.70" Telephone
number="01234 57912" Mobile number="0799 2266555" />
<Person Last Name="Bland" First Name ="Brian" Position="Programmer" Street="13
Castle Street" City/Town="Doncaster DN3 4BC" Date of birth="12.23.75" Telephone
number="01234 13579" Mobile number="0799 2266556" />
</Department>
- <Department Name="Application software department">
Person Last Name="Sowerby" First Name ="Sidney" Position="Department head"
Street="98 Station Street" City/Town="Bronfield DN90 9DN" Date of birth="10.30.74"
Telephone number="01237 46810" Mobile number="0799 2266554" />
Person Last Name="Mustard" First Name ="Michael" Position="Programmer" Street="32
Finkel Street" City/Town="Waterfield DN66 N77" Date of birth="06.17.77" Telephone
number="01238 91011" Mobile number="0799 2266557" />
Person Last Name="Tattle" First Name ="Tina" Position="Programmer" Street="17a
Waterside" City/Town="Doncaster DN3 4JJ" Date of birth="09.01.79" Telephone
number="01234 98765" Mobile number="0799 2266558" />
</Department>
</Company>
```

Figure 3.6 *Data in the personnel file using attributes*

3.4 Valid XML

Unlike HTML, XML has virtually no predefined tags. Instead you have the option to customize your own tags or elements. So that elements are not created arbitrarily, XML has a few rules that you have to follow. An XML document that follows these rules is said to be well-formed, or valid. This well-formed characteristic is necessary in order that XML processors and XML browsers can read such documents.

3.4.1 XML declaration

When an XML declaration is present it must be the first item to appear in the document. This is because the XML processor looks for the first bytes in the file to determine which character set is going to be used. Even leading spaces ahead of the XML declaration could cause problems.

3.4.2 Root elements

A well-formed XML document has a root element since XML allows only one element at the highest level. All the other elements must appear between the starting tag `<ROOT>` and the closing tag `</ROOT>`. You may of course give your root element a quite different name if you wish.

3.4.3 Elements

As you know, an element consists of a starting tag, its content and a closing tag. A starting tag begins with < followed by its name, and ends with >. A closing tag differs from a starting tag by beginning with </. Since XML assumes that an opening angled bracket (<) always marks the beginning of a tag and a closing angled bracket (>) always marks the end of a tag, it is important that you only use these characters for that purpose.

Whereas web browsers are very tolerant in the case of HTML and still display a document even if a closing tag is missing, you will not be so lucky with an XML document. If you forget a closing tag, the browser will simply display an error as the output.

You have already met the concept of a child element. Here again XML differs from HTML. In HTML elements or tags are allowed to overlap:

```
<center>
<h1>
Hello World!
</center>
</h1>
```

An XML browser is not so lenient in the same circumstances. The above code is not permitted in XML since the closing tag `</center>` comes before the closing tag `</h1>`. The browser would simply return an error. It should be written correctly as follows:

```
<center>
  <h1>
    Hello World
  </h1>
</center>
```

Naturally you can insert an empty tag in an element at any time:

```
<h1>
  Hello <br/>World
</h1>
```

Tip You are not allowed to choose the name of an element completely arbitrarily. The name of an element must start with a letter or an underscore. The rest of the name can consist of letters, numbers, underscores, hyphens and points. The name must not include a space or a colon. Similarly all names beginning with `xml` or `XML` are forbidden because these character strings are reserved for subsequent XML names and designations. Here are some examples of permissible names for XML elements:

```
<COMPANY>    </COMPANY>
<_root>    </_root>
<Carl_Computer>    </Carl_Computer>
<Name-Company>    </Name-Company>
<A00>    </A00>
```


Another difference compared to HTML is that XML distinguishes between capital letters and lower case letters. Though you are allowed to use capital and small letters, the starting tag and the closing tag must be absolutely identical. For instance the element `<A00>` cannot be closed with `</a00>`.

3.4.4 Attributes

In the case of attributes too, there are some rules for you to observe. The rules for attribute names are exactly the same as those for element names.

Tip The name of an attribute must start with a letter or an underscore. The rest of the name can consist of letters, numbers, underscores, hyphens and points. As with the names of elements, attribute names must not include spaces or colons. Similarly all names beginning with the character strings xml or XML are forbidden because these are reserved for subsequent XML names and designations.

Names of attributes must appear only once per element. For example, the following element is not permitted:

```
<Department_Name="Database department" Name="Application
software department"/>
```

On the other hand, because XML makes a distinction between capital and small letters the following element would be allowed:

```
<Department_Name="Database department" name="Application
software department"/>
```

However, this notation is not recommended because you could soon get into a muddle with it.

There are less restrictions in the case of attribute values. Attribute values can include spaces and begin with a number or contain virtually any punctuation mark. Since XML attributes are delimited by quotation marks, use an apostrophe for each of the opening and closing quotation marks if they are needed within an attribute value.

3.4.5 Comments

The contents of comments are handled as if they are not there. This fact can be used, for example, to write yourself reminders or to comment out sections of your XML document that are not yet finished. XML comments always begin with `<!--` and end with `-->`. They must not be inserted in a tag:

```
<?xml version="1.0" standalone="yes"?>
<A00 <!-- Element A00 starts here -->>
  Hello World
</A00 <!-- Element A00 ends here -->>
```

When you wish to comment out a section the whole element must be enclosed by the comment, not just a tag, since the XML browser would then have an opening or closing tag too many. The whole document would then no longer be well-formed and would produce an error. The following text would be permissible, for example:

```
<?xml version="1.0" standalone="yes"?>
<ROOT>
  <A00>
    Hello World
  </A00>
<!--
  <B00>
    Hello XML
  </B00>
-->
</ROOT>
```

Because the string (--) within a comment must occur only at the start and close of a comment, the following nested comments are not allowed:

```
<?xml version="1.0" standalone="yes"?>
<ROOT>
  <A00>
    Hello World
  </A00>
<!--
  <B00>
    <!-- Hello XML -->
  </B00>
-->
</ROOT>
```


3.4.6 Entity references

As you have already found out, XML will interpret certain characters incorrectly if you use them in the wrong place. Another such character is the ampersand (&) which must only be used at the beginning of an entity reference. However, if you do have to use any of the "forbidden" characters you can use entity references instead.

Entity references are markups which are replaced by these characters when your document is parsed. For example if you want to use the "less than" sign (<), which XML would interpret as the start of a tag, use the entity reference `<` instead, otherwise the document is not well-formed.

Entity reference	Character
&	&
<	<
>	>
"	"
'	'

If you have already used HTML you will already know about entity references. Unlike the entity references in HTML, those in XML must end with a semicolon. Another difference compared to HTML is that in XML only these five entity references are predefined.

3.4.7 CDATA

Suppose you had to write an XML document containing a lot of these entity reference characters, such as an XML document about an XML document:

```
&lt;?xml version="1.0" standalone="yes"?&gt;
&lt;A00&gt;
  Hello World
&lt;/A00&gt;
```

You would have to replace every `<`, `>`, `&`, `"` and `'` sign. Pretty complicated, wouldn't you say? And that's just for our "Hello World!" example. You would have the same bother with a source text written in C or Java. Help is at hand in the shape of a `CDATA` section, which lets you enter plain text as its content. This means that the characters `<`, `>`, `&`, `"` and `'` are all represented as themselves. A CDATA section begins with the tag `<![CDATA[` and ends with `]]>`. You can use a CDATA section to represent the above example as follows:

```
<![CDATA[
<?xml version="1.0" standalone="yes"?>
<A00>
  Hello World
</A00>
]]>
```

Note that a CDATA section ends with the closing tag `]]>`. This particular tag is therefore the only text that can never be included in a CDATA section. As soon as you use this text you will have to revert to using entity references for the entire text section.

3.5 Character sets

In the course of our previous examples it may have occurred to you that some alphabets use special characters such as the umlaut characters ä, ö, ü and ß which are used in German. It matters because we create XML documents in ASCII format. ASCII is the acronym for `American Standard Code for Information Interchange` and this includes the characters and signs needed for writing American English. The technique for encoding ASCII characters uses the numbers from 0 to 127. But additional characters need to use numbers from 128 and above. These requirements are fulfilled by the character set known as Latin-1. This encodes additional characters in the range 128 to 255 and enables letters such as ä, ö, ü and ß to be represented. But not even Latin-1 can represent all the characters and signs that exist throughout the world.

If you wish to retain the ability to use letters such as ä, ö, ü and ß, you can tell your XML processor that you are working in the Latin-1 character set. To do this you have to extend your XML declaration as follows:

```
<?xml version="1.0" encoding="ISO-8859-1" standal-
one="yes"?>
```

Another way is to put your encoding declaration on a separate line straight after the XML declaration:

```
<?xml encoding="ISO-8859-1"?>
```

The XML processor now knows that you are working in the Latin-1 character set. This is not always problem-free, since not all XML processors can process all forms of encoding. At all events, you can now use ä, ö, ü and ß if you wish:

```
<?xml version="1.0" standalone="yes"?>
<?xml encoding="ISO-8859-1"?>
<Company>
  <Name_Company> ComputerSoftware plc</Name_Company>
  <Department>
    <Name_Department> Geschäftsführung[1]</Name_Department>
    <Person>
      <Last_Name> Computer</Last_Name>
      <First_Name> Carl</First_Name>
      <Job_Title> Geschäftsführer[2]</Job_Title>
      <Street> 10 Eastfield</Street>
      <City_Town> Doncaster DN1 AB2</City_Town>
      <Date_of_Birth> 07.19.69</Date_of_Birth>
      <Telephone_Number> 01234 56789</Telephone_Number>
      <Mobile_Number> 0799 2266551</Mobile_Number>
    </Person>
...
```

Most browsers recognize the diffrent encodings and should display the text accordingly.

1. Geschäftsführung= Management. This is used as an example of working in the Latin- 1 character set.
2. Geschäftsführer= Managing director.

Name of character set	Language/countries
US-ASCII	English
UTF-8	Compressed Unicode
ISO-10646-UCS-2	Raw Unicode
ISO-8859-1	Latin-1, Western Europe
ISO-8859-2	Latin-2, Eastern Europe
ISO-8859-3	Latin-3, Southern Europe
ISO-8859-4	Latin-4, Northern Europe
ISO-8859-5	ASCII plus Cyrillic
ISO-8859-6	ASCII plus Arabic
ISO-8859-7	ASCII plus Greek
ISO-8859-8	ASCII plus Hebrew
ISO-8859-9	Latin-5, Turkish
ISO-8859-10	Latin-6, ASCII plus Nordic languages
ISO-8859-11	ASCII plus Thai
ISO-8859-13	Latin-7, ASCII plus Baltic languages such as Latvian
ISO-8859-14	Latin-8, ASCII plus Gaelic and Welsh
ISO-8859-15	Latin-9, Latin-0, Western Europe
ISO-2022-JP	Japanese
ISO-2022-CN	Chinese
ISO-2022-KR	Korean
Big5	Chinese, Taiwan
GB2312	Chinese, Mainland China
KOI6-R	Russian

Table 3.2 ***A selection of extended character sets***

Another possibility would be to use the Unicode character set, which does not need an encoding declaration. Unicode supports 65535 different characters and therefore includes a huge range of characters and signs. XML itself works with the Unicode character set or with UTF-8, a compressed version of the Unicode character set that allows you to easily identify and specify the required characters. Your documents have to be saved in Unicode. Documents in Unicode are about twice the size of documents written and saved in ASCII or Latin-1, since Unicode uses two bytes for each character.

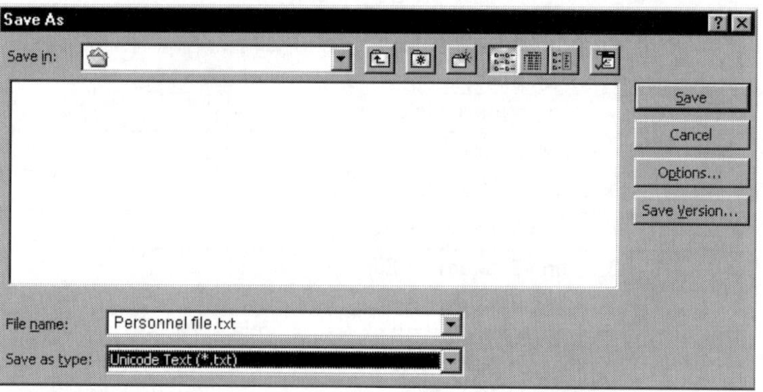

Figure 3.7 ***Save As ... Unicode format***

If you would rather not have such large documents or you cannot save in Unicode format, you can leave the document in its original character set.

Each Unicode character is represented by a number between 0 and 65535, which you can insert with the aid of the Unicode character reference number. This character reference number consists of the two characters `&#`, the character code and a closing semicolon. For example the umlaut character ä is represented as follows: `ä`. You can also represent the character code in hexadecimal notation (base 16). The hexadecimal notation uses `x` as a prefix.

```
<?xml version="1.0" standalone="yes"?>
<?xml-stylesheet type="text/css" href="personnelfile.css"?>
<Company>
  <Name_Company>ComputerSoftware plc</Name_Company>
  <Department>
    <Name_Department>
      Gesch&#x00E4;ftsf&#x00FC;hrung[3]
    </Name_Department>
    <Person>
      <Last_Name>Computer</Last_Name>
      <First_Name>Carl</First_Name>
      <Position>Gesch&#x00E4;ftsf&#x00FC;hrer[4]</Position>
      <Street>10 Eastfield</Street>
      <City_Town>Doncaster DN1 AB2</City_Town>
      <Date_of_Birth>07.19.69</Date_of_Birth>
      <Telephone_Number>01234 56789</Telephone_Number>
```

3. Geschäftsführung= Geschäftsführung (management).
4. Geschäftsführer= Geschäftsführer (managing director).

```
      <Mobile_Number>0799 2266551</Mobile_Number>
    </Person>
...
```

As the above listing shows, you just need to insert the Unicode character reference number.

Character	Unicode character reference number in decimal	Unicode character reference number in hexadecimal
Ä	Ä	Ä
Ö	Ö	Ö
Ü	Ü	Ü
ß	ß	&#x;00DF
ä	ä	ä
ö	ö	ö
ü	ü	ü

Table 3.3 *Excerpt from the Unicode character table*

No matter which variant you use, your resulting output should look like Figure 3.8.

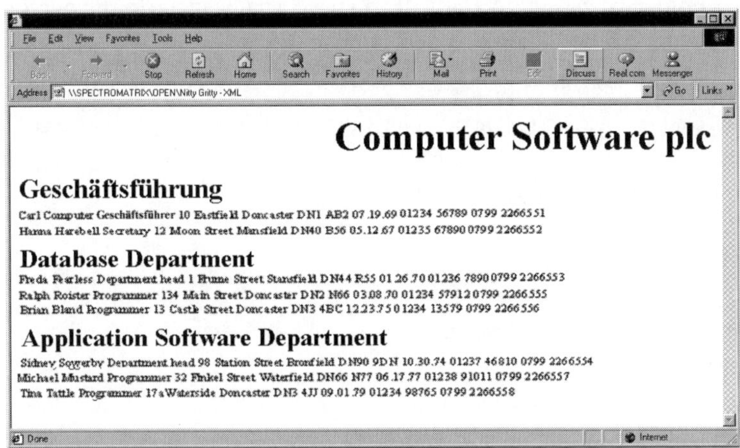

Figure 3.8 *Personnel file*

3.6 Namespaces in XML

In projects involving several programmers and public XML documents there is a big risk that problems will arise due to using duplicate element names. So namespaces were introduced to make quite certain that element names are unique and will not lead to confusion by being specified twice. Namespaces now make it possible to use parts of imported documents without the need for special conversion measures.

Just suppose that the company owned by Mr. Computer which featured in the personnel file in our example merges with another company and the other company also has an XML personnel file that has to be added. Due to the many options for configuring an XML document we can soon find that duplicate element names are starting to collide. Namespaces expand the element name and prevent collisions between elements.

A namespace can be defined as follows:

```
<Element_Name xmlns:Name="URL">
```

A namespace is declared in the root element. Thus the element name is the name of the root element. The name is followed by the prefix `xmlns:` which introduces the namespace declaration. This prefix assigns the name of the namespace, which is made unique by assigning a URL. If you used a namespace in the personnel list in our example it could look something like this:

```
<?xml version="1.0" standalone="yes"?>
<CompSoft:Company xmlns:CompSoft="http://www.ComputerSoft-
ware.com">
  <CompSoft:Name_Company>
    ComputerSoftware plc
  </CompSoft:Name_Company>
  <CompSoft:Department>
    <CompSoft:Name_Department>
      Management
    </CompSoft:Name_Department>
    <CompSoft:Person>
      <CompSoft:Last_Name>Computer</CompSoft:Last_Name>
      <CompSoft:First_Name>Carl</CompSoft:First_Name>
      <CompSoft:Job_Title>
        Managing Director
      </CompSoft:Job_Title>
      <CompSoft:Street> 10 Eastfield</CompSoft:Street>
      <CompSoft:City_Town>Doncaster DN1 AB2</Comp-
Soft:City_Town>
      <CompSoft:Date_of_Birth>
```

```
        07.19.69
      </CompSoft:Date_of_Birth>
      <CompSoft:Telephone_Number>
        01234 56789
      </CompSoft:Telephone_Number>
      <CompSoft:Mobile_Number> 0799 2266551</Comp-
Soft:Mobile_Number>
    </CompSoft:Person>
...
```

The major benefit is that we can use more than one namespace within a single XML document. For example:

```
<CompSoft:Company
 xmlns:CompSoft="http://www.ComputerSoftware.com"
xmlns:private="http://www.carl-computer.co.uk">
...
</CompSoft:Company>
```

4 Document type definition

The rules for the elements and attributes within an XML document are laid down in the `Document Type Definition`. The term Document Type Definition is often called DTD for short. It defines the relationship between elements as well as the data they are allowed or not allowed to contain. And since DTDs are conservative by nature, anything which is not expressly allowed is forbidden. An XML document that follows the DTD rules is said to be well-formed, or valid. Unfortunately the latest web browsers are still unable to check for validity.

4.1 Element declaration

In the DTD you must declare every element you intend to use in your XML document. You do this in an element declaration. But before you can start listing the elements you must identify the root element in a `Doctype` declaration. This must be in the following form:

```
<!DOCTYPE Name_of_Root_Element []>
```

> **Warning** Always take care to observe the distinction between upper and lower case in the Document Type Definition.

In our "Hello World!" example the relevant `DOCTYPE` declaration looks like this:

```
<!DOCTYPE A00 [
]>
```

It simply says that the root element is called `A00` and nothing more. Nor does it say anything about what an `A00` element can and cannot do. You now declare the individual elements between `[` and `]`. Do this by means of the element declaration `<!ELEMENT>` in the following format:

```
<!ELEMENT Name_of_Element RULE>
```

The simplest element rule ANY states that the element can contain anything at all. You are allowed to enter both character data and other valid tags between the starting tag and closing tag of this element. This rule is mostly used in unstructured documents, and should be avoided as much as possible since it is better to describe the contents as precisely as you can.

Because we only need character data for our "Hello World!" example, it would be better to use the rule (#PCDATA) (parsed character data). This means that all character data that is not an element can appear between the element tags. Our "Hello World!" example complete with DTD is a well-formed and valid XML document when it looks like this:

```
<?xml version="1.0" standalone="yes"?>
<!DOCTYPE A00 [
<!ELEMENT A00 (#PCDATA)>
]>
<!-- XML data starts here -->
<A00>
Hello World!
</A00>
```

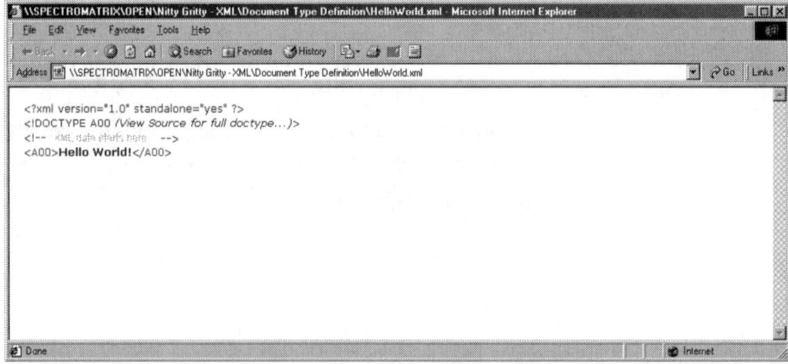

Figure 4.1 ***A well-formed, valid XML document***

Internet Explorer 5.5 is displaying the line `<!DOCTYPE A00 (View Source for full doctype...)>` to show that a DTD exists.

However, alter your XML document incorrectly on purpose:

```
<?xml version="1.0" standalone="yes"?>
<!DOCTYPE A00 [
<!ELEMENT A00 (#PCDATA)>
]>
<!-- XML data starts here -->

<B00>
```

```
Hello World!
</B00>
```

The XML document no longer obeys the rules defined in the DTD and is therefore no longer valid. As you can see, Internet Explorer does not check for validity and simply ignores the situation.

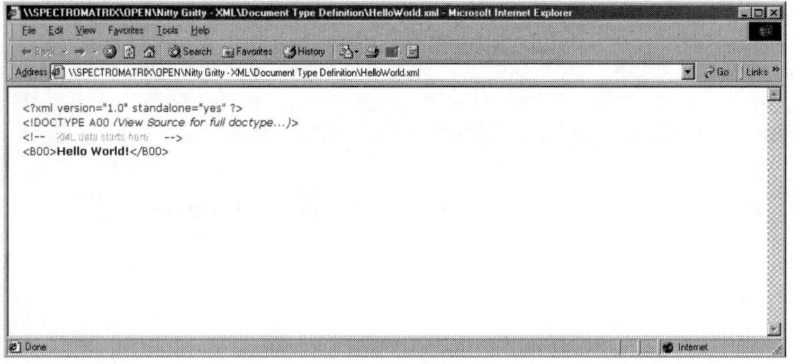

Figure 4.2 ***A well-formed but invalid XML document***

Now you can insert the stylesheet again:

```
<?xml version="1.0" standalone="yes"?>
<?xml-stylesheet type="text/css" href="helloworld.css"?>
<!DOCTYPE A00 [
<!ELEMENT A00 (#PCDATA)>
]>
<!-- XML data starts here -->
<A00>
Hello World!
</A00>
```

Since formatting is generally not reliant on the DTD, the document illustrations look the same with and without DTD.

Figure 4.3 ***XML document when using DTD and a stylesheet***

4.1.1 Child elements

An XML document does not contain only the root element, and this does not contain just `parsed character data`. It can also contain other elements, and these are then known as child elements. Since we want as far as possible to avoid an element declaration using the `ANY` rule, there needs to be another way of including child elements in the declaration of an element.

Let's go back to our personnel file for this problem. It contains thirteen elements that you have to declare in the DTD in order to obtain a well-formed, valid XML document:

```
<Company>
<Name_Company>
<Department>
<Name_Department>
<Person>
<Last_Name>
<First_Name>
<Job_Title>
<Street>
<City_Town>
<Date_of_Birth>
<Telephone_Number>
<Mobile_Number>
```

The simplest way would be to configure the DTD hierarchically and work our way from the outside in. Start in the usual way and declare the root element so that it can include further elements:

```
<!DOCTYPE Company [
<!ELEMENT Company ANY>
]>
```

However, the rule ANY merely states that the root element can contain other elements, not that other elements must be present. Because each company also has a name, you need to make sure that the Company element is also obliged to contain a Name_Company element. The way to deal with this is to replace the ANY rule with the name of the element in brackets which it is obligatory to include. Then you must also declare the new element. The Name_Company element contains character data only, so you only need to use the (#PCDATA) rule.

```
<!DOCTYPE Company [
<!ELEMENT Company (Name_Company)>
<!ELEMENT Name_Company (#PCDATA)>
]>
```


4.1.2 Logical operation AND

But the Company element has yet more child elements. In order to insert the three Department elements, insert them in the rule with an AND logical operation, that is to say a comma (,), after the Name_Company element.

```
<!ELEMENT Company (Name_Company, Department, Department,
Department)>
```

This AND operation has made sure that the Company element contains precisely one Name_Company element and three elements called Department. The comma separating the element names forces the elements into a precisely defined sequence, i.e. first comes the element Name_Company and then the three Department elements.

4.1.3 Indicators, repetition operators

There are other ways of nesting elements within the DTD. By using indicators or repetition operators you can control the way in which the individual nested elements are repeated. The table gives you an overview of the three possible indicators.

Indicator	Description
?	The element occurs not at all or once only.
+	The element occurs once or more than once.
*	The element occurs more than once, once only, or not at all.

Table 4.1 ***Indicators or repetition operator***

Elements with the `?` indicator do not have to be used if they are not needed, and can be used only once.

The + indicator makes sure that the element occurs at least once but it may occur more often. It is not acceptable to give an element a + indicator if you hardly ever use it.

The * indicator is the most flexible of the three. This variant allows you a free choice of whether and how often an element appears. On the other hand if you want an element to occur without fail, this is not the indicator to use.

For the `Company` element the * indicator is ideal because a company can contain any number of departments or even none at all. Simply enter the indicator after the element to which it refers:

```
<!ELEMENT Company (Name_Company, Department*)>
```

The declaration for the `Department` element is slightly different. A department must of course have a name, but it also has at least one dependent employee, represented by the element `Person`. The * indicator is not recommended for this task since you would then make it possible to have a department with no employees. The appropriate indicator for this situation is the + indicator. This makes at least one `Person` element compulsory but allows more.

```
<!ELEMENT Department (Name_Department, Person+)>
<!ELEMENT Name_Department (#PCDATA)>
```

We are still missing the following elements:

```
<Person>
<Last_Name>
<First_Name>
<Job_Title>
<Street>
<City_Town>
<Date_of_Birth>
<Telephone_Number>
<Mobile_Number>
```

The `Person` element has some child elements and you need to consider how these should be nested:

Child element	*Is the element absolutely essential?*	*What should be the possible number of elements?*	*Possible indicator*
`Last_Name`	Yes	One	None
`First_Name`	Yes	Multiple	+
`Job_Title`	Yes	One	None

Child element	Is the element absolutely essential?	What should be the possible number of elements?	Possible indicator
Street	Yes	One	None
City/Town	Yes	One	None
Date_of_Birth	Yes	One	None
Telephone_Number	No	Multiple	*
Mobile_Number	No	Multiple	*

Table 4.2 ***Child elements of the Person element***

According to our little table the declaration of the Person element now looks like this:

```
<!ELEMENT Person (Last_Name, First_Name+, Job_Title,
Street, City_Town, Date_of_Birth, Telephone_Number*,
Mobile_Number*)>
```

The remaining elements simply contain character data:

```
<!ELEMENT Last_Name (#PCDATA)>
<!ELEMENT First_Name (#PCDATA)>
<!ELEMENT Job_Title (#PCDATA)>
<!ELEMENT Street (#PCDATA)>
<!ELEMENT City_Town (#PCDATA)>
<!ELEMENT Date_of_Birth (#PCDATA)>
<!ELEMENT Telephone_Number (#PCDATA)>
<!ELEMENT Mobile_Number (#PCDATA)>
```

4.1.4 *Logical operation OR*

The DTD still offers a further two options for nesting elements, making the DTD more flexible still. One of these is the OR logical operation. This uses a vertical line (|) to link two or more rules together.

```
<!ELEMENT Telephone
(Home_Number|Mobile_Number|Car_Telephone)>
  <!ELEMENT Home_Number (#PCDATA)>
  <!ELEMENT Mobile_Number (#PCDATA)>
  <!ELEMENT Car_Telephone (#PCDATA)>
```

This declaration defines that within the element Telephone one of the elements Home_Number, Mobile_Number or Car_Telephone can appear. Please note that the Telephone element can contain one or other of the elements but not two or all three at the same time.

4.1.5 Logical operation AND/OR

You can use a combination of the AND operation and the OR operation to create an AND/OR operation.

```
<!ELEMENT Telephone
(Home_Number,(Mobile_Number|Car_Telephone))>
  <!ELEMENT Home_Number (#PCDATA)>
  <!ELEMENT Mobile_Number (#PCDATA)>
  <!ELEMENT Car_Telephone (#PCDATA)>
```

In this case the element `Telephone` must contain without fail a `Home_Number element` and either the `Mobile_Number element` or the `Car_Telephone element`. By skillful use of brackets, AND operations, OR operations and repetition operators you can configure virtually every conceivable combination of element declarations.

4

START UP!

4.1.6 Empty elements

As with non-empty elements, you must also declare empty elements in the DTD. But as we know, empty elements can contain neither child elements nor character data, so they are very easy to declare. Use the customary declaration `<!ELEMENT>` with the name of the empty element and the keyword `EMPTY`. For example:

```
<!ELEMENT Telephone EMPTY>
```

This would declare the element `Telephone` in the DTD as an empty element.

4.1.7 Comments

Comments in a DTD are subject to the same rules as in an XML document. Comments must not appear within a declaration. They begin with `<!--` and end with `-->`, and must not contain a double dash (`--`).

As in XML documents, they help the understanding of the source text and are ignored by the browser.

4.1.8 DTD for personnel file without attributes

Using the completed and compiled DTD your personnel file now looks like this:

```
<?xml version="1.0" standalone="yes"?>
<?xml-stylesheet type="text/css" href="personnelfile.css"?>
<!DOCTYPE Company [
<!ELEMENT Company (Name_Company, Department*|Person+)>
<!ELEMENT Name_Company (#PCDATA)>
```

```
  <!ELEMENT Department (Name_Department, Person+)>
    <!ELEMENT Name_Department (#PCDATA)>
    <!ELEMENT Person (Last_Name, First_Name+, Job_Title,
Street, City/Town, Date_of_Birth, Telephone_Number*,
Mobile_Number*)>
      <!ELEMENT Last_Name (#PCDATA)>
      <!ELEMENT First_Name (#PCDATA)>
      <!ELEMENT Job_Title (#PCDATA)>
      <!ELEMENT Street (#PCDATA)>
      <!ELEMENT City/Town (#PCDATA)>
      <!ELEMENT Date_of_Birth (#PCDATA)>
      <!ELEMENT Telephone_Number (#PCDATA)>
      <!ELEMENT Mobile_Number (#PCDATA)>
]>
<Company>
  <Name_Company> ComputerSoftware plc</Name_Company>
  <Department>
    <Name_Department> Management</Name_Department>
    <Person>
      <Last_Name> Computer</Last_Name>
      <First_Name> Carl</First_Name>
      <Job_Title> Managing Director</Job_Title>
      <Street> 10 Eastfield</Street>
      <City_Town> Doncaster DN1 AB2</City_Town>
      <Date_of_Birth> 07.19.69</Date_of_Birth>
      <Telephone_Number> 01234 56789</Telephone_Number>
      <Mobile_Number> 0799 2266551</Mobile_Number>
    </Person>
...
```

Note that indentations have no effect in the DTD either.

4.2 Internal/External DTD

You can use a Document Type Definition to define a particular form in which you want data to be saved in XML. You will first become aware of the power of these rules when you work with this DTD in several documents, or work on documents in collaboration with a number of people, or exchange data and this data stays compatible.

4.2.1 Internal DTD

So far you have defined the DTD within the XML document. You have used `<!DOCTYPE>` to define the root element and then, within square brackets `[ ]`, used the element declaration `<!ELEMENT>` to declare the root element and the rest of the elements.

```
<?xml version="1.0" standalone="yes"?>
<!DOCTYPE Name_of_Root_Element [
<!ELEMENT Name_of_Root_Elements Rule>
<!ELEMENT Name Rule>
...
]>
<Company>
  <Name_Company> ComputerSoftware plc</Name_Company>
...
```

However, you cannot work in other documents if you use this kind of DTD.

4.2.2 External DTD

If you want to use the same DTD when working in other documents, you must save the DTD to its own file. The customary file extension in this case is `.dtd`. It is also appropriate to name the personnel file as a .dtd file. Please make sure that you also save this file in text format. Insert the following listing in this file and delete this section from your XML document:

```
<!ELEMENT Company (Name_Company, Department*)>
<!ELEMENT Name_Company (#PCDATA)>
  <!ELEMENT Department (Name_Department, Person+)>
    <!ELEMENT Name_Department (#PCDATA)>
    <!ELEMENT Person (Last_Name, First_Name+,
Job_Title, Street, City_Town,
Date_of_Birth, Telephone_Number*, Mobile_Number*)>
      <!ELEMENT Last_Name (#PCDATA)>
      <!ELEMENT First_Name (#PCDATA)>
      <!ELEMENT Job_Title (#PCDATA)>
```

```
<!ELEMENT Street (#PCDATA)>
<!ELEMENT City_Town (#PCDATA)>
<!ELEMENT Date_of_Birth (#PCDATA)>
<!ELEMENT Telephone_Number (#PCDATA)>
<!ELEMENT Mobile_Number (#PCDATA)>
```

Your XML document should now have only this part left:

```
<?xml version="1.0" standalone="yes"?>
<!DOCTYPE Company [
]>
<Company>
  <Name_Company> ComputerSoftware plc</Name_Company>
...
```

Instead of inserting the original DTD into the now empty square brackets `[ ]`, you enter the location of the new file containing the old DTD:

```
<!DOCTYPE Company SYSTEM "Personnelfile.dtd">
```

The XML keyword `SYSTEM` indicates that an external DTD will be used. The keyword `SYSTEM` also indicates that this is a private DTD which will be used by only one author or group.

It is assumed that the DTD is in the same folder as the XML document. If this is not the case, you will need to enter a relative or absolute path at this point:

```
<!DOCTYPE Company SYSTEM "c:\Data\XML\Personnelfile.dtd">
```

or:

```
<!DOCTYPE Company SYSTEM "http://www.MyDomain.co.uk/Person-
nelfile.dtd">
```

This is mostly the case when you are also using the file with other XML documents or with other people.

You still need to make another change to the XML declaration `<?xml>`.

```
<?xml version="1.0" standalone="no"?>
```

Previously the XML document was not reliant on other files, but now that you have relocated the DTD this is no longer the case. This means you need to change the attribute `standalone="yes"` to `standalone="no"`. Since we are assuming that the DTD and the XML document are in the same folder, the XML document now looks like this:

```
<?xml version="1.0" standalone="no"?>
<!DOCTYPE Company SYSTEM "Personnelfile.dtd">
<Company>
  <Name_Company> ComputerSoftware plc</Name_Company>
  <Department>
```

```
    <Name_Department> Management</Name_Department>
    <Person>
...
```

4.2.3 Public DTD

The keyword `SYSTEM` states that this DTD is being used by one or more users, but the distribution of this DTD is kept within limits.

Use the keyword `PUBLIC` if a DTD is for general use. In similar instances, associations, branches of industry and the like have published their DTDs in order to arrive at a common standard for XML data.

Public DTDs are defined in a slightly different way:

```
<!DOCTYPE Name_of_Root_Element PUBLIC "DTD_Name" "DTD_URL">
```


The name of the root element and the DTD_URL are entered in the usual way. The new feature is the name of the DTD (DTD_Name). For the generalized use of DTDs the DTD is assigned a unique name which the XML processor uses to download the DTD. If this fails, the procedure falls back on the URL of the DTD.

4.2.4 Multiple DTDs

You can also attach several DTDs to an XML document. If, say, you are using an external DTD that you did not create personally in your own XML document and need to declare some more elements, there is no need for you to rewrite the whole of the DTD!

Suppose that someone has kindly created a DTD called `Person.dtd` which is just what you need and you are allowed to use it:

```
<!ELEMENT Person (Last_Name, First_Name+, Job_Title,
Street, City/Town, Date_of_Birth, Telephone_Number*,
Mobile_Number*)>
  <!ELEMENT Last_Name (#PCDATA)>
  <!ELEMENT First_Name (#PCDATA)>
  <!ELEMENT Job_Title (#PCDATA)>
  <!ELEMENT Street (#PCDATA)>
  <!ELEMENT City_Town (#PCDATA)>
  <!ELEMENT Date_of_Birth (#PCDATA)>
  <!ELEMENT Telephone_Number (#PCDATA)>
  <!ELEMENT Mobile_Number (#PCDATA)>
```

You now insert this DTD as usual into your XML document, but with the difference that you insert the element declarations you still need in `<!DOCTYPE>`.

The external DTD `Person` is known as an external DTD subset and the DTD you insert is known as an internal DTD subset.

```
<?xml version="1.0" standalone="no"?>
<!DOCTYPE Company SYSTEM "Person.dtd" [
  <!ELEMENT Name_Company (#PCDATA)>
    <!ELEMENT Department (Name_Department, Person+)>
      <!ELEMENT Name_Department (#PCDATA)>
]>
<Company>
  <Name_Company> ComputerSoftware plc</Name_Company>
  <Department>
    <Name_Department> Management</Name_Department>
    <Person>
...
```

Warning If the declarations overlap, perhaps intentionally in order to overwrite the imported declarations with your own, or perhaps unintentionally, only the declaration loaded first remains valid and the other one is ignored.

In the above example your own DTD comes second and would be ignored in this situation. In order to make sure that your own DTD remains valid you should separate the internal and external DTD subsets:

```
<?xml version="1.0" standalone="no"?>
<!DOCTYPE Company [
  <!ELEMENT Name_Company (#PCDATA)>
    <!ELEMENT Department (Name_Department, Person+)>
      <!ELEMENT Name_Department (#PCDATA)>
]>
<!DOCTYPE Company SYSTEM "Person.dtd">
<Company>
  <Name_Company> ComputerSoftware plc</Name_Company>
  <Department>
    <Name_Department> Management</Name_Department>
    <Person>
...
```

In this case your DTD will definitely be read first and your declarations remain valid.

4.3 Attribute declaration

In the previous chapter you learnt that you can also add attributes to elements. Just as with elements, attributes are also subject to DTD rules and you have to include in the DTD every attribute that you intend to use, but not every attribute declared in the DTD necessarily has to appear in the XML document.

4.3.1 Declaring attributes

You declare attributes with the aid of the declaration `<!ATTLIST>`. This must be in the following form:

```
<!ATTLIST Element_Name Attribute_Name Data_Type Default_
Value>
```

The element name is the name for which the attribute was declared, and the attribute name is the name of the declared attribute. The data type is the possible type of data which the attribute can assume. In the DTD you can choose one of 10 data types: CDATA, ID, IDREF, IDREFS, ENTITY, ENTITIES, NMTOKEN, NMTOKENS, NOTATION and a list attribute. The default value is either the value which the attribute receives when no other value is assigned, or one of the following default values #REQUIRED, #IMPLIED, #FIXED

The attribute declaration is valid only for the element concerned. If, for example, more than one element contains the attribute Name, it must be individually defined for each element in its own <!ATTLIST> declaration. The sequence is not important in this declaration, even if you declare the attribute first followed by the element. You may even declare an attribute more than once, but only the attribute declared first remains valid.

If an element has more than one attribute, these can be declared in a single <!ATTLIST> declaration. When doing so you must separate the values as follows:

```
<!ATTLIST Element_Name
   Attribute_Name Data_Type Default_Value
   Attribute_Name Data_Type Default_Value
   Attribute_Name Data_Type Default_Value
>
```

Here is an example: You have an empty element Triangle with the length of its three sides and its color as attributes. Let's use for this example the data type CDATA, which can contain character data as determined in the element declaration.

```
<!ELEMENT Triangle EMPTY>
<!ATTLIST Triangle
   SideA CDATA "12cm"
   SideB CDATA "8cm"
   SideC CDATA "15cm"
   Color CDATA "red"
>
```

We have now declared an empty element that possesses the attributes `SideA`, `SideB`, `SideC` and `Color`. Unless you subsequently assign other values to the element, it retains the values that we have declared as its default values.

4.3.2 Default value #REQUIRED

As you know, not every attribute that has been declared must necessarily be defined. However, if you use the default value `#REQUIRED`, the XML processor demands the value and returns an error if it is missing.

```
<!ELEMENT Triangle EMPTY>
<!ATTLIST Triangle
   SideA CDATA #REQUIRED
   SideB CDATA #REQUIRED
   SideC CDATA #REQUIRED
   Color CDATA #REQUIRED
>
```

This alteration makes the attributes forget their specific values and you are obliged to input the values required.

4.3.3 Default value #IMPLIED

When you use the default value `#IMPLIED` things behave differently. This default value demands no information and can even be left unspecified.

```
<!ELEMENT Triangle EMPTY>
<!ATTLIST Triangle
   SideA CDATA #REQUIRED
   SideB CDATA #REQUIRED
   SideC CDATA #REQUIRED
   Color CDATA #IMPLIED
>
```

If you change the default value of the attribute `Color` you are not required to enter any value here. There is not even any need to use it at all. The default values for `SideA`, `SideB` and `SideC` have not been changed because they are important to the definition of a triangle, and the XML processor would indeed not return an error, but in certain circumstances the specifications would give a meaningless result. You can also see that you are allowed to mix default values.

4.3.4 Default value #FIXED

If you declare an attribute with the default value `#FIXED`, the element receives an attribute with a fixed value. This has to be declared in a slightly different way:

```
<!ATTLIST Element_Name Attribute_Name Data_Type #FIXED
Default_Value>
```

This value can then no longer be changed. It does not even have to be specified at the same time, since it is automatically added to the element.

```
<!ELEMENT Triangle EMPTY>
<!ATTLIST Triangle
   SideA CDATA #FIXED "10cm"
   SideB CDATA #REQUIRED
   SideC CDATA #REQUIRED
   Color CDATA #IMPLIED
>
```

By changing the default value of attribute `SideA`, the `Triangle` element automatically receives this attribute with the value `10cm` assigned.

4.3.5 Attribute type CDATA

In the example of the default values we were working with the attribute type `CDATA`. This attribute type allows all characters with just one or two exceptions. The forbidden characters are the "less-than" sign (<), the double quotation mark (") and the ampersand (&). If you need these characters you must insert them either with the aid of the relevant entity reference or as a Unicode value.

4.3.6 The list attribute

A list attribute is not so much an attribute type as a list of possible specific values for the attribute. This list separates the individual possibilities with a vertical bar and returns a value by default if no other value is specified.

```
<!ATTLIST Element_Name Attribute_Name (X|Y) "X">
```

In this case you have only two values to choose from, `X` and `Y`; unless you specify otherwise, the attribute will be automatically transferred to the element and assigned the value `X`.

```
<!ELEMENT Triangle EMPTY>
<!ATTLIST Triangle
```

```
    SideA CDATA #FIXED "10cm"
    SideB CDATA #REQUIRED
    SideC CDATA #REQUIRED
    Color (red|yellow|green) "red"
>
```

In our triangle example you have the option to choose from three colors. There is no maximum number of options.

4.3.7 Attribute types NMTOKEN and NMTOKENS

The attribute type `NMTOKEN` is basically the `CDATA` attribute type, but it restricts the possible attribute values still further. The permitted characters here are only the same as those which may be used in an XML name. An `NMTOKEN` value must start with a letter or an underscore. The rest of the characters can be letters, numbers, underscores, hyphens and points. Similarly it must not contain spaces or colons.

```
<!ATTLIST Element_Name Attribute_Name NMTOKEN Default_
Value>
```

It is also possible to input a list of possible values separated by spaces instead of an individual value. To do this you need to use the plural form of the attribute type, `NMTOKENS`.

4.3.8 Attribute type ID

Attribute type `ID` is used to identify an element unambiguously. For this you must give the attribute a name which must not appear a second time or more as `ID`. If you use the `ID` more than once, the XML processor returns an error. The name must begin with a letter and may contain letters, numbers and underscores. The name must not include a space. Additionally the attribute type `ID` needs the default value `#REQUIRED`. No other values are allowed.

```
<!ELEMENT Triangle EMPTY>
<!ATTLIST Triangle
    SideA CDATA #FIXED "10cm"
    SideB CDATA #REQUIRED
    SideC CDATA #REQUIRED
    Color (red|yellow|green) "red"
    Number ID #REQUIRED
>
```

You can now use this `Number` to identify a particular `Triangle` element from among many, for example.

4.3.9 *Attribute types IDREF and IDREFS*

In combination with attribute type `ID` you can use attribute types `IDREF` and `IDREFS` to provide a link between elements where none exists already through the XML tree structure.

Here is a further example: We shall take our previously declared empty `Triangle` element and a new empty `Rectangle` element which are related to one another in a graphic.

```
<?xml version="1.0" standalone="yes"?>
<!DOCTYPE Graphic [
<!ELEMENT Graphic (Triangle*, Rectangle)>
   <!ELEMENT Triangle EMPTY>
   <!ELEMENT Rectangle EMPTY>
<!ATTLIST Triangle
   SideA CDATA #FIXED "10cm"
   SideB CDATA #REQUIRED
   SideC CDATA #REQUIRED
   Color (red|yellow|green) "red"
   Number ID #REQUIRED>
<!ATTLIST Rectangle
   SideA CDATA #REQUIRED
   SideB CDATA #REQUIRED
   SideC CDATA #REQUIRED
   SideD CDATA #REQUIRED
   Color #FIXED "black"
   Triangle IDREFS #REQUIRED>
]>
<Graphic>
  <Triangle SideB="4cm" SideC="8cm" Number="d1"/>
  <Triangle SideB="7cm" SideC="7cm" Color="green" Num-
ber="d2"/>
  <Rectangle SideA="7cm" SideB="7cm" SideC="6cm"
SideD="6cm" Triangle="d1 d2"/>
</Graphic>
```

We have created a link between the triangles and the rectangle. You have now also learnt how it differs from `IDREF`. `IDREFS` is the plural form of `IDREF` and you separate multiple values with a space. If your rectangle has to be linked to a large number of triangles, it would probably be easier if you gave the rectangle the `ID` attribute and entered the `IDREF` attribute of the rectangle in each of the triangles, rather than entering all the `ID`s for the triangles in the rectangle.

4.3.10 Attribute types ENTITY and ENTITIES

You can use an ENTITY attribute to incorporate external binary data into your XML document. The value of this attribute type corresponds to the name of the unparsed entity which we have defined with the aid of the <!ENTITY> declaration.

Tip The procedure for declaring entities and especially the unparsed entities will be explained in more detail in the "Entities" section.

```
<!ATTLIST Entity_Name Attribute_Name ENTITY #REQUIRED>
```

The plural form of the attribute ENTITY is ENTITIES. In this the names of the ENTITIES separated by spaces are entered as values for the attribute.

```
<!ATTLIST Entity_Name Attribute_Name ENTITIES #REQUIRED>
```

Warning The incorporation of non-XML data is not yet supported by the majority of XML browsers.

4.3.11 Attribute type NOTATION

Attribute NOTATION specifies that the value of this attribute is the name of a notation that has been declared with the aid of <!NOTATION> in the DTD. You need notations in order to use non-XML data in your XML document.

```
<!ATTLIST Entity_Name Attribute_Name NOTATION #REQUIRED>
```

Tip The procedure for declaring notations will be explained in more detail in the "Entities" section under Notations.

4.3.12 xml:lang

The attribute xml:lang is an attribute predefined by XML and can be used in any element. It indicates the language of the element concerned. This is particularly advantageous in multilingual documents. The standard language identifier in each case is currently represented as two letters; however, these do not give enough options to include all languages. The attribute declaration looks like this:

```
<!ATTLIST Element_Name xml:lang NMTOKEN Default Value>
```

The language then applies to the element and all its child elements.

If you want to assign a language to an element, simply insert the attribute `xml:lang` complete with language code (`ISO_639_Identifier`) in the appropriate element:

```
<Name_of_Element xml:lang="language_code"> ... </
Name_of_Element>
```

You can also define a language for yourself, but the language code must then begin with `X-`.

Language code	Language	Language code	Language
ar	Arabic	ga	Irish
bg	Bulgarian	hu	Hungarian
cs	Czech	is	Icelandic
da	Danish	it	Italian
de	German	ja	Japanese
el	Greek	no	Norwegian
en	English	pl	Polish
es	Spanish	pt	Portuguese
fi	Finnish	sv	Swedish
fr	French	tr	Turkish

Table 4.3 ***Excerpt from ISO 639***

4.3.13 xml:space

The attribute `xml:space` is also an attribute predefined by XML and can be used in any element. It can take either of two values and is declared as follows:

```
<!ATTLIST Element_Name xml:space(default|preserve)"pre-
serve">
```

XML understands the significance of whitespace, such as spaces, carriage returns or tabulator characters, and forwards these to the relevant program as well, but the programs themselves handle whitespace characters in very different ways unless they are specially told otherwise.

Value	Description
`preserve`	Whitespace is transferred to the program concerned as important.
`default`	No further significance is attached to the whitespace.

4.3.14 DTD for the personnel file with attributes

For our personnel file in attribute style the DTD looks like this:

```
<?xml version="1.0" standalone="yes"?>
<!DOCTYPE Company [
<!ELEMENT Company (Department*|Person+)>
  <!ELEMENT Department (Person+)>
    <!ELEMENT Person EMPTY>
<!ATTLIST Company Name CDATA #REQUIRED>
<!ATTLIST Department Name CDATA #REQUIRED>
<!ATTLIST Person
   Last_Name CDATA #REQUIRED
   First_Name CDATA #REQUIRED
   Job_Title CDATA #REQUIRED
   Street CDATA #REQUIRED
   City_Town CDATA #REQUIRED
   Date_of_Birth CDATA #REQUIRED
   Telephone_Number CDATA #IMPLIED
   Mobile_Number CDATA #IMPLIED
]>
<Company Name="ComputerSoftware plc">
  <Department Name="Management">
    <Person City_Town="Doncaster DN1 AB2"
Date_Of_Birth="07.19.69" First_Name="Carl"
JobTitle="Managing Director" Last_Name="Computer"
Mobile_Number="0799 2266551" Street="10 Eastfield"
Telephone_Number="01234 56789"/>
    </Person>
    <Person City_Town="Mansfield" DN40 B56"
Date_Of_Birth="05.12.67" First_Name="Hanna"
JobTitle="Secretary" Last_Name="Harebell"
Mobile_Number"0799 2266552" Street="12 Moon Street"
Telephone_Number="01235 67890"/>
    </Person>
  </Department>
```

4 START UP!

4.4 Entities

In the previous chapter you found out a few things about well-formed XML documents and got to know entity references. We explained that there are only five predefined entity references. Now you will learn how to define entities for yourself.

4.4.1 Internal entities

When using internal entities you can define short cuts that you can use later on in your XML document as internal entity references. To define such an entity reference, insert an <!ENTITY> tag in your DTD containing the name of the reference and the text that you want to replace.

```
<!ENTITY CoSo "ComputerSoftware plc">
```

It is important that the text to be substituted is in quotation marks since it can also contain spaces. The name of the tag is the text that you want to use later in order to call out the reference. No special characters other than underscores are allowed in the name and a distinction is made between upper and lower case.

Entities are declared in the same way as element declarations in the DTD:

```
<!DOCTYPE Company [
  <!ENTITY CoSo "ComputerSoftware plc">
  <!ELEMENT Name_Company (#PCDATA)>
    <!ELEMENT Department (Name_Department, Person+)>
      <!ELEMENT Name_Department (#PCDATA)>
]>
```

An entity reference consists of an ampersand (&), the name of the entity and a closing semicolon (;). This entity reference is then simply inserted like the five predefined entity references into an XML element that permits parsed character data (#PCDATA) or everything (ANY).

```
...
<Company>
  <Name_Company>&CoSo;</Name_Company>
  <Department>
    <Name_Department> Management</Name_Department>
    <Person>
...
```

One of the great advantages of these entity references can be appreciated when there is frequently used data. If a value changes there is no need to change it x times in the document, because you just change it once in the DTD.

4.4.2 External entities

When using external entities you can define entire XML documents as external entity references. You can then use a short cut to add all the details about a person into the actual XML document, for instance:

```
<?xml version="1.0"?>
<Person>
  <Last_Name>Computer</Last_Name>
  <First_Name>Carl</First_Name>
  <Job_Title>Managing Director</Job_Title>
  <Street>10 Eastfield</Street>
  <City_Town>Doncaster DN1 AB2</City_Town>
  <Date_of_Birth>07.19.69</Date_of_Birth>
  <Telephone_Number>01234 56789</Telephone_Number>
  <Mobile_Number>0799 2266551</Mobile_Number>
</Person>
```

External entities are formed in the same way as internal entities:

```
<!ENTITY CComputer SYSTEM "Person.xml">
```

This assumes that the XML document is in the same folder. If this is not the case, you will need to enter a relative or absolute path at this point.

A reference to an external entity is formed in the same way as an internal entity reference:

```
...
<Company>
  <Name_Company>&CoSo;</Name_Company>
  &Ccomputer;
<Company>
```

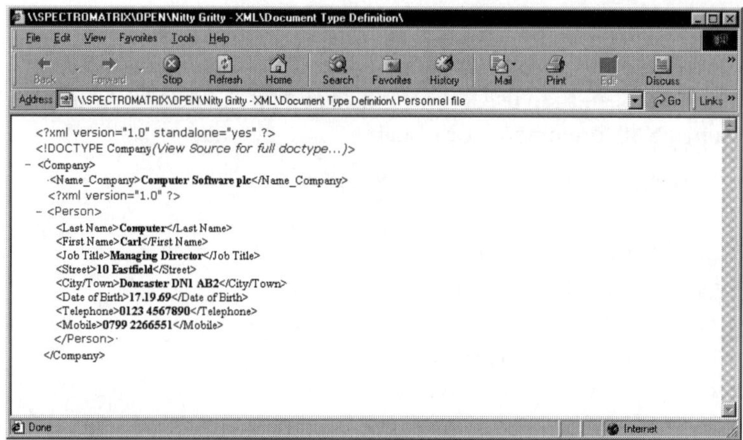

Figure 4.4 ***The personnel file using a relocated XML document***

4.4.3 Internal parameter entities

When using internal parameter entities you can even use entity references within your DTD short cuts. They differ from ordinary internal entities and their references only in that they need a percentage sign with your definition (`%`):

```
<!ENTITY % Name "Text">
```

Also the reference begins with a percentage sign (`%`) rather than an ampersand. Here is a conceivable example:

```
<!ENTITY % PCD "(#PCDATA)">
  <!ELEMENT Last_Name %PCD>
  <!ELEMENT First_Name %PCD>
  <!ELEMENT Job_Title %PCD>
  <!ELEMENT Street %PCD>
  <!ELEMENT City_Town %PCD>
  <!ELEMENT Date_of_Birth %PCD>
  <!ELEMENT Telephone_Number %PCD>
  <!ELEMENT Mobile_Number %PCD>
```

Tip However, you have to define parameter entities before you can use them. With other entities it was different, since the XML processor reads in the whole DTD anyway before examining the XML document.

4.4.4 External parameter entities

As you saw in the section on multiple DTDs, you can extend a DTD by means of an internal and an external DTD subset. In very large documents, however, that may well be too unsightly. You can use external parameter entities just as you would normal external entities to insert relocated document sections into the DTD (in this case a part of the DTD).

The principle is the same as for ordinary external entities, but with a slightly altered definition: they need a percentage sign with your definition (`%`):

```
<!ENTITY % Name SYSTEM "URL_DTD">
```

This assumes that the DTD is in the same folder. If this is not the case, you will need to enter a relative or absolute path at this point.

A reference to an external parameter entity is formed in the same way as an internal parameter entity reference:

```
...
<!ENTITY % Person SYSTEM "Person.dtd">
%Person;
...
```

Tip However, you have to define parameter entities before using them. With other entities it was different, since the XML processor reads in the whole DTD anyway before examining the XML document.

4.4.5 Notations

Not all data exists in XML format. Unparsed entities and the different elements available do not make it possible to insert such data into an XML document. Since in principle XML does not recognize any other data format, you have to make it understand.

Warning This method of identifying non-XML files is at the present time not properly supported, if at all.

A notation is declared in the DTD. It consists of the tag `<!NOTATION>` and contains the name that will be used subsequently for such file types, and the URL for the location of the program that handles this file type. Instead of a URL you can enter an `externalID` that describes this file type.

```
<!NOTATION Name SYSTEM "URL/externalID">
```

4.4.6 *Unparsed entities*

You can use `Notation` to incorporate unparsed entities into your XML document. This entity is also formed in the same way as ordinary entities and parameter entities:

```
<!ENTITY Name SYSTEM "URL" NDATA Name_of_Notation>
```

In addition to the name that you want this entity reference to have, and the location where the file resides, it also needs the keyword `NDATA` (Notation Data) along with the name given in the notation.

To insert an unparsed entity reference into your XML document, you have to declare an empty element together with an attribute containing only the name of the entity reference, so that later on you will have an empty element for the entity reference alone:

```
<Name_Empty_Element Name_Attribute="Name_Entity_Reference"/
>
```

4.5 Including and ignoring sections

You know how to comment out sections of an XML source text. In a DTD you can not only use comments for this purpose but also the declaration `<![ IGNORE [ ]]>`, which does the same job:

```
<![ IGNORE [
  DTD section that you wish to be omitted/ignored
]]>
```

If you use `<![ IGNORE [ ]]>` you can ignore any declarations of elements, attributes and entities you choose, even including `<![ IGNORE [ ]]>` blocks. Just as when you comment out XML elements, you must always comment out the entire declaration.

There is also the declaration `<![ INCLUDE [ ]]>`. This makes sure that a section is included:

```
<![ INCLUDE [
  DTD section that you wish to be included
]]>
```

However, an `INCLUDE` declaration does not take precedence over an `IGNORE` declaration. This means that an `INCLUDE` declaration incorporated into an `IGNORE` declaration will actually be ignored.

The use for this declaration is not yet obvious, so please have a look at this example. You define a parameter entity for `IGNORE`:

```
<!ENTITY % INIG "IGNORE">
```

You then use this in an `IGNORE` declaration:

```
<![ %INIG [
...
    Declarations
...
]]>
```

Now just by converting the parameter entity to `INCLUDE` you can once again include the ignored block in the DTD without having to make large scale changes to the DTD. An example such as this is useful for DTDs that are frequently used, but at the same time some documents in this section either have no need for it or are disrupted by it.

CSS and XSL and XSLT

As already mentioned, you can use XML to structure the data in your document but not how you want it to be displayed. As a result the majority of XML documents are not particularly attractive to look at. Internet Explorer displays your data in the form of a tree structure. Netscape 6 and Opera 5 show no structure at all and reproduce XML documents as running text.

Since XML is not responsible for how data should be displayed, you need a stylesheet with formatting rules for each separate element. The stylesheet then instructs your browser how to display each element, and in this way affects how your XML document will look.

You have three options for formatting data written in XML. One is known as Cascading Stylesheets (CSS). The others are known as Extensible Stylesheet Language (XSL) and XSL Transformation (XSLT). CSSs are simpler than XSL or XSLT as far as syntax is concerned, but less powerful.

5.1 CSS

Cascading Stylesheets have been available ever since HTML began. Their formatting capabilities work with both HTML and XML. However, XML elements are much better suited to CSS formatting than HTML elements since you can assign rules to any element in XML, whereas HTML allows this only for the elements `P`, `PRE`, `LI`, `DIV` and `SPAN`.

CSS syntax is really so simple that we shall give you only a brief introduction to it at this point. You can then try out the other features and options for yourself with the aid of the reference material.

5.1.1 Attaching and defining a stylesheet

A cascading stylesheet is saved to a file of its own with the extension .css. Make sure that you save the file in pure text format without including any form of control character whatsoever.

To attach a stylesheet to your XML document, use the stylesheet declaration `<?xml-stylesheet ?>` within your XML document.

```
<?xml-stylesheet href="file" type="text/css"?>
```

The attribute `href` defines the stylesheet file. Just quote the file name and extension if the file is in the same folder as the XML document. If this is not the case, use a relative or absolute path at this point. The type of stylesheet is defined by the attribute `type`, and in this example `text/css` stands for a cascading stylesheet. And that is all you need to include in your XML document in order to attach a stylesheet.

To define a stylesheet, first give the element name and then write the stylesheet rule within curly brackets ({ }). A rule consists of two things. The first is the keyword that describes the rule, in effect the type of formatting. The second is the value which the keyword can take, separated by a colon.

```
Element name
  {
  Keyword:Value
  }
```

You can even assign more than one formatting property to an element by separating the rules by a semicolon and listing all the rules you need.

```
Element name {
  Keyword:Value;
  Keyword:Value;
  Keyword:Value;
...}
```

The various stylesheets for the elements are simply listed one below the other and then saved as a stylesheet with the file extension .css.

5.1.2 *Font family, font size and font color*

The keywords for font family, font size and font color are `font-family`, `font-size` and `color`. To format a text you have to assign values to these keywords.

Here is an example:

```
<?xml version="1.0" standalone="yes"?>
<?xml-stylesheet type="text/css" href="example1.css"?>
<ROOT>
   <A00>serif 18pt red</A00>
   <B00>italic 14pt green</B00>
   <C00>fantasy 24pt blue</C00>
</ROOT>
```

Here is an example of how you can assign three elements one stylesheet each:

```
A00 {
  font-family:serif;
  font-size:18pt;
  color:red;}
B00 {
  font-family:italic;
  font-size:14pt;
  color:green;}
C00 {
  font-family:fantasy;
  font-size:24pt;
  color:blue;}
```

Ideally your output is in color. In all other respects it should look like Figure 5.1.

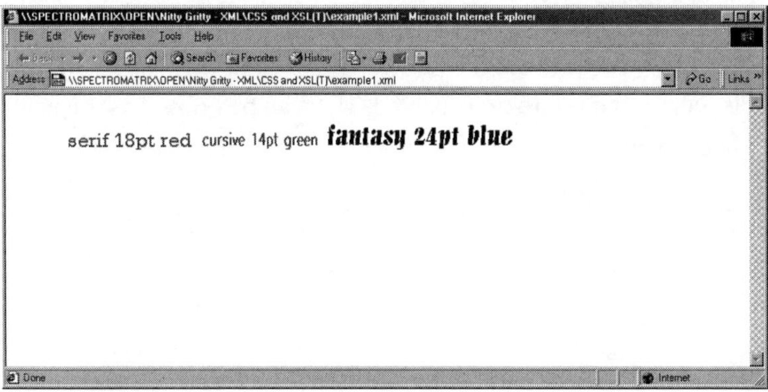

Figure 5.1 ***Font formatting***

5.1.3 CSS units

The above example used certain units for the keyword values. These values vary according to the type of value required.

Some keywords need units of quantity such as inch, centimeter, millimeter, point and pica.

	Unit	Inch	Centimeter	Millimeter	Point	Pica
Inch	in	1.00	2.54	25.40	72.00	6.00
Centimeter	cm	0.39	1.00	10.00	28.35	4.72
Millimeter	mm	0.04	0.10	1.00	2.83	0.47
Point	pt	0.01	0.04	0.35	1.00	0.83
Pica	pc	0.17	0.42	4.23	12.00	1.00

Table 5.1 ***Absolute specifications***

Numerical fractions always use a point as the decimal separator, not a comma as is customary in some countries.

You can also specify the size using quantities which are relative to a particular element of the browser display.

Unit	Effect
em	Refers to the width of the letter m in the current font.
ex	Refers to the height of the letter x in the current font.
px	Specifies the size in pixels, the smallest units on your screen.
%	Refers to a percentage of the element size.

Table 5.2 ***Relative specifications***

Other keywords require a color to be specified. This can be quoted as the name of the color in English, as a decimal or hexadecimal value, or as a percentage.

Color	English value	Decimal value	Hexadecimal value	Percentage
Black	black	rgb(0,0,0)	#000000	rgb(0%,0%, 0%)
White	white	rgb(255,255,255)	#FFFFFF	rgb(100%, 100%,100%)
Red	red	rgb(255,0,0)	#FF0000	rgb(100%,0%,0%)
Green	green	rgb(0,128,0)	#008000	rgb(0%,50%, 0%)

Color	English value	Decimal value	Hexadecimal value	Percentage
Blue	blue	rgb(0,0,255)	#0000FF	rgb(0%,0%, 100%)
Yellow	yellow	rgb(255,255,0)	#FFFF00	rgb(100%, 100%,0%)

Table 5.3 ***Extract from a color table***

5.1.4 Position

The keywords `top`, `right`, `bottom` and `left` are used in conjunction with the keyword `position` to define the absolute or relative position of an element. Please amend your stylesheet as follows:

```
A00,B00,C00 {
  position:absolute;}
A00 {
  top:15%;
  left:1cm;
  font-family:serif;
  font-size:18pt;
  color:red;}
B00 {
  top:5cm;
  left:30%;
  font-family:italic;
  font-size:14pt;
  color:green;}
C00 {
  top:15mm;
  left:90%;
  font-family:fantasy;
  font-size:24pt;
  color:blue;}
```

Assigning the value `absolute` to the keyword `position` gives you an absolute position for the element in relation to the edge of the browser. Using absolute values for the keywords `top` and `left` would also give you absolute values, but due to using some relative sizes, namely percentages, the distance is recalculated every time the size of the browser window changes.

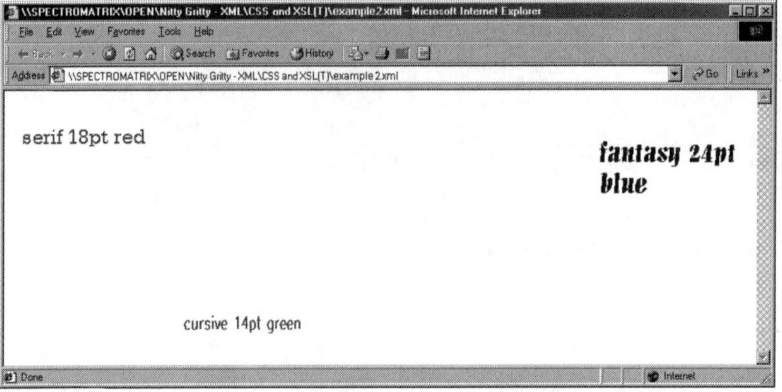

Figure 5.2 ***Example showing the use of position specifications***

5.1.5 Selectors

You have already used a selector in the previous example. With the aid of selectors you can assign the same stylesheet to more than one element at the same time.

```
A00,B00,C00 {
  position:absolute;}
```

This instruction assigns the keyword `position` to all three elements. In this way you can summarize certain standard properties of several or even all elements in a single instruction without having to carry out the same step for each element individually.

5.1.6 Background

The following example shows among other things how the very same stylesheet definition can appear differently from one browser to another. Add the following line to your stylesheet:

```
ROOT {background-color: silver;}
```

This line assigns a background color to the element concerned. This background color should normally extend only over the area of the element in each case. Since the root element in fact contains no characters, Internet Explorer displays the page precisely as defined, that is without a background color. On the other hand Netscape 6 interprets this stylesheet as the background for the whole document. Even if you completely clear the root element and even delete the child element it adopts the background color.

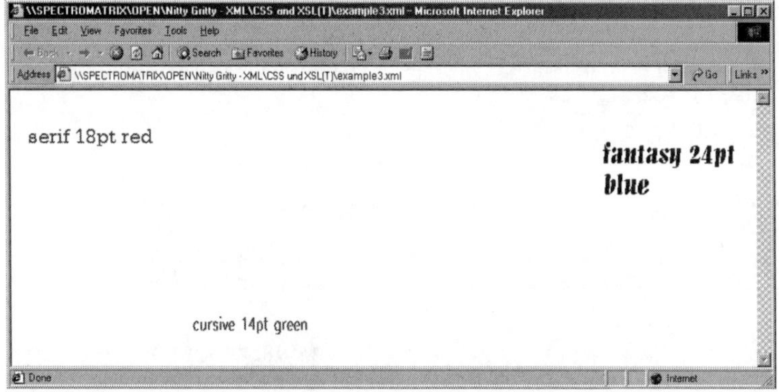

Figure 5.3 ***Example of the background in Internet Explorer***

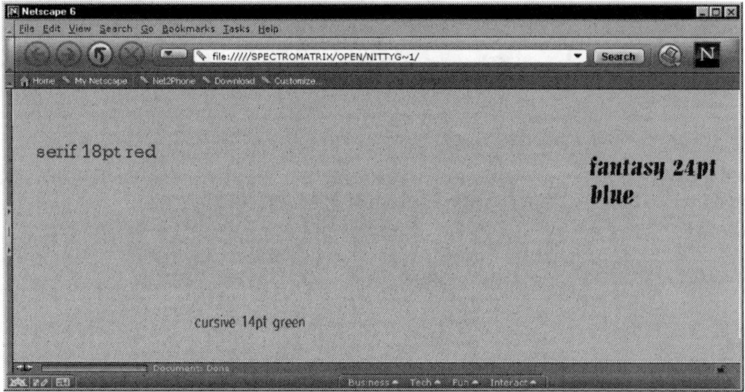

Figure 5.4 ***Example of the background in Netscape 6***

Now delete the stylesheet for the root element and change the selector:

```
A00,B00,C00 {
  background-color: silver;
  position:absolute;}
```

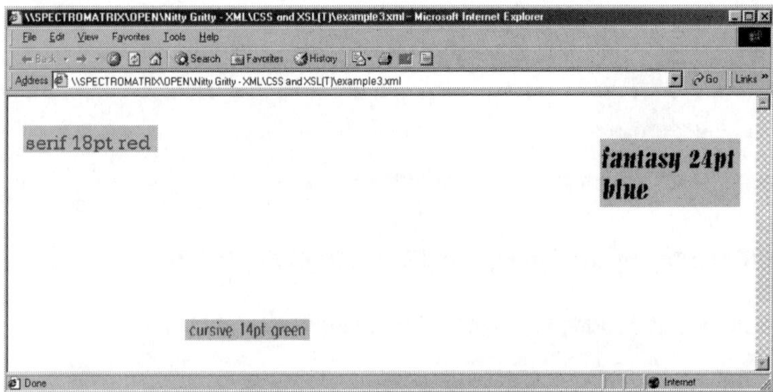

Figure 5.5 *Example of an amended background in Internet Explorer*

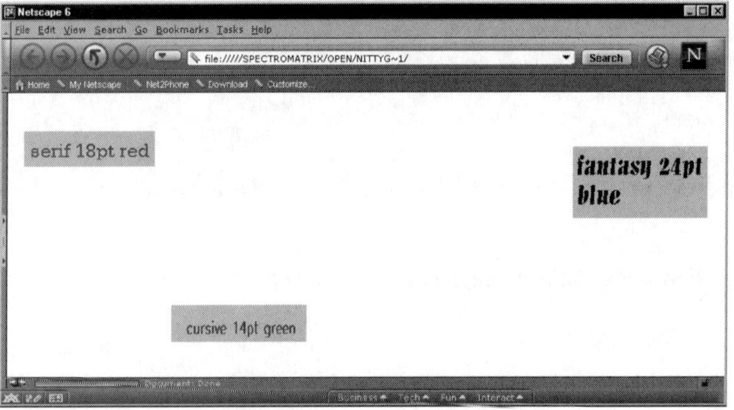

Figure 5.6 *Example of an amended background in Netscape 6*

Now both browsers look the same again. This sort of difference in the way stylesheets are interpreted may well crop up. You should therefore always test your results on more than one browser.

5.1.7 Comments

You can also enter comments in CSS stylesheets. These are not formed in the same way as in XML documents, which use `<!--` and `-->`, but in the way you would enter a remark or comment in programming language C, using `/*` and `*/`.

```
/* This is a comment */
```

5.2 XSLT

This section will show you the essential features of XSLT. You can use the transformation area of XSL, known as XSLT, to replace one tag by another. For instance you can transform an XML document into perfectly written HTML code. To be precise it is the style of XML that Internet Explorer supports. In fact you can use all HTML tags in conjunction with XSL in this way.

As was the case with CSS stylesheets, this section concentrates only on the essentials because full coverage of XSLT stylesheets would go far beyond the bounds of this book. However, if you make use of these basic facts and the reference section in this book you will have no problem getting further into the subject.

5.2.1 Attaching a stylesheet

XSLT stylesheets are every bit as easy to attach as CSS stylesheets.

An XSLT stylesheet is saved to a file with the extension .xsl. Make sure that you save the file in pure text format without including any form of control character whatsoever.

To attach a stylesheet to your XML document, use the stylesheet declaration `<?xml-stylesheet ?>` within your XML document.

```
<?xml-stylesheet href="file" type="text/xsl"?>
```

The attribute `href` defines the stylesheet file. Just quote the file name and extension if the file is in the same folder as the XML document. If this is not the case, use a relative or absolute path at this point. The type of stylesheet is defined by the attribute `type`, and in this example `text/xsl` stands for an XSLT stylesheet. And that is all you need to include in your XML document in order to attach a stylesheet.

5.2.2 Defining a stylesheet

In the case of XSLT stylesheets it is not enough just to enter the individual instructions in a text file. It is also important to keep to the rules that apply to validly written XML documents. An XSLT stylesheet is therefore also a properly constructed XML document. The best way to start is with a really simple stylesheet:

```
<?xml version="1.0"? encoding="ISO-8859-1">
<xsl:stylesheet xmlns:xsl="http://www.w3.org/TR/WD-xsl">
  <xsl:template match="/">
    <HTML>
      <HEAD>
        <TITLE>Personnel file ComputerSoftware plc</TITLE>
      </HEAD>
      <BODY>
        The information in the file will be displayed here
      </BODY>
    </HTML>
  </xsl:template>
</xsl:stylesheet>
```

An XSLT stylesheet is an XML document in all respects, so it begins with an XML declaration, but in the case of an XSLT stylesheet you also have to use an XSL namespace.

Now we should take a look at the two new elements. One of these is the root element of an XSLT stylesheet `<xsl:stylesheet>`. It includes amongst other things the location for the definition of the XSL namespace.

Tip Internet Explorer requires this namespace in order to display XSL stylesheets.

The other is the element `<xsl:template>`, which is the actual formatting instruction to the elements in the XML document. Each `xsl:template` element possesses a `match` attribute defining the input document area. The value of the attribute is `"/"` which in this case defines the root element of the XML document.

Now save your document and look at the result. If you view the stylesheet in Internet Explorer, you will once again recognize the familiar tree structure that you have already seen in a validly written XML document.

But the only way you can see the actual effects of the stylesheet is to view the XML document to which the XSLT stylesheet has been applied.

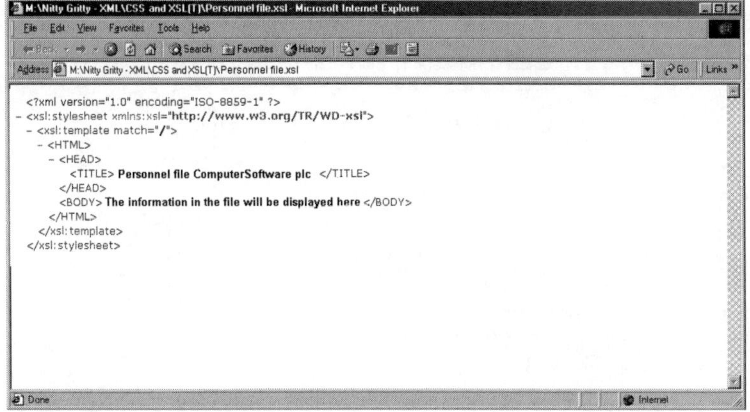

Figure 5.7 ***The tree structure of the XSLT stylesheet***

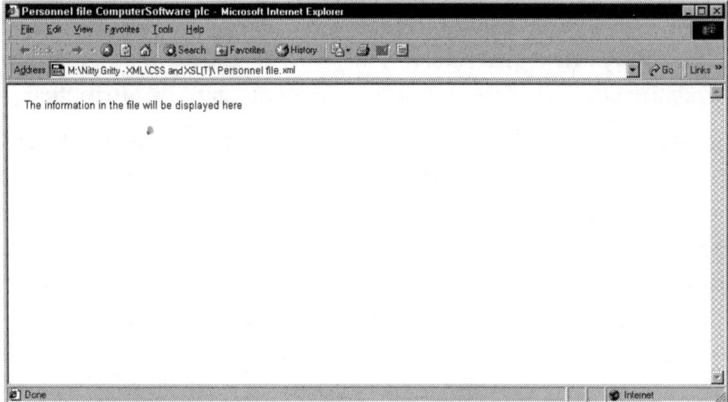

Figure 5.8 ***The personnel file when this XSLT stylesheet is used***

5.2.3 *Choosing elements and attributes*

In the previous section you certainly created an XSLT stylesheet, but so far you have seen none of the data from the XML document. To put this right the first step is to choose the data you want to display. The data includes an example of a personnel list in attribute style. A quick reminder: When a CSS stylesheet was being used the XML document looked the way it appears in Figure 5.9.

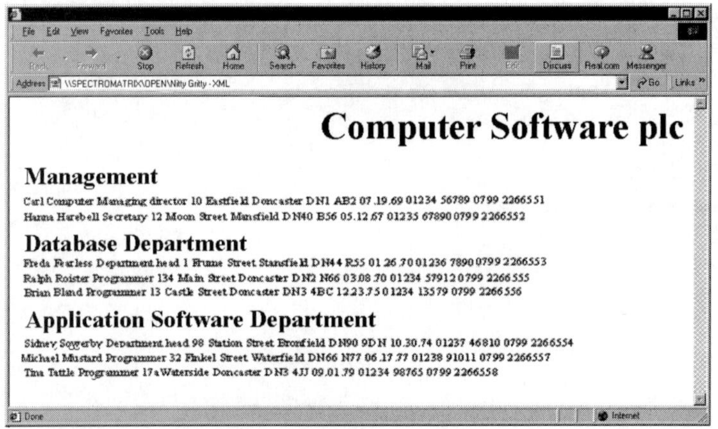

Figure 5.9 ***The personnel file when the CSS stylesheet is used***

If you had used the CSS stylesheet on the personnel list in attribute style, you would have had an empty browser screen for output. This is because the CSS stylesheet affects only the content of the individual elements, not the attributes.

To capture the data, use the two XSL elements `<xsl:value-of/>` and `<xsl:for-each>`. The empty element `<xsl:value-of/>` determines the content of the elements which are controlled by formatting. But the definition of the first of these two elements applies only to the output of an individual XML element, which is why you need the element `<xsl:for-each>`. This element repeats the selection for all the elements defined by `select`.

```
<?xml version="1.0" encoding="ISO-8859-1"?>
<xsl:stylesheet xmlns:xsl="http://www.w3.org/TR/WD-xsl">
  <xsl:template match="/">
    <HTML>
      <HEAD>
        <TITLE>
          <xsl:for-each select="Company">
            <xsl:value-of select="@Name"/>
          </xsl:for-each>
        </TITLE>
      </HEAD>
      <BODY>
          <xsl:for-each select="Company">
            <xsl:value-of select="@Name"/>
          </xsl:for-each>
          <xsl:for-each select="Company/Department">
            <xsl:value-of select="@Name"/>
```

```
            <xsl:for-each select="Person">
              <xsl:value-of select="@First_Name"/>
              <xsl:value-of select="@Last_Name"/>
              <xsl:value-of select="@Job_Title"/>
              <xsl:value-of select="@Street"/>
              <xsl:value-of select="@City_Town"/>
              <xsl:value-of select="@Date_of_Birth"/>
              <xsl:value-of select="@Telephone_Number"/>
              <xsl:value-of select="@Mobile_Number"/>
            </xsl:for-each>
        </xsl:for-each>
      </BODY>
    </HTML>
  </xsl:template>
</xsl:stylesheet>
```

As you can see, if you use `<xsl:for-each>` to select elements, you must also specify the individual tree elements in the form if a path (`Company/Department`) before you can work with the elements you want. For so long as the `for-each-element` remains open you stay within this element and can use another `for-each-element` to access the next child element.

Another difference with respect to CSS is that you can also use `<xsl:value-of/>` elements to access the attributes of XML elements. To access an attribute, prefix the name of the attribute with an `@` sign.

As the result shows, you have certainly retrieved all the data but there is still no formatting.

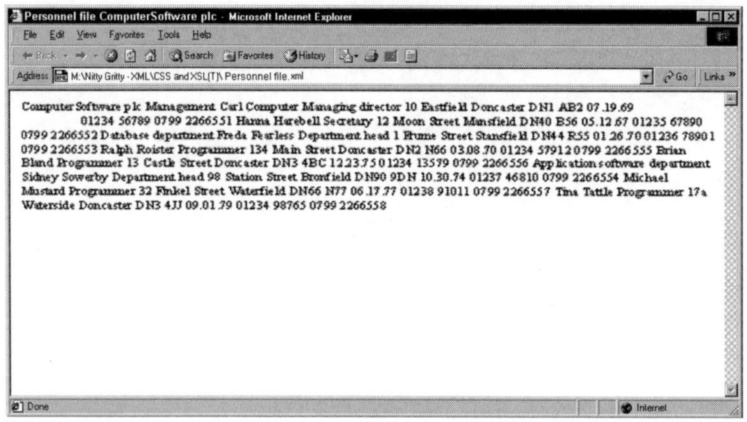

Figure 5.10 ***The unformatted personnel file produced by the XSLT stylesheet***

5.2.4 *Attaching HTML formatting*

As previously mentioned, you can use any and every HTML tag. For this reason it is useful to change your stylesheet a little, as shown below. You can then display the same contents in a number of different ways.

```
<?xml version="1.0" encoding="ISO-8859-1"?>
<xsl:stylesheet xmlns:xsl="http://www.w3.org/TR/WD-xsl">
  <xsl:template match="/">
    <HTML>
      <HEAD>
        <TITLE>
          <xsl:for-each select="Company">
            <xsl:value-of select="@Name"/>
          </xsl:for-each>
        </TITLE>
      </HEAD>
      <BODY>
        <xsl:for-each select="Company">
          <H1 ALIGN="RIGHT">
            <xsl:value-of select="@Name"/>
          </H1>
        </xsl:for-each>
        <TABLE>
          <THEAD>
            <TR>
              <TH>FIRST_NAME</TH>
              <TH>LAST_NAME</TH>
              <TH>JOB_TITLE</TH>
              <TH>DEPARTMENT</TH>
              <TH>STREET</TH>
              <TH>CITY/TOWN</TH>
              <TH>DATE_OF_BIRTH</TH>
              <TH>TELEPHONE_NUMBER</TH>
              <TH>MOBILE_NUMBER</TH>
            </TR>
          </THEAD>
          <TBODY>
            <xsl:for-each select="Company/Department/Per-
son">
              <TR>
                <TD >
                  <xsl:value-of select="@First_Name"/>
```

```
                </TD>
                <TD>
                  <xsl:value-of select="@Last_Name"/>
                </TD>
                <TD>
                  <xsl:value-of select="@Job_Title"/>
                </TD>
                <TD>
                  <xsl:value-of select="../@Name"/>
                </TD>
                <TD><xsl:value-of select="@Street"/></TD>
               <TD><xsl:value-of select="@City_Town"/></TD>
                <TD>
                  <xsl:value-of select="@Date_of_Birth"/>
                </TD>
                <TD>
                 <xsl:value-of select="@Telephone_Number"/>
                </TD>
                <TD><xsl:value-of select="@Mobile_Number"/
></TD>
              </TR>
            </xsl:for-each>
          </TBODY>
        </TABLE>
      </BODY>
    </HTML>
  </xsl:template>
</xsl:stylesheet>
```

Note that you have to access the parent element in order to access the attribute belonging to the element Department. You can do this by specifying a path:

```
<xsl:value-of select="../@Name"/>
```

To access a child element, simply complete the path specification.

```
<xsl:value-of select="Name_Child Element"/>
```

Or in the case of an attribute:

```
<xsl:value-of select="Name_Child_Element/@Name_Attribute"/>
```

The HTML tag best suited to formatting your XML data is `<div>`. It is so good for the reason that it has no formatting of its own and you therefore have a free hand to format the element. Here is an example:

```
...
<xsl:for-each select="Company">
  <div style="font-size: 32pt; color:black; text-
align:right">
    <xsl:value-of select="@Name"/>
  </H1>
</xsl:for-each>
...
```

The HTML tag <span> is very similar to the <div> tag except that it does not provide a line break.

It is also important for the HTML code to be fully valid. As mentioned in the case of XML documents, your browser will not permit the slightest error in this case either.

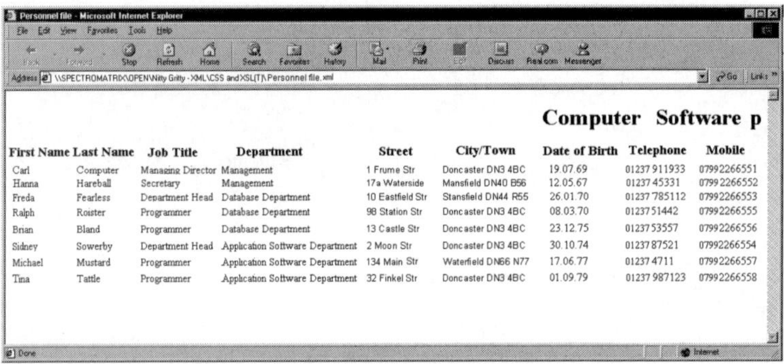

First Name	Last Name	Job Title	Department	Street	City/Town	Date of Birth	Telephone	Mobile
Carl	Computer	Managing Director	Management	1 Frume Str	Doncaster DN3 4BC	19.07.69	01237 911933	07992266551
Hanna	Hareball	Secretary	Management	17a Waterside	Mansfield DN40 B56	12.05.67	01237 45331	07992266552
Freda	Fearless	Department Head	Database Department	10 Eastfield Str	Stansfield DN44 R55	26.01.70	01237 785112	07992266553
Ralph	Roister	Programmer	Database Department	98 Station Str	Doncaster DN3 4BC	08.03.70	01237 51442	07992266555
Brian	Bland	Programmer	Database Department	13 Castle Str	Doncaster DN3 4BC	23.12.75	01237 53557	07992266556
Sidney	Sowerby	Department Head	Application Software Department	2 Moon Str	Doncaster DN3 4BC	30.10.74	01237 87521	07992266554
Michael	Mustard	Programmer	Application Software Department	134 Main Str	Waterfield DN66 N77	17.06.77	01237 4711	07992266557
Tina	Tattle	Programmer	Application Software Department	32 Finkel Str	Doncaster DN3 4BC	01.09.79	01237 987123	07992266558

Figure 5.11 ***The personnel file displayed as a table***

If you think that you could have got the same result just by using HTML, see what happens when you alter the following line.

```
<xsl:for-each select="Company/Department/Person" order-by"+
@Job_Title">
```

You can use this method to sort the table by any of the criteria you wish. You would have had to completely rewrite an HTML document and the actual XML data would not have changed.

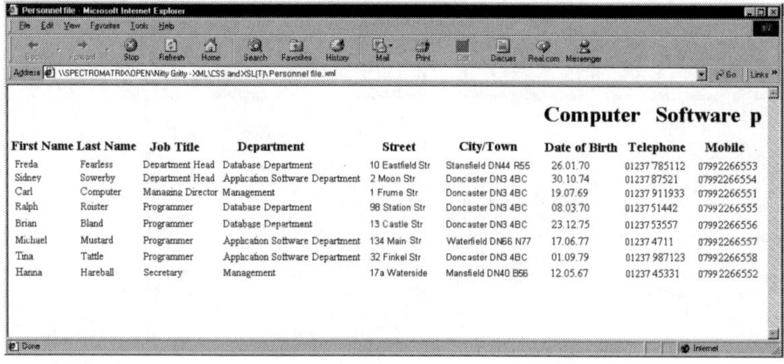

Computer Software p

First Name	Last Name	Job Title	Department	Street	City/Town	Date of Birth	Telephone	Mobile
Freda	Fearless	Department Head	Database Department	10 Eastfield Str	Stansfield DN44 R55	26.01.70	01237 785112	07992266553
Sidney	Sowerby	Department Head	Application Software Department	2 Moon Str	Doncaster DN3 4BC	30.10.74	01237 87521	07992266554
Carl	Computer	Managing Director	Management	1 Frume Str	Doncaster DN3 4BC	19.07.69	01237 911933	07992266551
Ralph	Roister	Programmer	Database Department	98 Station Str	Doncaster DN3 4BC	08.03.70	01237 51442	07992266555
Brian	Bland	Programmer	Database Department	13 Castle Str	Doncaster DN3 4BC	23.12.75	01237 53557	07992266556
Michael	Mustard	Programmer	Application Software Department	134 Main Str	Waterfield DN66 N77	17.06.77	01237 4711	07992266557
Tina	Tattle	Programmer	Application Software Department	32 Finkel Str	Doncaster DN3 4BC	01.09.79	01237 987123	07992266558
Hanna	Hareball	Secretary	Management	17a Waterside	Mansfield DN40 B56	12.05.67	01237 45331	07992266552

Figure 5.12 ***The personnel file sorted by job title***

5.2.5 Inserting JavaScript

You can also insert JavaScript in an XSLT stylesheet. Simply include the content within a `<![CDATA[ ]]>` section. Please amend your stylesheet as follows:

```
<?xml version="1.0" encoding="ISO-8859-1"?>
<xsl:stylesheet xmlns:xsl="http://www.w3.org/TR/WD-xsl">
  <xsl:template match="/">
    <HTML>
      <HEAD>
        <TITLE>
          <xsl:for-each select="Company">
            <xsl:value-of select="@Name"/>
          </xsl:for-each>
        </TITLE>
        <script language="JavaScript">
          <![CDATA[
            function Greetings()
              {
                alert("Hello XML!");
              }
          ]]>
        </script>
      </HEAD>
      <BODY onLoad="Greetings()">
...
```

Now when you open your XML document a little pop-up window will greet you.

5 START UP!

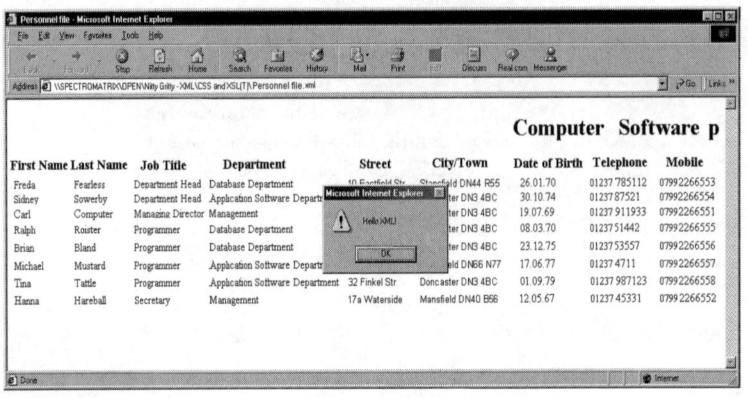

Figure 5.13 *The personnel file with JavaScript*

5.3 XSL

The second part of XSL is the formatting language. This is another instance of an XML application that describes how you want the contents of an XML document to be output. XSL carries out its formatting role with the aid of features known as formatting objects. Among other things these include footnotes, margin notes and page numbers with cross-referencing. Whereas CSS and XSLT are chiefly intended for web applications, formatting objects have been designed for a broader range of options. In due course an XSL stylesheet will be able to define the layout of an entire book.

The expression "in due course" was deliberately chosen because XSL formatting objects, or `XSL-FO` for short, are not yet a valid standard and in fact are still being worked on. Actually there are only a very few programs and as yet no browser which can support formatting objects and display documents containing them. For this reason the next section just gives a brief overview without going into detail.

5.3.1 Formatting objects

XSL-FO is very comprehensive and consists at the present time of 51 formatting objects with an even greater number of properties. Most of these 51 formatting objects relate to various kinds of rectangular areas or their containers. The whole formatting model is based on *areas*. These are rectangular areas which can contain text, blank space and other formatting objects. Formatting objects differ mainly in their content and are divided into a hierarchy of four types of rectangular areas:

- Area containers
- Block areas
- Line areas
- Inline areas

An area container is the highest level of container in XSL. It can be precisely positioned and can contain smaller area containers or a number of block areas.

A block area represents a block element and can also contain further block areas. Block areas are inserted sequentially into an area container. If another container is inserted or removed before or after a container, it changes its position accordingly.

A line area represents a line of text within a block area and can contain inline areas.

An inline area is part of a line area, for example an individual character or a mathematical formula. Inline areas can also contain further inline areas.

5.3.2 The namespace

Like an XSLT stylesheet, an XSL-FO also needs a special namespace. This is saved to `http://www.w3.org/XSL/Format/1.0`:

```
<xsl:stylesheet
  xmlns:xsl="http://www.w3.org/TR/WD-xsl"
..xmlns:fo="http://www.w3.org/XSL/Format/1.0"
  result-ns="fo">
```

5.3.3 Formatting properties

Formatting objects define the sequence in which content will be stored on the various pages of an XSL document. However, the details are determined by the properties of the formatting objects. Formatting properties are handled like attributes of the individual formatting objects. Many of these attributes are also used by CSS stylesheets. Efforts are being directed toward standardizing attribute names in CSS and XSL stylesheets so that attributes with the same name are identical in both.

XLink

6

One of the advantages of HTML is that different documents, texts, points in texts, etc. can be combined together. This is also possible in XML. Here, XLink undertakes this task. In XML, you will learn about two kinds of links: simple links and extended links. The simple link undertakes the same task as a link in HTML, but the extended XLink differs greatly from the HTML link. There is a further difference from HTML in that XLink is not yet supported by the browsers.

6.1 XLink attributes

In addition to the division into the simple and the extended XLink, the extended link is again divided into four groups. More on this later. What is important right now is that different attributes are necessary (N) or optional (O), depending on the type of link:

	simple	***extended***	***locater***	***arc***	***resource***	***title***
type	N	N	N	N	N	N
href	O		N			
role	O	O	O		O	
arcrole	O			O		
title	O	O	O	O	O	
show	O			O		
actuate	O			O		
from				O		
to				O		

Table 6.1 ***Attributes in XLink***

The attribute `type` is the only thing that has to appear for all link elements. It determines the nature of the link and can thereby assume the values: `simple`, `extended`, `locater`, `arc`, `resource` and `title` .

An href attribute, on the other hand, is needed only by the link element locater and takes as its value an address input.

The attributes role, arcrole and title are a description of the function of the link and title.

The attributes show and actuate determine how the link behaves. The following values are possible for the attribute show :

new	Opens a new window.
replace	Replaces the old contents of the browser window.
embed	Shows the contents of the link in the old document.
undefined	Leaves the choice of behavior to the application.

Table 6.2 ***Values of the attribute: show***

actuate can also assume several values:

onLoad	The link is loaded automatically.
OnRequest	The link waits for a request.
undefined	Leaves the loading to the application.

Table 6.3 ***Values of attribute: actuate***

The attributes from and to nominate from where to where you can jump. They are allowed only in the arc element.

6.2 Namespace

The XLink also needs its own namespace. This is located under http://www.w3.org/1999/xlink and is defined in the usual way:

```
<Element xmlns:xlink="http://www.w3.org/1999/xlink">
  ...
  Contents
  ...
</Element>
```

6.3 Simple link

Before a link can be used, it also has to be declared in the DTD with all its attributes, and this is done in the usual way:

```
...
<!ELEMENT alink (#PCDATA)>
<!ATTLIST alink
  xlink:type CDATA #FIXED "simple"
  xlink:href CDATA #REQUIRED
  xlink:title CDATA #IMPLIED
  xlink:show (new|replace|embed|undefined) #IMPLIED
  xlink:actuate (onLoad|onRequest|undefined) "onRequest">
...
```

Once this is done, the link can be embedded in the XML document, but without the attribute `xlink:type`, because, in the declaration, we have already set this attribute to `#FIXED` and have thereby defined a simple link:

```
...
<alink xmlns:xlink="http://www.w3.org/1999/xlink"
  xlink:href="http://www.myDomain.co.uk/my.xml"
  xlink:title="XML rules!"
  xlink:show="new"
  xlink:actuate="onRequest">
Here is a link!
</alink>
...
```


6.4 Extended link

Extended links are actually an improvement on an HTML link.
By contrast with the simple XLinks and the HTML links, extended links can combine more than one resource. One of the special features of extended links is as follows:

- ➔ It is possible to set up references from read-only media, for instance, the data on a CD ROM, to other media.
- ➔ It is also possible to generate links from and to data which itself does not support any linking.

You can recognize extended links from the value: `extended` of the attribute `xlink:type`. This XLink element also contains further child elements. They have the attribute values `locator`, `arc`, `title` and `resource`.

type value	Description
locator	Localizes a remote resource.
arc	Defines the jump rules.
title	Describes the XLink.
resource	Localizes a local resource.

Table 6.4 ***Further attribute values of xlink:type***

To set up an extended link, it must again be declared in the DTD; when you do this, don't forget to declare its child elements too:

```
...
<!ELEMENT alink (anotherlink+)>
<!ELEMENT anotherlink (#PCDATA)>
<!ATTLIST alink
  xlink:type CDATA #FIXED "extended"
  xlink:title CDATA #IMPLIED
  xlink:show (new|replace|embed|undefined) #IMPLIED
  xlink:actuate (onLoad|onRequest|undefined) "onRequest">
<!ATTLIST anotherlink
  xlink:type CDATA #FIXED "locater"
  xlink:role CDATA #IMPLIED
  xlink:title CDATA #IMPLIED
...
```

First of all, the extended (`extended`) link is created and then the child elements are added to this element, enabling several resources to be operated.

```
...
<alink xmlns:xlink="http://www.w3.org/1999/xlink"
  xlink:title="XML rules!"
  xlink:show="new"
  xlink:actuate="onRequest">
    <anotherlink
      xlink:href="http://www.myDomain.co.uk/my.xml"
      xlink:role="co.uk"/>
    <anotherlink
      xlink:href="http://www.myDomain.ac.uk/my.xml"
      xlink:role="ac.uk"/>
    <anotherlink
      xlink:href="http://www.myDomain.com/my.xml"
      xlink:role="com"/>
</alink>
```

Embedding the child elements also makes it possible to access various resources via a link. In reality, it is not yet clear right now how such a link is achieved.

7 XHTML

XHTML is the abbreviation of `Extensible Hypertext Markup Language`. The very name XHTML hints at a similarity with HTML.

7.1 What is XHTML?

XHTML is an attempt by W3C to rewrite HTML in XML code.
So XHTML 1.0 is a reformulation of the HTML 4 standard into an XML 1.0 application. Its contents are intended to be XML compliant and to be capable of running on HTML 4 compliant browsers provided a few rules are observed.

7.2 Strictly compliant documents

In order to be both XML compliant and capable of being viewed on HTML 4 compliant browsers, XHTML must observe a few rules:

1. It must check out against one of the three DTDs, in other words it must be valid:
   - XHTML 1.0 Strict
   - XHTML 1.0 Transitional
   - XHTML 1.0 Frameset
2. The root element must be `<html>`.
3. The standard namespace must be defined in the root element as http://www.w3.org/1999/xhtml.
4. The DTD must be declared before the root element by defining the `PUBLIC-DTD`. The `SYSTEM-DTD` may be changed.

```
<!DOCTYPE html
  PUBLIC "-//W3C/DTD XHTML 1.0 Strict//EN"
  "DTD/xhtml1-strict.dtd
<!DOCTYPE html
  PUBLIC "-//W3C/DTD XHTML 1.0 Transitional//EN"
  "DTD/xhtml1-transitional.dtd
<!DOCTYPE html
  PUBLIC "-//W3C/DTD XHTML 1.0 Frameset//EN"
  "DTD/xhtml1-frameset.dtd
```

Here is some typical syntax:

```
<?xml version="1.0" encoding="UTF-8"?>
<!DOCTYPE html
  PUBLIC "-//W3C/DTD XHTML 1.0 Strict//EN"
  "DTD/xhtml1-strict.dtd">
<html xmlns="http://www.w3.org/1999/xhtml" xml:lang="en">
  <head>
    <title>Hello World!</title>
  </head>
  <body>
    <h1>Hello World!</h1>
  </body>
</html>
```


This screen should look familiar to you:

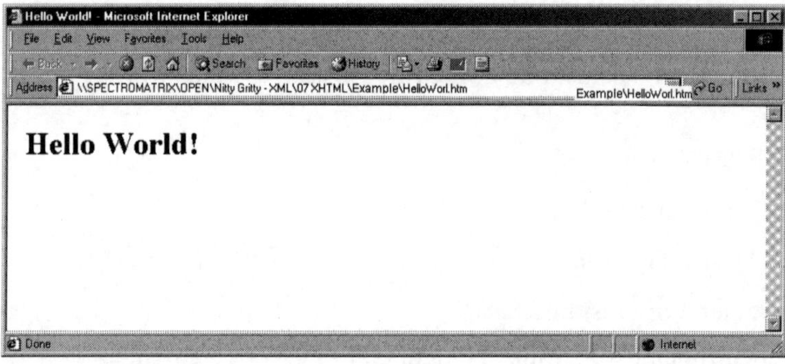

Figure 7.1 ***Hello World! in XHTML***

7.3 Differences compared to HTML 4

An XHTML document must also meet the requirements of XML, so you must give up the "bad habits" of HTML. If you have never worked with HTML that will probably be easy.

7.3.1 XHTML documents must be well-formed

As in the case of an XML document, an XHTML document must also be properly constructed, or well-formed. This means you must nest the elements correctly.

```
<h2>This line is <h1>wrongly nested!</h2></h1>
<h2>And this line is <h1>correctly nested!</h1></h2>
```

Also every starting tag that is not an empty element must have a corresponding closing tag.

7.3.2 Element and attribute names

Since XML distinguishes between upper and lower case, all attribute names and element names must be written in lower case.

7.3.3 Element restrictions

The following elements have a restriction regarding which elements they are allowed to contain:

Element	Restriction
`a`	`a`
`pre`	`img, object, big, small, sub and sup`
`button`	`input, select, textarea, label, button, form, fieldset, iframe and isindex`
`label`	`label`
`form`	`form`

Table 7.1 ***Element restrictions***

These restrictions apply to all dependent elements.

7.3.4 Attribute values

Attribute values that are not written in quotation marks are not permitted in XML and neither is attribute minimizing. Therefore these are also forbidden in XHTML. The following syntax must be strictly observed:

```
Attributename="value"
```

7.3.5 *Script elements and style elements*

Since script elements and style elements are declared in XHTML with a #PCDATA value, you should among other things not use the characters "<" and "&" Instead of replacing such characters with the aid of entities you should use a CDATA section.

```
<script>
  <![CDATA[
    Content
  ]]>
</script>
```

Another consists of using external script documents and style documents.

7.3.6 *The attributes ID and name*

In HTML 4 you can assign not only the attribute `ID` but also the attribute `name` in order to identify an element. This is not the case in XML, where as you know, only the attribute `ID` is used. In XHTML 1.0 both these are possible at the moment in order to retain compatibility with HTML. However, from now on it would be better to use the attribute `ID`, since the `name` attribute will probably be dropped in a forthcoming version of XHTML.

7.4 Future developments

XHTML provides the basis for document types intended to enhance and subdivide XHTML. This will enable many new devices and applications to be supported. The use of modularity will make the following functionalities possible, among others:

- ➔ XHTML support for handheld devices and mobile telephones.
- ➔ Moves to enhance and/or subdivide XHTML.
- ➔ Simplify transformation between document types.
- ➔ Encourage the reuse of modules in new document types.

Part II

Take that!

Quick reference guide for XML

XML gains from its expandability, but at the same time there are virtually no predefined elements that can be summarized in a quick reference guide. This section therefore tries to explain the main features of XML as concisely as possible.

8.1 XML declaration

An XML declaration must be in the following form:

```
<!xml version="1.0">
```

The attribute `version` stands for the XML specification you are using. An XML declaration can contain other attributes as well as the `version` attribute:

Attribute	Description
`encoding`	Description of the character set you are using.
`standalone`	Defines whether the Document Type Definition (DTD) is located in a separate file or in the XML document itself.

Table 8.1 ***Attributes in the XML declaration***

8.2 Elements

An element consists of a starting tag, its content and a closing tag. The starting and closing tags must have the same name.

```
<Name> Content </Name>
```

The name of an element must start with a letter or an underscore. The rest of the name can consist of letters, numbers, underscores, hyphens and points. The name must not include a space or a colon. Similarly all names beginning with `xml` or `XML` are forbidden because they are reserved for subsequent XML names and designations.

8.3 Root element

A root element covers all the other elements since XML allows only one element at the highest level. The same rules that apply to ordinary elements also apply to the root element.

```
<Name_Root_Element>
...
Content
...
</Name_Root_Element>
```

8.4 Attributes

The content of any element can also include additional attributes. Attributes are a name-value pair and always form part of the starting tag.

```
<Element_name Attribute_name="value"> ...
```

An element can always possess more than one attribute; attributes must be separated by a space and their names must be unique within the element concerned.

The name of an attribute, like that of an element, must start with a letter or an underscore. The rest of the name can consist of letters, numbers, underscores, hyphens and points. The name must not include a space or a colon. Similarly all names beginning with `xml` or `XML` are forbidden because they are reserved for subsequent XML names and designations.

8.5 Empty elements

Empty elements consist of a starting tag only, which has to be in the following form:

```
<Name_Empty_Element/>
```

An empty element has no contents of its own but can contain attributes.

The name of an empty element must start with a letter or an underscore. The rest of the name can consist of letters, numbers, underscores, hyphens and points. The name must not include a space or a colon. Similarly all names beginning with `xml` or `XML` are forbidden because they are reserved for subsequent XML names and designations.

8.6 CDATA section

The XML processor handles the contents of a CDATA section as plain text. These contents are not examined for the possible presence of XML instructions.

```
<![CDATA[
...
Content
...
]]>
```

The only string of characters that a CDATA section is not allowed to contain is the closing tag]]>.

8.7 Internal DTD

The Document Type Definition, or DTD for short, defines the rules to which the elements and attributes in an XML document must adhere. An internal DTD has to be located ahead of the root element. Enter the actual content of the DTD between square brackets.

```
<!xml version="1.0" standalone="yes">
<!DOCTYPE Name_Root_Element [
  ...
  DTD content
   ...
]>
<ROOT>
  ...
  XML content
  ...
</ROOT>
```

8.8 External DTD

The Document Type Definition, or DTD for short, defines the rules to which the elements and attributes in an XML document must adhere. Save an external DTD to a file with the extension .dtd. In this case simply enter the address of the DTD ahead of the root element.

```
<!xml version="1.0" standalone="no">
<!DOCTYPE Name_Root_Element SYSTEM "URL">
<ROOT>
  ...
  XML content
  ...
</ROOT>
```

8.9 Public DTD

The Document Type Definition (DTD) defines the rules to which the elements and attributes in an XML document must adhere. Save a public DTD to a file with the extension .dtd. In this case simply enter the name and address of the DTD ahead of the root element.

```
<!xml version="1.0" standalone="no">
<!DOCTYPE Name_Root_Element PUBLIC "Name_DTD" "URL">
<ROOT>
  ...
  XML content
  ...
</ROOT>
```

8.10 DTD subsets

The Document Type Definition, or DTD for short, defines the rules to which the elements and attributes in an XML document must adhere. Besides internal and external DTDs you can also mix both DTD types. They are then internal and external DTD subsets. Show the internal DTD subset in square brackets. Create a link to an external DTD for the external DTD subset.

```
<!xml version="1.0" standalone="yes">
<!DOCTYPE Name_Root_Element PUBLIC "Name_DTD" "URL"[
  ...
  Internal DTD subset content
   ...
]>
<ROOT>
  ...
  XML content
  ...
</ROOT>
```

If the two DTD subset declarations overlap, only the one declared first is valid. For this reason the instructions are also separable.

8.11 Element declaration

For your XML document to be valid you must declare in the DTD every element you intend to use in the document.

```
<!ELEMENT Name_Element RULE>
```

Rule	Description
`ANY`	The content of the element can be another element, any string of characters, or both.
`EMPTY`	Elements with this rule are empty elements.
`(#PCDATA)`	The content of the element cannot be anything other than a freely chosen character string (Parsed Character Data).
`(Name_Element)`	The content of this element can be another element.

Table 8.2 ***Rules when declaring elements***

If the contents of an element consist of parsed character data or other elements, you can link them to a logical operation. You can do this by means of an AND operation:

```
<!ELEMENT Name_Element (X,Y)>
```

or by means of an OR operation:

```
<!ELEMENT Name_Element (X|Y)>
```

Logical operation	Description
`And (X,Y)`	An AND operation specifies that the elements in brackets occur in precisely that sequence.
`Or (X|Y)`	An OR operation chooses only one of the elements in brackets.
`And/Or (X,(Y|Z))`	By skillful use of brackets you can create an AND/OR operation.

Table 8.3 ***Options for logical operations using AND / OR***

You can use indicators or repetition operators to bring about repeated occurrences of elements.

```
<!ELEMENT Name_Element (X+,Y)*>
```

Indicator	Description
?	The element occurs not at all or once only.
+	The element occurs once or more than once.
*	The element occurs more than once, once only, or not at all.

Table 8.4 *Possible indicators for elements*

8.12 Attribute declaration

For your XML document to be valid you must declare in the DTD every attribute you intend to use in the document.

```
<!ATTLIST Element_Name Attribute_Name Data_Type
Default_Value>
```

All the attributes for an element can also be declared in an instruction:

```
<!ATTLIST Element_Name
  Attribute_Name Data_Type Default_Value
  Attribute_Name Data_Type Default_Value
  Attribute_Name Data_Type Default_Value
>
```

The data type specifies what sort of data is allowed as the value for an attribute:

Data type	Description
CDATA	Parsed character data.
enumerated	A list of values from which only one will be chosen.
ENTITY	An entity declared in the DTD.
ENTITIES	Multiple entities separated by a space.
ID	A unique element character.
IDREF	The value of an element ID.
IDREFS	Multiple element IDs separated by a space.
NMTOKEN	An XML name token.
NMTOKENS	Multiple XML name tokens separated by a space.
NOTATION	A notation declared in the DTD.

Table 8.5 *Possible data types for attributes*

A standard value can be entered as the default value.

```
<!ATTLIST Element_Name Attribute_Name Data_Type "standard
value">
```

If a standard value is not suitable, one of the following default values can be used:

Modifier	Description
#REQUIRED	The value of the attribute must be specified with the element.
#IMPLIED	The value of the attribute can be left unspecified.
#FIXED "X"	The value of the attribute is defined, will be quoted with the attribute declaration and from then on cannot be changed by the user.

Table 8.6 ***Possible attribute modifiers***

8.13 Entity reference

An entity reference consists of an ampersand, the name of the entity and a semicolon. You can use one of the five predefined entity references in place of the following characters:

Entity reference	Character
&	&
<	<
>	>
"	"
'	'

Table 8.7 ***Predefined entities***

8.14 Internal entities

When using internal entities you can define short cuts that you can use later on in your XML document as internal entity references.

```
<!ENTITY Entity_Name "any_text">
```

An entity reference consists of an ampersand, the name of the entity and a semicolon.

8.15 External entities

When using external entities you can define entire XML documents as external entity references.

```
<!ENTITY Entity_Name SYSTEM "XML_file">
```

This assumes that the XML document is in the same folder. If this is not the case, you will need to enter a relative or absolute path at this point.

8.16 Internal parameter entities

When using internal parameter entities, you can even use entity references within your DTD short cuts.

```
<!ENTITY % Entity_Name "any_text">
```

This sort of reference begins with a percentage sign (%) rather than an ampersand. You have to define parameter entities before you can use them.

8.17 External parameter entities

You can use external parameter entities to insert DTD components into your DTD.

```
<!ENTITY % Entity_Name SYSTEM "URL_DTD">
```

This assumes that the DTD is in the same folder. If this is not the case, you will need to enter a relative or absolute path at this point.

This sort of reference begins with a percentage sign (%) rather than an ampersand. You have to define parameter entities before you can use them.

8.18 Unparsed entities

You can use notation to incorporate unparsed entities, that is to say non-XML files, into your XML document.

```
<!ENTITY Entity_Name SYSTEM "URL_ File" NDATA Name_Notation>
```

This assumes that the file is in the same folder. If this is not the case, you will need to enter a relative or absolute path at this point.

8.19 Notations

A notation simply links the value of an NDATA keyword to the specific information that the unparsed entity is intended to use.

```
<!NOTATION Name SYSTEM "URL/externalID">
```

8.20 IGNORE section

If you use `<![IGNORE [ ]]>` you can ignore any declarations of elements, attributes or entities you choose. Just as when you comment out XML elements, you must always comment out an entire declaration.

```
<![ IGNORE [
  DTD section that you wish to be omitted/ignored
]]>
```

8.21 INCLUDE

Use an `<![ INCLUDE [ ]]>` declaration to make sure that a section is incorporated into the DTD:

```
<![ INCLUDE [

  DTD section that you wish to be included

]]>
```

However, an `INCLUDE` declaration does not take precedence over an `IGNORE` declaration. This means that an `INCLUDE` declaration incorporated into an `IGNORE` declaration will actually be ignored.

8.22 Comments

The contents of comments are handled as if they are not there. This fact can be used, for example, to write yourself reminders or to comment out sections of your XML document or DTD.

```
<!--
...
  Contents of a comment
...
-->
```

A comment which comments out an area must always consist of a complete XML element or a DTD declaration.

Quick reference guide for XSLT

This XSLT quick reference guide should help you get acquainted with the more extensive features of XSLT and write sophisticated XSLT stylesheets. Together with the earlier introduction to XSLT, we hope that we have answered most of the questions that you had when you first looked into XSLT.

9.1 xsl:apply-imports

This XSLT element lets you form an XML element complete with all its child elements with the aid of an imported stylesheet rule.

```
<xsl:apply-imports/>
```

9.2 xsl:apply-templates

This lays down that the child elements of a specific XML element are to be processed further.

```
<xsl:apply-templates/>
```

Use a `select` attribute to choose a particular element from among the child elements of the specified XML element.

```
<xsl:apply-templates select="Sample"/>
```

9.3 xsl:attribute

This XSLT element adds an attribute complete with a value to the current XML element.

```
<xsl:attribute name="Name_Attribute">
  Value_Attribute
</xsl:attribute>
```

9.4 xsl:attribute-set

Use this to insert one or more formatting attributes which can then be used by means of a formatting object.

```
<xsl:attribute-set name="Value">
...
Formatting attributes
...
</xsl:attribute-set>
```

9.5 xsl:call-template

Selects an XML element by its name.

```
<xsl:call-template name="Value"/>
```

9.6 xsl:choose

In conjunction with XSL elements `xsl:when` and `xsl:otherwise`, this element provides a means of carrying out conditional tests.

```
<xsl:choose>
  <xsl:when test="Value">
    ...
  </xsl:when>
  <xsl:otherwise>
    ...
  </xsl:otherwise>
</xsl:choose>
```

9.7 xsl:comment

This XSLT element inserts a comment into your XML document.

```
<xsl:comment>... Comment ...</xsl:comment>
```

This comment is then inserted in an XML document as follows:

```
<!-- ... Comment ... -->
```

9.8 xsl:copy

Copies the current element into the output.

```
<xsl:copy> ... </xsl:copy>
```

The attribute `use-attribute-sets` enables formatting previously defined with the element `<xsl:attribute-set>` to be used.

```
<xsl:copy use-attribute-set="Name"> ... </xsl:copy>
```


9.9 xsl:copy-of

This element copies the elements selected by `select`.

```
<xsl:copy-of select="Path/Name"/>
```

9.10 xsl:element

This XSLT element creates an XML element in the resulting document.

```
<xsl:element name="Name"> ... </xsl:element>
```

Possible attributes:

Attribute	*Description*
`namespace`	Defines the namespace for the element.
`use-attribute-sets`	Uses formatting previously defined with `<xsl:attribute-set>`.

Table 9.1 ***Possible attributes with*** `<xsl:element>`

9.11 xsl:fallback

This XSLT element guarantees the downward compatibility of XSL stylesheet instructions.

```
<xsl:fallback> ... </xsl:fallback>
```

9.12 xsl:for-each

This XSLT element enables you to select between all identical peer elements that correspond to the attribute value for `select`.

```
<xsl:for-each select="Value"/>
```

9.13 xsl:if

This XSLT element provides a simple dependency query.

```
<xsl:if test="Value"> ... </xsl:if>
```


9.14 xsl:import

This XSLT element lets you import an external XSLT stylesheet. This element must be positioned ahead of every other element. If there is conflict between stylesheets, the imported stylesheet has a lesser significance. If several stylesheets are imported, the one imported first has the least significance.

```
<xsl:import href="Address"/>
```

9.15 xsl:include

This XSLT element specifies an XSL stylesheet which has to be inserted. In contrast to the element `<xsl:import>`, where the imported stylesheet has a lesser significance, this stylesheet has the same significance as the current stylesheet.

```
<xsl:include href="Address"/>
```

9.16 xsl:message

Sends a text message either to the message buffer or to a message dialog box.

```
<xsl:message terminate="YES|NO"> ... </xsl:message>
```

The attribute `terminate` specifies whether the XSLT stylesheet should be terminated.

9.17 xsl:namespace-alias

This XSLT element replaces the name prefix passed on by another name prefix.

```
<xsl:namespace-alias
  stylesheet-prefix="Prefix"
  result-prefix="Prefix"/>
```

9.18 xsl:otherwise

In conjunction with XSL elements `xsl:when` and `xsl:choose`, this element provides a means of carrying out conditional tests.

```
<xsl:choose>
  <xsl:when test="Value">
    ...
  </xsl:when>
  <xsl:otherwise>
    ...
  </xsl:otherwise>
</xsl:choose>
```

9.19 xsl:output

Use this XSLT element to define the output method.

```
<xsl:output/>
```

There are certain attributes which you can use to determine the output method:

Attribute	Description
method	Defines the output method (xml | html | text).
version	Defines the version for the XML declaration.
omit-xml-declaration	Defines whether an XML declaration is incorporated in the output document (yes | no).
standalone	Defines the value for standalone in the XML declaration (yes | no).
encoding	Defines the character set for the XML declaration.
doctype-system	Defines the possible external DTD for the XML declaration ("Name.dtd").
doctype-public	Defines the possible external public DTD for the XML declaration ("Name of DTD").
cdata-section-elements	Defines the elements that you want to be inserted in a CDATA section in the output.
indent	Defines indenting in your output document (yes | no).
media-type	Defines the media type of the output document; MIME type will be used (text/xml | text/html | text/plain | text/rtf | etc.).

Table 9.2 ***Attributes of the*** `output` ***method***

9.20 xsl:param

This XSLT element declares a parameter with a name that can be used in `xsl:stylesheet` or `xsl:template`.

```
<xsl:param name="Name"></xsl:param>
```

9.21 xsl:preserve-space

This XSL element protects all the spaces for the element between the starting tag and the closing tag.

```
<xsl:preserve-space element="Name"/>
```

9.22 xsl:processing-instruction

This element inserts an instruction into your output document. Use the `name` attribute to define the name of the instruction.

```
<xsl:processing-instruction name="PI-Name">
</xsl:processing-instruction>
```

9.23 msxsl:script

This XSLT element is a Microsoft element and is intended for a script. It defines global variables and functions for it. You can use the `language` attribute to define the script language type, and the `implements-prefix` attribute to define a namespace for the script block.

```
<msxsl:script
  language="JScript"
  implements-prefix="user">
 ...
Script
 ...
</msxsl:script>
```

9.24 xsl:sort

This XSLT element defines the criteria for sorting elements.

```
<xsl:sort />
```

The following attributes are needed for sorting:

Attribute	Description
`select`	Defines the sort key for the element. The value "." is used as the default. This sets the current value of the element as the sort key.

`data-type`	Specifies the data type of the string.
	`text`
	means that values will be sorted in alphabetical order.
	`number`
	means that values will be converted to numbers and then sorted according to their resulting values.

`order`	This determines whether values will be sorted in *ascending* order or *descending* order.
`case-order`	Determines the sort sequence when there is a mixture of capital letters and lower case. The default sort sequence is by capital letters.
`lang`	Determines the alphabet by which values will be sorted. The default is the alphabet for the system environment you are currently using.

Table 9.3 ***Possible attributes for*** `xsl:sort`

9.25 xsl:strip-space

This XSLT element removes all insignificant spaces from an element. The target of the instruction is an element.

```
<xsl:strip-space element="Name"/>
```

9.26 xsl:stylesheet

This element is the root element of a stylesheet. It contains all the stylesheet elements.

```
<xsl:stylesheet>
...
</xsl:stylesheet>
```

Possible attributes:

Attribute	Description
`version`	This attribute is required. It specifies the stylesheet version.
`id`	Specifies a unique identification character which makes it easier to attach stylesheets.

Table 9.4 ***Attributes for the*** `stylesheet` ***method***

9.27 xsl:template

This XSLT element locates various XML elements in order to apply stylesheet rules to them. The `match` attribute defines the element that needs to be found.

```
<xsl:template>
...
Formatting rules
...
</xsl:template>
```

9.28 xsl:text

This XSLT element inserts a text into your output document.

```
<xsl:text>
...
text
...
</xsl:text>
```

9.29 xsl:transform

This element is a synonym for the XSLT root element `xsl:stylesheet`. It too contains all the stylesheet elements.

```
<xsl:stylesheet>
...
</xsl:stylesheet>
```

Possible attributes:

Attribute	Description
`version`	This attribute is required. It specifies the stylesheet version.
`id`	Specifies a unique identification character which makes it easier to attach stylesheets.

Table 9.5 ***Possible attributes with*** `xsl:transform`

9.30 xsl:value-of

This XSLT element extracts the value of an XML element or XML attribute chosen by means of `select` and inserts this value in the output element. You may also specify a path:

```
<xsl:value-of select="Element"/>
<xsl:value-of select="@Attribute"/>
<xsl:value-of select="Element/@Attribute"/>
```

9.31 xsl:when

In conjunction with XSLT elements `xsl:otherwise` and `xsl:choose`, this element provides a means of carrying out conditional tests.

```
<xsl:choose>
  <xsl:when test="Value">
    ...
  </xsl:when>
  <xsl:otherwise>
    ...
  </xsl:otherwise>
</xsl:choose>
```

Quick reference guide for CSS

10

This reference gives you all the important information you need for writing a CSS stylesheet for an XML document. You should bear in mind, however, that not all stylesheet rules are supported yet. By this we mean in particular the CSS 2.0 instruction, but while the book was being written, a first draft was published for CSS 3.0 by W3C.

10.1 Text formatting

In this section, you will discover the options you have for formatting text. Text formatting covers information on font types, sizes, colors and weights, plus character and word spacing.

10.1.1 font-family (CSS 1.0)

The keyword `font-family` defines the font type to be used for an element. Some examples of font types are Arial, Helvetica, Times Roman and Sans Serif.

```
Element {font-family: Arial}
```

If a font type is unavailable or cannot be displayed, then `font-family` has no effect. If you define several font types, separated by commas, the order you use is the deciding factor. The first font type available is the one that will be used.

```
Element {font-family: "Old Bookman", Arial, Century}
```

Font names containing a space character must be put inside quotation marks. The following font families are predefined: `serif`, `sans serif`, `italics`, `fantasy` and `monospace`.

10.1.2 font-style (CSS 1.0)

With `Element {font-style: value}` you are defining the font style, which depends on the availabilty within the font type. The following can be input:

Value	*Meaning*
`italic`	The font style is italic.
`oblique`	The font style is oblique (italic).
`normal`	The font style is normal.

Table 10.1 ***How do you want the font to appear?***

10.1.3 font-variant (CSS 1.0)

The keyword `font-variant` enables you to produce small capitals:

```
Element {font-variant: value}
```

The following can be used:

Value	*Meaning*
`small-caps`	Small capitals.
`normal`	Normal font variant.

Table 10.2 ***Do you want the font to appear in small capitals?***

10.1.4 font-size (CSS 1.0)

With the keyword `font-size` you can change the font size of the element. You can define the font size:

```
Element {font-size: 48pt}
```

And you can select the font size relative to the normal font size:

```
Element {font-size: 140%}
```

Or, you can select one of the following imprecise values:

Value	Meaning
`xx-small`	Tiny.
`x-small`	Very small.
`small`	Small.
`medium`	Medium.
`large`	Large.
`x-large`	Very large.
`xx-large`	Enormous.
`smaller`	Visibly smaller than normal.
`larger`	Visibly larger than normal.

Table 10.3 ***Possible values for the font size***

A combination of font size and line height is also possible:

```
Element {font-size: 12pt/14pt}
```

In this example, the font size is 12pt and the line height is 14pt.

10.1.5 font-weight (CSS 1.0)

With `font-weight` you can set the degree of boldness of the element. Several values are available to you here, but not all font types support all the possible entries allowed:

```
Element {font-weight: value}
```

Value	Meaning
`bold`	Bold.
`bolder`	Extra bold.
`lighter`	Lighter.
`100, 200, 300, ..., 800, 900`	Extra light (100), medium (500) to extra bold (900).

Table 10.4 ***How bold do you want the font to be?***

10.1.6 font (CSS 1.0)

This keyword covers the keywords `font-family`, `font-style`, `font-variant`, `font-size` and `font-weight` . The values are listed one after another – the order in which they are entered has no significance.

```
Element {font: italic 24pt arial, serif}
```

10.1.7 word-spacing (CSS 1.0)

Inputting this defines the spacing between the individual words, but it is not yet supported by Internet Explorer 5.5. An example:

```
Element {word spacing: 10mm}
```


10.1.8 letter-spacing (CSS 1.0)

Inputting this defines the spacing between the individual letters or the individual characters. An example:

```
Element {letter-spacing: 3mm}
```

10.1.9 text-decoration (CSS 1.0)

When you input this, you define the text decoration with the following entries:

```
Element {text-decoration: value}
```

Value	Meaning
`underline`	Underlining.
`overline`	Overlining.
`line-through`	Line-through.
`blink`	Blinking.
`none`	No text decoration.

Table 10.5 ***Possible values for the text appearance***

`blink` is not supported by Internet Explorer 5.5.

10.1.10 text-transform (CSS 1.0)

You can use the following words to set capital and small letters:

```
Element {text-transform: value}
```

Value	Meaning
`capitalize`	First letters of words in capitals.
`uppercase`	Capital letters only.
`lowercase`	Small letters only.
`none`	No text transformation.

Table 10.6 ***Possible text transformations***

`text-transform` is not supported by Internet Explorer 5.5.

10.1.11 color (CSS 1.0)

With `color` you define the font color. You can select the color by name:

```
Element {color: green}
```

Or with a corresponding hex value:

```
Element {color: #008000}
```

10.1.12 text-shadow (CSS 2.0)

With this keyword, you can generate a shadow effect for the text. You can select the shadow color by name:

```
Element {text-shadow: gray}
```

by the corresponding hex value:

```
Element {text-shadow: #808080}
```

or by `none` for no text shadow:

```
Element {text-shadow: none}
```

10.2 Spacings, margins and alignment

In this section, we tell you how to set the spacings, margins and the alignment with the adjacent element.

10.2.1 margin-top (CSS 1.0)

This keyword defines the top distance from the preceding element or border. One numeric entry is allowed:

```
Element {margin-top: 15mm}
```

Bear in mind that Internet Explorer and Netscape will react differently to the distance set if the preceding element has defined a distance with `margin-bottom` Internet Explorer compares the size of the two entries and then reacts to the larger value. With Netscape, the top distance `margin-top` always takes priority.

10.2.2 margin-bottom (CSS 1.0)

This keyword defines the bottom distance from the succeeding element or border. One numeric entry is allowed:

```
Element {margin-bottom: 10mm}
```

Bear in mind that Internet Explorer and Netscape will react differently to the distance set if the succeeding element has defined a distance with `margin-top` .

Internet Explorer compares the size of the two entries and then reacts to the larger value. With Netscape, the top distance `margin-top` always takes priority.

10.2.3 margin-left (CSS 1.0)

This keyword defines the left-hand distance from the adjacent element or window border. One numeric entry is allowed:

```
Element {margin-left: 12mm}
```

10.2.4 margin-right (CSS 1.0)

This keyword defines the right-hand distance from the adjacent element or window border. One numeric entry is allowed:

```
Element {margin-right: 12mm}
```

10.2.5 margin (CSS 1.0)

The keyword `margin` covers the following keywords: `margin-top`, `margin-bottom`, `margin-left`, `margin-right`.

```
Element {margin: 1cm}
```

If one value is entered, the same distance is assigned to all four edges.

```
Element {margin: 1cm 2cm}
```

Two entries mean: the first entry determines the distance for the top and bottom, and the second for right and left.

```
Element {margin: 1cm 2cm 3cm}
```

With three entries, the first value determines the top distance, the second the distance for right and left, and the third determines the bottom margin.

```
Element {margin: 1cm 2cm 3cm 4cm}
```

With four entries, the order is top, right, left, bottom.

10.2.6 text-indent (CSS 1.0)

With `text-indent` you define an indent for the first line of a continuous text. One numeric entry is allowed:

```
Element {text-indent: 5mm}
```

Using a negative value moves the text outwards:

```
Element {text-indent: -5mm}
```

10.2.7 line-height (CSS 1.0)

The keyword `line-height` is used to set the height of a line. One numeric entry is allowed:

```
Element {line-height: 16pt}
```

10.2.8 vertical-align (CSS 1.0)

With `vertical-align` you can set the vertical alignment. The following can be entered:

```
Element {vertical-align: value}
```

Value	Meaning
`top`	Align top flush.
`middle`	Align centrally.
`bottom`	Align bottom flush.
`baseline`	Align with the baseline.
`sub`	Position lower.
`super`	Position higher.
`text-top`	Align with top edge of text.
`text-bottom`	Align with bottom edge of text.

Table 10.7 ***Possible values for*** `vertical-align`

10.2.9 text-align (CSS 1.0), alignment (CSS 2.0)

These two keywords are used to align texts. The following inputs are possible:

```
Element {text-align: value}
Element {alignment: value}
```

Value	Meaning
`left`	Left justify.
`right`	Right justify.
`center`	Centered.
`justify`	Block justify.

Table 10.8 ***Possible values with*** `text-align` ***or*** `alignment`

10.2.10 white-space (CSS 2.0)

You can set what happens with a line wrap by using `white-space`. The options are as follows:

```
Element {white-space: value}
```

Value	Meaning
normal	Automatic line wrap.
pre	Line wrap as input.
nowrap	No automatic line wrap.

Table 10.9 ***Possible line wraps***

10

TAKE THAT!

10.3 Border and internal spacing

This section tells you how to set the borders and internal spacings of the individual elements.

10.3.1 border-top-width (CSS 1.0)

This keyword defines the thickness of the line above an element. One numeric input or one of the following inputs is allowed:

```
Element {border-top-width: value}
```

Value	Meaning
thin	Thin.
medium	Medium.
thick	Thick.

Table 10.10 ***Line width for the top border line***

Internet Explorer also needs to be told the `border-top-style`, for example `solid`:

```
Element{
border-top-width: value;
border-top-style:solid
}
```

10.3.2 border-bottom-width (CSS 1.0)

This keyword defines the thickness of the line below an element. One numeric input or one of the following inputs is allowed:

```
Element {border-bottom-width: value}
```

Value	Meaning
thin	Thin.
medium	Medium.
thick	Thick.

Table 10.11 ***Line thickness for the bottom border line***

Internet Explorer also needs to be told the `border-bottom-style`, for example `solid`:

```
Element{
border- bottom-width: value;
border bottom-style:solid
}
```

10.3.3 border-left-width (CSS 1.0)

This keyword defines the thickness of the line to the left of an element. One numeric input or one of the following inputs is allowed:

```
Element {border-left-width: value}
```

Value	Meaning
thin	Thin.
medium	Medium.
thick	Thick.

Table 10.12 ***Line thickness for left-hand border line***

Internet Explorer also needs to be told the `border-left-style`, for example `solid`:

```
Element{
border-left-width: value;
border-left-style:solid
}
```

10.3.4 border-right-width (CSS 1.0)

This keyword defines the thickness of the line to the right of an element. One numeric input or one of the following inputs is allowed:

```
Element {border-right-width: value}
```

Value	Meaning
thin	Thin.
medium	Medium.
thick	Thick.

Table 10.13 ***Line thickness for right-hand border line***

Internet Explorer also needs to be told the `border-right-style`, for example solid:

```
Element{
border-right-width: value;
border-right-style:solid
}
```

10.3.5 border-width (CSS 1.0)

This keyword defines the thickness of the line around an element. One numeric input or one of the following inputs is allowed:

```
Element {border-width: value}
```

Value	Meaning
thin	Thin.
medium	Medium.
thick	Thick.

Table 10.14 ***Line thickness for the border***

Internet Explorer also needs to be told the `border-style`, for example `solid`:

```
Element{
border-width: value;
border-style:solid
}
```

10.3.6 border-color (CSS 1.0)

You set the border color with `border-color`. You can select the color by name:

```
Element {border-color: green}
```

or with the corresponding hex value:

```
Element {border-color: #008000}
```

Internet Explorer also needs to be told the `border-style`, for example `solid`:

```
Element{
border-color: value;
border-style:solid
}
```

10.3.7 border-style (CSS 1.0)

With `border-style` you define the border type. The following inputs are allowed:

```
Element {border-style: value}
```

Value	Meaning
`dotted`	Dotted.
`dashed`	Dashed.
`solid`	Line.
`double`	Double line.
`groove`	Three-dimensional effect.
`ridge`	Three-dimensional effect.
`inset`	Three-dimensional effect.
`outset`	Three-dimensional effect.
`none`	No border.

Table 10.15 ***Possible values for the appearance of the border***

For some of the effects, the color cannot be black.

Internet Explorer also needs to be told the border width `border-width`:

```
Element{
border-width: medium;
border-style: value
}
```

10.3.8 border-top (CSS 1.0)

The keyword `border-top` covers the keywords `border-top-width`, `border-top-style` and `border-color` and defines the appearance of the line above the element. The inputs for line width, border type and color are separated with a space:

```
Element {border-top: value value value}
```

10.3.9 border-bottom (CSS 1.0)

The keyword `border-bottom` covers the keywords `border-bottom-width`, `border-bottom-style` and `border-color` and defines the appearance of the line below the element. The inputs for line width, border type and color are separated with a space:

```
Element {border-bottom: value value value}
```

10.3.10 border-left (CSS 1.0)

The keyword `border-left` covers the keywords `border-left-width`, `border-left-style` and `border-color` and defines the appearance of the line to the left of the element. The inputs for line width, border type and color are separated with a space:

```
Element {border-left: value value value}
```

10.3.11 border-right (CSS 1.0)

The keyword `border-right` covers the keywords `border-right-width`, `border-right-style` and `border-color` and defines the appearance of the line to the right of the element. The inputs for line width, border type and color are separated with a space:

```
Element {border-right: value value value}
```

10.3.12 border (CSS 1.0)

The keyword `border` covers the keywords `border-width`, `border-style` and `border-color` and defines the appearance of the line around the element. The inputs for line width, border type and color are separated with a space:

```
Element {border: value value value}
```

10.3.13 padding-top (CSS 1.0)

The keyword `padding-top` defines the distance between element content and the top limit of the element. One numeric input is allowed:

```
Element {padding-top: 7px}
```

10.3.14 padding-bottom (CSS 1.0)

The keyword `padding-bottom` defines the internal distance between the element content and the bottom limit of the element. One numeric input is allowed:

```
Element {padding-bottom: 7px}
```


10.3.15 padding-left (CSS 1.0)

The keyword `padding-left` defines the internal distance between the element content and the left-hand limit of the element. One numeric input is allowed:

```
Element {padding-left: 7px}
```

10.3.16 padding-right (CSS 1.0)

The keyword `padding-right` defines the internal distance between the element content and the right-hand limit of the element. One numeric input is allowed:

```
Element {padding-right: 7px}
```

10.3.17 padding (CSS 1.0)

The keyword `padding` defines the internal distance between the content of the element and the top, bottom, left-hand and right-hand limits of the element. One numeric input is allowed:

```
Element {padding: 7px}
```

10.4 Background color and background images

In this section, we tell you how to define the background to the individual elements.

10.4.1 background-color (CSS 1.0)

The keyword `background-color` defines the background color of the element. You can input one color:

```
Element {background-color: red}
```

or make one numeric input:

```
Element {background-color: #FF0000}
```

10.4.2 background-image (CSS 1.0)

The keyword `background-image` defines an image as the background to the element. The following input is allowed:

```
Element {background-image: url(IMAGE)}
```

It is assumed that the background image is located in the same directory as the stylesheet. If this is not the case, a relative or absolute path must be used.

10.4.3 background-repeat (CSS 1.0)

The keyword `background-repeat` is used to define the repetition behavior of background graphics. Without this input, the graphic will repeat itself over the entire available space. The following inputs are allowed:

```
Element {background-repeat: value}
```

Value	Meaning
`no-repeat`	No repetition.
`repeat`	Normal repetition as per default setting.
`repeat-x`	Repetition over one line only.
`repeat-y`	Repetition over one column only.

Table 10.16 ***Possible options for behavior of the background***

10.4.4 background-attachment (CSS 1.0)

With `background-attachment` you can fix the background graphics. The following inputs are allowed:

```
Element {background-attachment: value}
```

Value	Meaning
`scroll`	Scroll (standard).
`fixed`	Background graphic is fixed.

Table 10.17 ***How do you want the background to behave?***

10.4.5 background-position (CSS 1.0)

With `background-position` you can define the position of the top left-hand corner of the background graphic. Numeric values are allowed:

```
Element {background-position: 5mm 8mm}
```

Here, the first value defines the left-hand distance, and the second value the top distance. The following inputs are also allowed:

```
Element {background-position: value}
```

Value	Meaning
`middle`	Vertical middle.
`top`	Vertical flush-top.
`bottom`	Vertical flush-bottom.
`center`	Horizontally centered.
`left`	Horizontally flush-left.
`right`	Horizontally flush-right.

Table 10.18 ***Possible alignments of the background***

10.4.6 background (CSS 1.0)

The keyword `background` covers the keywords `background-image`, `background-repeat`, `background-position` and `background-attachment` and defines the inputs for the background graphics of an element. The inputs are separated with a space; you do not need to enter something for all the inputs:

```
Element {background: value value value value}
```

10.5 Lists and tables

In this section we tell you how to create the enumerations and numbered lists.

10.5.1 list-style-type (CSS 1.0)

You define the way lists are numbered with `list-style-type`. The following inputs are allowed:

```
Element {list-style-type: value}
```

Value	Meaning
decimal	Numbering 1., 2., 3., 4., etc.
lower-roman	Numbering i., ii., iii., iv., etc.
upper-roman	Numbering I., II., III., IV., etc.
lower-alpha	Numbering a., b., c., d., etc.
upper-alpha	Numbering A., B., C., D., etc.
disc	Floppy symbol.
circle	Circle.
square	Square.
none	No character.

Table 10.19 ***What numbering do you want to use in the list?***

10.5.2 list-style-position (CSS 1.0)

You define the indenting of the numbering in lists with `list-style-position`. The following inputs are allowed:

```
Element {list-style-position: value}
```

Value	Meaning
inside	Indented.
outside	Move out (standard).

Table 10.20 ***Is the numbering indented?***

10.5.3 list-style-image (CSS 1.0)

With `list-style-image` you can define a graphic as a listing character. The following inputs are allowed:

```
Element {list-style-image: url(IMAGE}
```

It is assumed that the graphic is located in the same directory as the XML document. If this is not the case, a relative or absolute path must be used.

10.5.4 list-style (CSS 1.0)

The keyword `list-style` covers the keywords `list-style-image`, `list-style-position` and `list-style-type` and defines the inputs for listing characters. The inputs are separated with a space; you do not need to enter something for all the inputs:

```
Element {list-style: value value value}
```

10.5.5 column-span (CSS 2.0)

With this you make the cells of a table spread over several columns. Numeric inputs are allowed:

```
Element {column-span: 3}
```

10.5.6 row-span (CSS 2.0)

Use this to make the cells of a Table spread over several rows. Numeric inputs are allowed:

```
Element {row-span: 2}
```

10.5.7 caption-side (CSS 2.0)

With `caption-side` you determine the positioning of table headers and captions. The following inputs are allowed:

```
Element {caption-side: value}
```

Value	Meaning
`top`	Header centered.
`topleft`	Header flush left.
`topright`	Header flush right.
`bottom`	Caption centered.
`bottomleft`	Caption flush left.
`bottomright`	Caption flush right.

Table 10.21 ***Where do you want a table header or caption to go?***

10.5.8 speak-header-cell (CSS 2.0)

With `speak-header-cell` you can define repetition behavior for speech output. The following values are allowed:

```
Element {speak-header-cell: value}
```

Value	Meaning
`once`	Header cell is read out once only (standard).
`always`	Header cell is read out every time.

Table 10.22 ***How is the first line to be read out?***

10.6 Pseudo formats

In this section you will learn how to deal with pseudo formats.

10.6.1 :link, :visited, :active (CSS 2.0)

With `:link`, `:visited` and `:active` you define the displaying of links that you are now clicking on, or where you have already or not yet done so. Inputs for color, font and background are allowed within the braces:

```
Element:link {color: red; font-weight: bold}
Element:visited {color: green; font-weight: bold}
Element:active {color: black; font-weight: bold}
```

10.6.2 :first-line (CSS 2.0)

Using `:first-line` gives the first line of a new paragraph its own formatting. Inputs for color, font and background are allowed within the braces:

```
Element:first-line {font-weight: bold}
```

10.6.3 :first-letter (CSS 1.0)

Using `:first-letter` gives the first character in a new paragraph its own formatting. Inputs for color, font and background are allowed within the braces:

```
Element:first-letter {font-weight: bold}
```

10.6.4 :before, :after (CSS 2.0)

With `:before`, `:after` you can insert text before or after an element:

```
Element:before {content: "TEXT"}
Element:after {content: "TEXT"}
```

10.7 Position elements

In this section we tell you how to define the position of the elements.

10.7.1 position (CSS 2.0)

With `position` you can position an element. The following inputs are allowed:

```
Element {position: value}
```

Value	Meaning
absolute	Absolute positioning in relation to window border (can be scrolled).
fixed	Absolute positioning in relation to window border (cannot be scrolled).
relative	Relative position in relation to previous element.
static	Normal position.

Table 10.23 ***How is an element to be positioned?***

As it is not yet certain where the element is to begin, the keyword `position` is only of use if you input either `top`, `bottom`, `left` or `right` with it:

```
Element{
position: relative;
top: 20%;
}
```

10.7.2 top (CSS 2.0)

With `top` and in conjunction with the keyword `position` you define the top starting position of an element. For automatic positioning, you can input the value `auto`:

```
Element{
position: relative;
top: auto;
}
```

One numeric input is also allowed:

```
Element{
position: relative;
top: 2cm;
}
```

10.7.3 bottom (CSS 2.0)

With `bottom` and in conjunction with the keyword `position` you define the bottom starting position of an element. For automatic positioning, you can input the value `auto`:

```
Element{
position: relative;
bottom: auto;
}
```

One numeric input is also allowed:

```
Element{
position: relative;
bottom: 5%;
}
```


10.7.4 left (CSS 2.0)

With `left` in conjunction with the keyword `position` you define the left-hand starting position of an element. For automatic positioning, you can input the value `auto`:

```
Element{
position: relative;
left: auto;
}
```

One numeric input is also allowed:

```
Element{
position: relative;
left: 12px;
}
```

10.7.5 right (CSS 2.0)

With `right` in conjunction with the keyword `position` you define the right-hand starting position of an element. For automatic positioning, you can input the value `auto`:

```
Element{
position: relative;
right: auto;
}
```

One numeric input is also allowed:

```
Element{
position: relative;
right: 8mm;
}
```

10.7.6 width (CSS 2.0)

With `width` in conjunction with the keyword `position` you define the width of an element. One numeric input is allowed:

```
Element{
position: relative;
width: 80%;
}
```

10.7.7 min-width (CSS 2.0)

With `min-width` in conjunction with the keyword `position` you define the minimum width of an element. One numeric input is allowed:

```
Element{
position: relative;
min-width: 5cm;
}
```

10.7.8 max-width (CSS 2.0)

With `max-width` in conjunction with the keyword `position` you define the maximum width of an element. If the content is larger, it is shortened. One numeric input is allowed:

```
Element{
position: relative;
max-width: 5cm;
}
```

10.7.9 height (CSS 2.0)

With `height` in conjunction with the keyword `position` you define the height of an element. One numeric input is allowed:

```
Element{
position: relative;
height: 43mm;
}
```

10.7.10 min-height (CSS 2.0)

With `min-height` in conjunction with the keyword `position` you define the minimum height of an element. One numeric input is allowed:

```
Element{
position: relative;
min-height: 5cm;
}
```

10.7.11 max-height (CSS 2.0)

With `max-height` in conjunction with the keyword `position` you define the maximum height of an element. If the content is larger, it is shortened. One numeric input is allowed:

```
Element{
position: relative;
max-height: 5cm;
}
```

10.7.12 overflow (CSS 2.0)

With `overflow` you define what happens with the oversize if a child element is larger than its parent element. The following inputs are allowed:

```
Element {overflow: value}
```

Value	Meaning
`visible`	The parent element is matched to the oversize of the child element.
`hidden`	The child element is matched to the size of the parent element and is shortened.
`scroll`	The size of the parent element remains the same and the browser offers scroll bars.
`auto`	The size of the parent element remains the same and the browser offers scroll bars if necessary.

Table 10.24 ***Possible values for overflow***

With `direction` you can also define the direction in which the element is to run:

```
Element{
overflow: visible;
direction: rtl;
}
```

10.7.13 direction (CSS 2.0)

With `direction` you define the direction in which the element is to run if a child element is larger than its parent element. The following inputs are allowed:

```
Element {direction: value}
```

Value	Meaning
`ltr`	From left to right (standard).
`rtl`	From right to left.
`ltr-override`	Still unclear.
`rtl-override`	Still unclear.

Table 10.25 ***Possible values for direction***

With `overflow` you can also define what happens in the event of oversize:

```
Element{
overflow: visible;
direction: rtl;
}
```

10.7.14 float (CSS 2.0)

With `float` you determine the way in which the succeeding elements are to float around this element. The following inputs are allowed:

```
Element {float: value}
```

Value	Meaning
`left`	Element located on the left and the succeeding elements float around it to the right.
`right`	Element located on the right and the succeeding elements float around it to the left.
`none`	No floating around (standard).

Table 10.26 ***Possible values for float***

In order for this keyword to function, you must also input information on `width`:

```
Element{
float: right;
width: 3cm;
}
```

10.7.15 clear (CSS 2.0)

With `clear` you terminate the floating around an element initiated by `float`. The following inputs are allowed:

```
Element {clear: value}
```

Value	Meaning
`left`	In the case of `float: left` it forces a continuation below the element.
`right`	In the case of `float: right` it forces a continuation below the element.
`both`	Forces a continuation below the element in either case.
`none`	Forces no continuation below the element (standard).

Table 10.27 ***Possible values for clear***

10.7.16 z-index (CSS 2.0)

If you have used the keyword `position` to position several elements, and their display areas overlap, you must define the order in which they are to be stored one above the other. Numeric values are allowed:

```
Element{
position: absolute;
z-index: 3;
}
```

The higher the value for the keyword `z-index`, the further upwards the element will be stored.

10.7.17 display (CSS 2.0)

With `display` you determine the way an element is displayed. The following inputs are allowed:

```
Element {display: value}
```

Value	Meaning
`block`	The element is located in its own paragraph.
`inline`	The element is shown in the text.
`list-item`	As for `block`, but with listing character.
`run-in`	Still unclear.
`compact`	Still unclear.
`none`	Element is not displayed and does not occupy any space.

Table 10.28 ***Possible values for display***

10.7.18 visibility (CSS 2.0)

With `visibility` you determine the way an element is displayed. The following inputs are allowed:

```
Element {visibility: value}
```

Value	Meaning
`hidden`	Element is not displayed and does not occupy any space.
`visible`	Element is displayed (standard).

Table 10.29 ***Visible or invisible***

10.7.19 clip (CSS 2.0)

Irrespective of the information input on the size or automatic size of the elements, with `clip` you specify only a segment of the element display. At present, only a rectangle can be shown (`rect`), but polygons, circles and ellipses are also planned. Numeric values are allowed:

```
Element {clip:rect (A B C D)}
```

Value	Meaning
`A`	Top limit with reference to top limit of element.
`B`	Right-hand limit with reference to left-hand limit of element.
`C`	Bottom limit with reference to top limit of element.
`D`	Left-hand limit with reference to left-hand limit of element.

Table 10.30 ***How big is the element?***

It is a condition that the bottom value is larger than the top one, and the right-hand value larger than the left.

10.8 Multi-column text flow

Multi-column text flow is familiar from newspapers, for instance.

10.8.1 columns (CSS 2.0)

With `columns` you obtain a multi-column flow of text. The text is automatically distributed over the columns. You are allowed to input the number of columns you want:

```
Element {columns: 2}
```

10.8.2 column-gap (CSS 2.0)

With `column-gap` you define the column spacing. With more than two columns, the value input applies to all columns. One numeric input is allowed:

```
Element {column-gap: 12mm}
```

10.8.3 column-rule-width (CSS 2.0)

With `column-rule-width` you define the width of the separating line between the columns. With more than two columns, the value input applies to all columns. One numeric input is allowed:

```
Element {column-rule-width: 2mm}
```

A combination with `column-rule-style` is necessary.

```
Element{
column-rule-width: 1mm;
column-rule-style: dashed;
}
```

10.8.4 column-rule-style (CSS 2.0)

With `column-rule-style` you define the nature of the separating line between the columns. With more than two columns, the value input applies to all columns. One of the following can be input:

```
Element {column-rule-width: 2mm}
```

Value	Meaning
`dotted`	Dotted separating lines.
`dashed`	Dashed separating lines.
`solid`	Solid separating lines.
`double`	Double solid separating lines.
`groove`	Three-dimensional effect for separating lines.
`ridge`	Three-dimensional effect for separating lines.
`inset`	Three-dimensional effect for separating lines.
`outset`	Three-dimensional effect for separating lines.
`none`	No separating lines.

Table 10.31 ***Possible values for separating lines***

A combination with `column-rule-width` is necessary:

```
Element{
column-rule-width: 2mm;
column-rule-style: solid;
}
```

10.8.5 column-rule-color (CSS 2.0)

With `column-rule-color` you define the color of the separating line between the columns. With more than two columns, the value input applies to all columns. One color can be input:

```
Element {column-rule-color: blue}
```

A combination with `column-rule-style` and `column-rule-width` is necessary.

```
Element{
column-rule-width: 1mm;
column-rule-color: red;
column-rule-style: dashed;
}
```

10.8.6 column-rule (CSS 2.0)

The keyword `column-rule` brings together the keywords `column-rule-width`, `column-rule-style` and `column-rule-color`. With more than two columns, the value input applies to all columns. The inputs must be separated with a space and it is not necessary to input a color:

```
Element {column-rule: 1mm dotted}
```

10.9 Speech output

By defining speech output, you can also have the document contents output acoustically.

10.9.1 volume (CSS 2.0)

With `volume` you define the volume. Values from 0, for very soft, to 100, for very loud, are allowed:

```
Element {volume: 75}
```

The following inputs are also possible:

```
Element {volume: value}
```

Value	Meaning
`silent`	No sound, but pause in length of the element.
`x-soft`	Very soft, corresponds to 0.
`soft`	Soft, corresponds to 25.
`medium`	Medium, corresponds to 50.
`loud`	Loud, corresponds to 75.
`x-loud`	Very loud, corresponds to 100.

Table 10.32 ***Possible values for the volume***

10.9.2 speak (CSS 2.0)

With `speak` you can affect the pronunciation. The following inputs are allowed:

```
Element {speak: value}
```

Value	Meaning
`normal`	Normal pronunciation.
`spell-out`	Text is spelled out.
`none`	No speech output.

Table 10.33 ***Possible values for speak***

10.9.3 pause-before (CSS 2.0)

With `pause-before` you enforce a pause in speech before an element. You can enter one numeric value in seconds (`s`) or milliseconds (`ms`):

```
Element {pause-before: 35ms}
```

There is a further option in that a percentage can be input. The pause will then depend on the speaking rate `speech-rate`:

```
Element{
speech-rate: fast;
pause-before: 25%;
}
```

10.9.4 pause-after (CSS 2.0)

With `pause-after` you enforce a pause in speech after an element. You can enter one numeric value in seconds (`s`) or milliseconds (`ms`):

```
Element {pause-after: 15ms}
```

Another option is to input a percentage. The pause will then depend on the speaking rate speech-rate:

```
Element{
speech-rate: medium;
pause-after: 15%;
}
```


10.9.5 pause (CSS 2.0)

With pause you define a pause in speech before and after an element. With one numeric value entered in seconds (s) or milliseconds (ms) the same pause is inserted before and after the element:

```
Element {pause: 15ms}
```

If two values are input, the first determines the pause in speech before the element and the second determines the pause after the element:

```
Element {pause: 15ms 2s}
```

A further option is to input a percentage. The pause will then depend on the speaking rate speech-rate:

```
Element{
speech-rate: slow;
pause-after: 5%;
}
```

10.9.6 cue-before (CSS 2.0)

With cue-before a signal is played before an element. It is assumed that the sound file is located in the same directory as the stylesheet. If this is not the case, a relative or absolute path must be used.

```
Element {cue-before: url(sound file)}
```

Some of the sound formats allowed are .WAV, .AU and .AI.

10.9.7 cue-after (CSS 2.0)

With cue-after a signal is played after an element. It is assumed that the sound file is located in the same directory as the stylesheet. If this is not the case, a relative or absolute path must be used.

```
Element {cue-after: url(sound file)}
```

Some of the sound formats allowed are .WAV, .AU and .AI.

10

TAKE THAT!

10.9.8 cue (CSS 2.0)

With `cue` a signal is played before and after an element. It is assumed that the sound file is located in the same directory as the stylesheet. If this is not the case, a relative or absolute path must be used.

```
Element {cue: url(sound file)}
```

Some of the sound formats allowed are .WAV, .AU and .AI.

10.9.9 play-during (CSS 2.0)

With `play-during` a background piece is played during a speech output. It is assumed that the sound file is located in the same directory as the stylesheet. If this is not the case, a relative or absolute path must be used.

```
Element {play-during: url(sound file) mix}
```

If you leave out the word mix, the background piece drowns out the actual speech output. Some of the sound formats allowed are .WAV, .AU and .AI.

10.9.10 azimuth (CSS 2.0)

With `azimuth` a stereophonic impression is imposed on the speech output. The minimum requirement is stereo or surround hardware. With `deg` (degree) you can input values from 0 to 360 in order to define the position of the speaker:

```
Element {azimuth: 120deg}
```

You can also work with the following inputs:

```
Element {azimuth: value}
```

Value	Meaning
`left-side`	Left side.
`left-side behind`	Left side behind.
`far-left`	Far left.
`far-left behind`	Far left behind.
`left`	Left.
`left behind`	Left behind.
`center-left`	Center left.
`center-left behind`	Center left behind.
`center`	Center.
`center behind`	Center behind.
`center-right`	Center right.
`center-right behind`	Center right behind.

Value	Meaning
right	Right.
right behind	Right behind.
far-right	Far right.
far-right behind	Far right behind.
right-side	Right side.
right-side behind	Right side behind.

Table 10.34 ***Possible values for azimuth***

10.9.11 elevation (CSS 2.0)

With `elevation` a stereophonic impression is imposed on the speech output from above and below. The minimum requirement is stereo or surround hardware. With `deg` (degree) you can enter values from `-90` (bottommost) to `90` (topmost) in order to define the position of the speaker:

```
Element {elevation: -45deg}
```

You can also work with the following inputs:

```
Element {elevation: value}
```

Value	Meaning
below	Below.
lower	Lower.
level	Level.
above	Above.
higher	Higher.

Table 10.35 ***From what level does the speech take place?***

10.9.12 speech-rate (CSS 2.0)

With `speech-rate` the speed of the speech output is defined. A numeric value stands for the mean number of words per minute:

```
Element {speech-rate: 80}
```

You can also work with the following inputs:

```
Element {speech-rate: value}
```

Value	Meaning
`x-slow`	Very slow.
`slow`	Slow.
`slower`	Slower than normal.
`medium`	Normal.
`faster`	Faster than normal.
`fast`	Fast.
`x-fast`	Very fast.

Table 10.36 ***Values for the speech rate***

10.9.13 voice-family (CSS 2.0)

With `voice-family` you define the voice of the speech output. The following inputs are possible:

```
Element {voice-family: value}
```

Value	Meaning
`male`	Male voice.
`female`	Female voice.
`child`	Child's voice.

Table 10.37 ***Possible values for the speaker***

10.9.14 pitch (CSS 2.0)

With `pitch` you define the pitch of the speech output. As well as entering the frequency in Hertz (`hz`) or Kilohertz (`khz`) as the mean pitch, you can input the following:

```
Element {pitch: value}
```

Value	Meaning
`x-low`	Very low voice.
`low`	Low voice.
`medium`	Normal voice.
`high`	High voice.
`x-high`	Very high voice.

Table 10.38 ***Values for voice pitch***

10.9.15 pitch-range (CSS 2.0)

With `pitch-range` you define the modulation of the speech output. A value of 50 corresponds to a normal speaking manner. With a lower value, the voice sounds more monotonous and a higher value corresponds to an excitable voice:

```
Element {pitch-range: 75}
```


10.9.16 stress (CSS 2.0)

With `stress` you define the stress factor of the speech output. A value of 50 corresponds to a normal speaking manner. With a lower value, the voice is hasty and excitable, whereas a higher value defines a calm, self-assured voice:

```
Element {stress: 50}
```

10.9.17 richness (CSS 2.0)

With `richness` you define how confident the speaking manner for the speech output is to be. A value of 50 corresponds to a normal speaking manner. With a lower value, the voice is unsure, while a higher value gives a self-confident, commanding voice:

```
Element {richness: 35}
```

10.9.18 speak-punctuation (CSS 2.0)

With `speak-punctuation` you define whether or not the punctuation is to be included in the speech output. The following values are possible:

```
Element {speak-punctuation: value}
```

Value	Meaning
code	Punctuation is also read out.
none	Punctuation is not read out (standard).

Table 10.39 ***Is punctuation to be read out?***

10.9.19 speak-date (CSS 2.0)

With `speak-date` you define what date format will be read out for the speech output. The following values are possible:

```
Element {speak-date: value}
```

Value	Meaning
myd	Month, year, day.
dmy	Day, month, year.
ymd	Year, month, day.

Table 10.40 ***How is the date to be read out?***

10.9.20 speak-numeral (CSS 2.0)

With speak-numeral you define the way in which number sequences are to be read. The following values are possible:

```
Element {speak-numeral: value}
```

Value	Meaning
digit	Each digit individually (1,2,3).
continuous	As a whole number (123).

Table 10.41 ***How are numbers to be spoken?***

10.9.21 speak-time (CSS 2.0)

With speak-time you define the time format to be used in the speech output. The following values are possible:

```
Element {speak-time: value}
```

Value	Meaning
12	12-hour format (12am-12pm).
24	24-hour format (0-24 hrs).

Table 10.42 ***What time format is to be used for reading?***

10.10 Cursor and Microsoft special filters

In this section you will find out about the stylesheet keyword and also the special Microsoft filters.

10.10.1 cursor (CSS 2.0)

With the keyword cursor you can provide an element with its own cursor, in other words, when the cursor is located above this element, it changes its appearance. The options are as follows:

```
Element {cursor: value}
```

Value	Meaning
`auto`	Automatic cursor (standard).
`default`	Platform-dependent standard cursor.
`crosshair`	Crosshair.
`pointer`	Pointer.
`move`	Cross indicating movability.
`n-resize`	Arrow upwards.
`ne-resize`	Arrow upwards right.
`e-resize`	Arrow right.
`se-resize`	Arrow downwards right.
`s-resize`	Arrow downwards.
`sw-resize`	Arrow downwards left.
`w-resize`	Arrow left.
`nw-resize`	Arrow upwards left.
`text`	Text cursor.
`wait`	Wait symbol.
`help`	Help symbol.
`url (File)`	Own cursor, in GIF or JPG graphics.

Table 10.43 ***Possible values for cursor***

10.10.2 filter:Alpha() (CSS 2.0)

With this Microsoft special filter, you can merge the foreground elements with background elements. Suitable for this are graphics shown on a background graphic. The available options comprise the following parameters:

```
Element {filter: Alpha(parameter, parameter, ...);}
```

Paramenter	Meaning
`opacity=`	Degree of coverage at the start of merging. Values between 0 and 100 are allowed. A value of 0 means that the graphic is completely transparent and the background shows through fully. With a value of 100, there is no transparency and the background does not show through.
`finishopacity=`	Degree of coverage at the end of merging. Values between 0 and 100 are allowed. A value of 0 means that the graphic is completely transparent and the background shows through fully. With a value of 100, there is no transparency and the background does not show through.

Paramenter	Meaning
style=0	Background and foreground are added colorwise and the foreground element is changed accordingly. No further input is necessary.
style=1	Linear course from the self-defined starting point with startx= and starty= after a self-defined end point finishedx= and finishedy=. At the start, the value for opacity= is needed and at the end, the value of finishopacity=.
style=2	Elliptical course from inside to outside. Inside, the value for opacity= is needed and outside, that of finishopacity=.
style=3	Rectangular course from inside to outside. Inside, the value for opacity= is needed and outside, that of finishopacity=.
startx=	In conjunction with style=1, start point in pixels horizontally from left-hand margin of foreground graphics.
starty=	In conjunction with style=1, start point in pixels vertically from top margin of foreground graphics.
finishedx=	In conjunction with style=1, end point in pixels horizontally from left-hand margin of foreground graphics.
finishedy=	In conjunction with style=1, end point in pixels vertically from top margin of foreground graphic.

Table 10.44 ***Values for alpha***

You can also combine several filters, for example Alpha() and Blur(), to do this, simply leave a space between the filters and add a further filter with its parameters:

```
Element {filter: Alpha(...) Blur(...);}
```

10.10.3 filter:Blur() (CSS 2.0)

With this Microsoft special filter, you can achieve a blurred effect. Suitable for this are graphics. The available options comprise the following parameters:

```
Element {filter: Blur(parameter, parameter, ...);}
```

Parameter	Meaning
add=0	The contours of the original graphic are no longer recognizable.
direction=	Indicates the direction of the blurring. These values are allowed: 0, 45, 90, 135, 180, 225, 270, 315.
strength=	Indicates the strength of the effect. Here, 0 stands for no effect.

Table 10.45 ***Possible parameters for the Blur filter***

You can also combine several filters, for example `Alpha()` and `Blur()`, to do this, simply leave a space between the filters and add a further filter with its parameters:

```
Element {filter: Alpha(...) Blur(...);}
```

10.10.4 filter:Chroma() (CSS 2.0)

With this Microsoft special filter, you can achieve a transparent effect. Suitable for this are graphics. Unlike GIF graphics, the filter affects the whole of the graphic. The available options comprise the following parameters:

```
Element {filter: Chroma(parameter);}
```

Paramenter	Meaning
color=	Inputting of one hexadecimal color is allowed.

Table 10.46 ***What color do you want the filter to have?***

You can also combine several filters, for example `Alpha()` and `Blur()`, to do this, simply leave a space between the filters and add a further filter with its parameters:

```
Element {filter: Alpha(...) Blur(...);}
```

10.10.5 filter:DropShadow() (CSS 2.0)

With this Microsoft special filter, you can impose a shadow effect on the contours. Suitable for this are graphics with clear contours, e.g. clipart and text. The available options comprise the following parameters:

```
Element {filter: DropShadow(parameter, parameter, ...);}
```

Paramenter	Meaning
`color=`	Inputting of one hexadecimal color is allowed.
`offx=`	Shadow effect horizontally in pixels. With positive numbers, the shadow is thrown to the right and with negative numbers, it is thrown to the left.
`offy=`	Shadow effect vertically in pixels. With positive numbers, the shadow is thrown downwards and with negative numbers, it is thrown upwards.
`positive=1`	Produces a shadow for the transparent color of a GIF graphic.

Table 10.47 ***Parameter of filter:DropShadow( )***

You can also combine several filters, for example `Alpha()` and `Blur()`, to do this, simply leave a space between the filters and add a further filter with its parameters:

```
Element {filter: Alpha(...) Blur(...);}
```

10.10.6 filter:FlipH() (CSS 2.0)

With this Microsoft special filter, you can show the graphic reflected horizontally. This filter does not need any parameters:

```
Element {filter: FlipH();}
```

You can also combine several filters, for example `Alpha()` and `Blur()`, to do this, simply leave a space between the filters and add a further filter with its parameters:

```
Element {filter: Alpha(...) Blur(...);}
```

10.10.7 filter:FlipV() (CSS 2.0)

With this Microsoft special filter, you can show the graphic reflected vertically. This filter does not need any parameters:

```
Element {filter: FlipV();}
```

You can also combine several filters, for example `Alpha()` and `Blur()`, to do this, simply leave a space between the filters and add a further filter with its parameters:

```
Element {filter: Alpha(...) Blur(...);}
```

10.10.8 filter:Glow() (CSS 2.0)

With this Microsoft special filter, you can achieve a glowing border around an element. The available options comprise the following parameters:

```
Element {filter: Glow(parameter, parameter);}
```

Parameter	Meaning
color=	Inputting of one hexadecimal color is allowed.
strength=	Strength of effect (1 to 255).

Table 10.48 ***Parameters of glow filter***

You can also combine several filters, for example `Alpha()` and `Blur()`, to do this, simply leave a space between the filters and add a further filter with its parameters:

```
Element {filter: Alpha(...) Blur(...);}
```

10.10.9 filter:Gray() (CSS 2.0)

With this Microsoft special filter, you can show the graphic in gray stages. This filter does not need any parameters:

```
Element {filter: Gray();}
```

You can also combine several filters, for example `Alpha()` and `Blur()`, to do this, simply leave a space between the filters and add a further filter with its parameters:

```
Element {filter: Alpha(...) Blur(...);}
```

10.10.10 filter:Invert() (CSS 2.0)

With this Microsoft special filter, you can invert the colors of graphics and elements. This filter does not need any parameters:

```
Element {filter: Invert();}
```

You can also combine several filters, for example `Alpha()` and `Blur()`, to do this, simply leave a space between the filters and add a further filter with its parameters:

```
Element {filter: Alpha(...) Blur(...);}
```

10.10.11 filter:Mask() (CSS 2.0)

With this Microsoft special filter, you can replace the transparent color of a GIF graphic with the transferred color; all non-transparent colors are given the color that was defined as transparent:

```
Element {filter: Mask(Parameter);}
```

Paramenter	Meaning
`color=`	Inputting of one hexadecimal color is allowed.

Table 10.49 ***Possible parameters of the mask filter***

You can also combine several filters, for example `Alpha()` and `Blur()`, to do this, simply leave a space between the filters and add a further filter with its parameters:

```
Element {filter: Alpha(...) Blur(...);}
```

10.10.12 filter:Shadow() (CSS 2.0)

With this Microsoft special filter, you can place a shadow around an element. The available options comprise the following parameters:

```
Element {filter: Shadow(parameter, parameter);}
```

Parameter	Meaning
`color=`	Inputting of one hexadecimal color is allowed.
`direction=`	Indicates the direction of the shadow. The values allowed are 0, 45, 90, 135, 180, 225, 270, 315.

Table 10.50 ***Parameters for shadow***

You can also combine several filters, for example `Alpha()` and `Blur()`, to do this, simply leave a space between the filters and add a further filter with its parameters:

```
Element {filter: Alpha(...) Blur(...);}
```

10.10.13 filter:Wave() (CSS 2.0)

With this Microsoft special filter, you can place a shadow around an element. The available options comprise the following parameters:

```
Element {filter: Shadow(parameter, parameter);}
```

Parameter	Meaning
`freq=`	Wave frequency (the higher the value, the smaller the waves).
`light=`	Strength of light (0-100).
`phase=`	Start of sine wave phase (0-100).
`strength=`	Strength of overall effect (ca. 1-10).
`add=`	1= Original graphic is added to the effect. 2= Original graphic is not added to the effect.

Table 10.51 ***Possible parameters of the wave filter***

You can also combine several filters, for example `Alpha()` and `Blur()`, to do this, simply leave a space between the filters and add a further filter with its parameters:

```
Element {filter: Alpha(...) Blur(...);}
```

10.10.14 filter:XRay() (CSS 2.0)

With this Microsoft special filter, you can achieve an effect like a photonegative (gray stages and inverting) of graphics and elements. This filter does not need any parameters:

```
Element {filter: XRay();}
```

You can also combine several filters, for example `Alpha()` and `Blur()`, to do this, simply leave a space between the filters and add a further filter with its parameters:

```
Element {filter: Alpha(...) Blur(...);}
```

Alphabetical HTML reference

As XML and HTML operate closely together, we have decided to add an HTML reference section to this book. This quick reference guide shows you which attributes belong to the individual tags and what effects they achieve. One very important point in HTML programming is the compatibility of individual tags with different browsers. We have listed here, for all tags and their attributes, their availability in Microsoft Internet Explorer and in Netscape Navigator along with the associated HTML versions. A version specified as "4.0B1" relates to browser version 4.0 Beta 1. This reference contains information up to browser versions Microsoft Internet Explorer 5.02 (version 5.5 was released too close to the publication of the book to be considered) and Netscape Navigator 4.72 (here again, version 6.0 came out just before we went to print). This reference section is not exhaustive, depicting only the most important tags.

11.1 A

11.1.1 <a>

Tag/Attribute	2.0	3.0	3.2	4.0	Internet Explorer	Netscape
<a href>	X	X	X	X	1.0	1.0
accesskey				X	4.0B1	
charset				X		
coords				X		
hreflang				X		
methods	X	X				
name	X	X	X	X	1.0	1.0
rel	X	X	X	X		
rev	X	X	X	X		
shape		X		X		

Tag/Attribute	2.0	3.0	3.2	4.0	Internet Explorer	Netscape
tabindex				X	4.0B1	
target				X	3.0A1	2.0
title	X	X	X	X	4.0B1	
type				X		
urn	X	X				

Probably the most important tag in HTML is <a>, since it defines (with the attribute href) a link to other HTML pages or other data. An area of text or some other object is defined as the anchor for the link.

accesskey

With accesskey, you can define a keyboard shortcut by which you can access the link. Assign a unique letter to the attribute and it will be executed when you depress its key with the associated shortcut key, which depends on the browser and operating system.

charset

This attribute contains the character coding of the target. The standard value is ISO-8859-1.

coords

Specifies the coordinates for the anchor area of the link in an image map. Depending on the value of the attribute shape, the coordinates are indicated as follows (always in pixels starting from the top left-hand corner of the image):

Value of shape	Submission format to coords
rectangle	"left, top, right, bottom"
circle	"center point X, center point Y, radius"
polygon	"point1 X, point1 Y, point2 X, point2 Y, etc"

Table 11.1 *Submission format to coords depending on value of shape*

href

The target address of the link.

Warning Either href or name must be defined in <a> .

hreflang

This attribute specifies the main language of the target.

methods

Here, target keywords, separated by spaces, originally had to be input, but as none of the normal browsers supported this attribute, it was no longer listed from HTML 3.2 onwards.

name

Here, a designation is entered for the link (which then also operates as a read character), enabling you to jump directly to this point in the document.

Warning Either `href` or `name` must be defined in `<a>`.

rel

Here, keywords separated by spaces originally had to be input, clarifying the connection between the page and target. Unfortunately, none of the usual browsers support this attribute.

rev

This attribute corresponds to the reversal of `rel`. Here, keywords separated by spaces originally had to be input, clarifying the connection between the page and target. Unfortunately, none of the usual browsers support this attribute.

shape

Here, the geometric shape of the anchor area in the image map is defined. Possible values are `default` (standard value), `rectangle` `circle` and `polygon`.

tabindex

Specifies the tab index of the link. Positive values stand for the position of the link in the list of objects that can be activated with [Tab]. Negative values mean that the link does not appear in the tab index.

target

Here, you input the name of the target frame in which the link's target is to be displayed.

title

Specifies the title of the target, which is displayed when you move the mouse over the link without clicking on it.

type

Specifies the MIME type of the target.

urn

This attribute was originally meant to enhance `name`, but was never supported by the normal browsers, and therefore disappeared from the language from HTML 3.2 onwards.

Example:

```
<a href="http://www.address.co.uk/directory/
index.htm#pointA" target="Center Frame">Click here!</a>
```

Tag/Attribute	*2.0*	*3.0*	*3.2*	*4.0*	*Internet Explorer*	*Netscape*
<a name>	X	X	X	X	1.0	1.0
href	X	X	X	X	1.0	1.0
methods	X	X				
name	X	X	X	X	1.0	1.0
rel	X	X	X	X		
rev	X	X	X	X		
title	X	X	X	X	4.0B1	
urn	X	X				

Probably the most important tag in HTML is `<a>`, since it defines (with the attribute `name`) a read character.

href

The target address of the link.

Warning Either `href` or `name` must be defined in `<a>`.

methods

Here, target keywords separated by spaces originally had to be input. However, as none of the normal browsers supported this attribute, it was no longer listed from HTML 3.2 onwards.

name

Here, a designation for a read character is input, enabling you to jump directly to this point in the document.

> **Warning** Either `href` or `name` must be defined in `<a>`

rel

Here, keywords separated by spaces originally had to be input, clarifying the connection between the page and target. Unfortunately, none of the usual browsers support this attribute.

rev

This attribute corresponds to the reversal of `rel`. Here, keywords separated by spaces originally had to be input, clarifying the connection between the page and target. Unfortunately, none of the usual browsers support this attribute.

title

Specifies the title of the target, which is displayed when you move the mouse over the link without clicking on it.

urn

This attribute was originally intended to enhance `name` but was never supported by any of the normal browsers and therefore disappeared from the language from HTML 3.2 onwards.

Example:

```
<a name="PointA">
```

11.1.2 <applet>

Tag/Attribute	2.0	3.0	3.2	4.0	Internet Explorer	Netscape
<applet>			X	X	3.0B2	2.0
align			X	X	3.0B2	2.0
alt			X	X	3.0B2	2.0
archive				X	4.0	3.0B7
code			X	X	3.0B2	2.0
codebase			X	X	3.0B2	2.0
height			X	X	3.0B2	2.0
hspace			X	X	3.0B2	2.0
mayscript						3.0
name			X	X	3.0B2	2.0
object				X		
src					4.0	
vspace			X	X	3.0B2	2.0
width			X	X	3.0B2	2.0

This tag enables Java applets to be embedded. Browsers that support Java ignore all information enclosed by `<applet>` ... `</applet>` with the exception of the `<param>` tag. Conversely, browsers that do not support Java ignore `<applets>` and the `<param>` tags contained in them. They display all other information contained in `<applet>` ... `</applet>`, and this applies even if the Java applet should cause an error and cannot be loaded.

align

Specifies the alignment of the subsequent text with the applet. Possible values are: `baseline`, `bottom`, `left`, `middle`, `right`, `textbottom`, `textmiddle`, `texttop` and `top`.

alt

The value of this attribute is output if the browser does not recognize `<applet>` This can sometimes apply in the case of old text browsers, for instance.

archive

Refers to a .zip file which contains all classes of applet. The URL is indicated either relative to `codebase` or absolute.

code

Refers to the class of applet. The URL is indicated either relative to `codebase` or absolute.

codebase

Specifies the directory in which the code is located and to which `archive`, `code` and `src` are to refer.

height

Specifies the height of the applet in pixels so that a wildcard of the appropriate size can be displayed even at the stage of downloading the code.

hspace

Specifies the left and right-hand space between the applet and all other HTML components in pixels.

mayscript

This attribute does not contain a value. When it is specified, the applet obtains JavaScript functionality. If the attribute should be missing and the applet attempts to access JavaScript elements, an error is output.

name

This attribute contains the name of the applet. This is needed to identify itself in comparison with other applets on this page.

object

Specifies the name of a data source containing applets.

src

Points to the source of the applet's class file. The URL is indicated either relative to `codebase` or absolute.

vspace

Specifies the top and bottom space between the applet and all other HTML components in pixels.

width

Specifies the width of the applet in pixels so that a wildcard of the appropriate size can be displayed even at the stage of downloading the code.

Example:

```
<applet codebase="http://www.address.co.uk/java/"
code="an_applet.class" >
  <param name="Line1" value="Textline 1">
  <param name="Line2" value="Textline 2">
  <param name="Line2" value="Textline 2">
  You do not have a Java-compatible browser!<br>
</applet>
```


See also:

`<param>`, `<embed>`, `<noembed>`, `<noscript>`, `<param>`, `<script>`

11.1.3 <area>

Tag/Attribute	2.0	3.0	3.2	4.0	Internet Explorer	Netscape
<area>			X	X	1.0	2.0
accesskey				X		
alt			X	X	4.0B2	3.0
coords			X	X	1.0	2.0
href			X	X	1.0	2.0
nohref			X	X	1.0	2.0
shape			X	X	1.0	2.0
tabindex				X	4.0B1	
target				X	3.0A1	2.0

This tag is needed in order to produce client's own image maps. You can generate hot areas within them.

accesskey

With `accesskey`, you can define a keyboard shortcut by which you can access the link. Assign a unique letter to the attribute and it will be executed when you depress its key with the associated shortcut key, which depends on the browser and operating system.

alt

The value of this attribute is output if the browser does not recognize `<area>`. This can sometimes apply in the case of old text browsers, for instance.

coords

Specifies the coordinates for the anchor area of the link in an image map. Depending on the value of the attribute `shape`, the coordinates are indicated as follows (always in pixels starting from the top left-hand corner of the image):

Value of `shape`	*Submission format to* `coords`
rectangle	"left, top, right, bottom"
circle	"center point X, center point Y, radius"
polygon	"point1 X, point1 Y, point2 X, point2 Y, etc"

Table 11.2 ***Submission format to coords depending on value of shape***

href

Specifies the target of the link.

Warning Must not be set together with `nohref` !

nohref

If you want to turn an `<area>` link off for a short time, instead of `href`, you can use this stand-alone attribute.

shape

Here, the geometric shape of the anchor area in the image map is defined. Possible values are `default` (standard value), `rectangle`, `circle` and `polygon` .

tabindex

Specifies the tab index of the hot area. Positive values stand for the position of the area in the list of objects that can be activated with [Tab] . Negative values mean that the hot area does not appear in the tab index.

11 TAKE THAT!

target

Here, the name of the target frame in which the link's target is to be displayed is entered.

Example:

```
<map name="An Image Map">
  <area shape="rectangle" coords="10,20,30,40"
  href="http://www.address.co.uk/a.htm">
  <area shape="circle" COORDS="60,50,20"
 href="http://www.address.co.uk/b.htm">
  <area shape="polygon" coords="5,100,10,110,0,110"
 href="http://www.address.co.uk/c.htm">
</map>
```

See also:

`<bgsound>, <img>, <map>, <object>`

11.2 B

11.2.1 <b>

Tag/Attribute	2.0	3.0	3.2	4.0	Internet Explorer	Netscape
`<b>`	X	X	X	X	1.0	1.0

Text enclosed by `<b>` ... `</b>` is displayed in bold typeface.

Example:

```
<b>This text is printed in bold,</b> but this is not.
```

See also:

`<big>, <font>, <i>, <q>, <s>, <small>, <strong>, <sub>, <sup>, <tt>, <u>`

11.2.2 <base>

Tag/Attribute	2.0	3.0	3.2	4.0	Internet Explorer	Netscape
`<base>`	X	X	X	X	1.0	1.0
`href`	X	X	X	X	1.0	1.0
`target`				X	3.0A1	2.0

This tag enables you to specify a basic preset for `href` and `target` for all HTML elements on the page.

href

Specifies the basic address to which all relative URL information on the page is related.

target

Specifies the standard target frame to which all HTML elements on the page automatically refer.

Example:

```
<base href="http://www.address.co.uk"
target="Center frame">
```

See also:

`<isindex>, <meta>, <scripts>, <style>, <title>`

11.2.3 <basefont>

Tag/Attribute	2.0	3.0	3.2	4.0	Internet Explorer	Netscape
<basefont>			X	X	1.0	1.0
color				X	1.0	
face				X	1.0	
size			X	X	1.0	1.0

This tag sets the standard font type.

color

Here, the color of the text is defined. You can use RGB values and color values predefined for many browsers (see Appendix B).

face

Expects a list of names of font types, separated by commas. The first font type found (and installed on the user's system) is used as the output font type for the text enclosed by this tag.

size

Represents the font size. Possible values are `1` to `7`. If you put a `+` or a `-` in front of the value, the size will be calculated relative to the current font size.

Example:

```
<basefont color="#ff0000" face="Arial" size=4>
```

11.2.4 <bgsound>

Tag/Attribute	2.0	3.0	3.2	4.0	Internet Explorer	Netscape
<bgsound>					2.0	
balance					4.0B1	
delay					2.0	
loop					2.0	
src					2.0	
volume					2.0B1	

This tag enables you to play background music.

balance

You can use this attribute to affect the stereo adjustment of the music reproduction. Values between `-10000` (left) and `10000` (right) are allowed. Centralized stereo output is achieved with the value `0`.

delay

Specifies the delay before playing and between repetitions in milliseconds.

loop

Specifies the number of repetitions. You can use positive integers or `infinite` for endless repetition.

src

Expects the URL of an audio file (.au, .mid or .wav).

volume

Specifies the loudness of the music reproduction. Values you can use are: `-10000` (quiet or off) to `0` (full volume).

Example:

```
<bgsound src="a_song.mid" loop=infinite>
```

See also:

```
<area>, <img>, <map>, <object>
```

11.2.5 <big>

Tag/Attribute	2.0	3.0	3.2	4.0	Internet Explorer	Netscape
<big>		X	X	X	3.0A1	1.1

Text enclosed by <big> ... </big> is shown in a larger font size.

Example:

```
<big>This text is printed in big,</big> but this is not.
```

See also:

```
<b>, <font>, <i>, <q>, <s>, <small>, <strong>, <sub>,
<sup>, <tt>, <u>
```

11 TAKE THAT!

11.2.6 <blockquote>

Tag/Attribute	2.0	3.0	3.2	4.0	Internet Explorer	Netscape
<block-quote>	X	X	X	X	1.0	1.0
cite				X		

Identifies quotes. These are normally provided with left and right-hand parentheses.

cite

Specifies the original address of the quote as a URL.

Example:

```
<blockquote cite="http://www.spectrosoftware.de">...and
life becomes colorful</blockquote>.
```

See also:

```
<center>, <code>, <h1>, <h2>, <h3>, <h4>, <h5>, <h6>, <mul-
ticol>, <p>, <pre>.
```

11.2.7 <body>

Tag/Attribute	2.0	3.0	3.2	4.0	Internet Explorer	Netscape
<body>	X	X	X	X	1.0	1.0
alink			X	X	4.0B1	1.1
background		X	X	X	1.0	1.1

Tag/Attribute	2.0	3.0	3.2	4.0	Internet Explorer	Netscape
bgcolor			X	X	1.0	1.1
bgproperties					2.0	
bottommargin					4.0B1	
leftmargin					2.0	
link			X	X	1.0	1.1
marginheight						4.0
marginwidth						4.0
nowrap					4.0	
rightmargin					4.0B1	
scroll					4.0B1	
text			X	X	1.0	1.1
topmargin					2.0	
vlink			X	X	1.0	1.1

This tag is responsible for the structuring of the HTML page at the highest level. All text and image elements should be enclosed by `<body>` ... `</body>` since global attributes affecting the entire HTML body are defined.

alink

Here, the color of the current link (link on the page itself) is defined. You can use RGB values and color values predefined for many browsers (see Appendix B).

background

Specifies the address of an image that is to be loaded into the background of the HTML page.

bgcolor

Here, the background color of the document is defined. You can use RGB values and color values predefined for many browsers (see Appendix B).

bgproperties

Indicates background properties. The only value you can use presently is `fixed`, which leaves the background unchanged even when scrolling. The contents of the page then move over the background like on a transparent film.

bottommargin

Specifies the bottom border left free in the document in pixels.

leftmargin

Specifies the left-hand border left free in the document in pixels.

link

Here, the color of a link is defined. You can use RGB values and color values predefined for many browsers (see Appendix B).

marginheight

Specifies the top and bottom borders left free in the documents in pixels.

marginwidth

Specifies the left and right-hand borders left free in the document in pixels.

nowrap

Indicates whether the usual HTML conventions for linewrap apply or will be ignored.

Value	*Meaning*
false	The normal conventions apply: text that reaches the end of a line is automatically wrapped.
true	Text that reaches the end of a line is not wrapped. Only explicitly specified formatting (` `, `<p>`, ...) will be followed.

Table 11.3 ***The values of nowrap in <body>***

rightmargin

Specifies the right-hand border left free in the document in pixels.

scroll

Indicates whether scroll bars are to be shown.

Value	*Meaning*
auto	Insert scroll bars if required.
no	Never insert scroll bars.
yes	Always insert scroll bars.

Table 11.4 ***The values of scroll in <body>***

text

Here, the color of the text is defined. You can use RGB values and color values predefined for many browsers (see Appendix B).

topmargin

Specifies the top border of the document left free in pixels.

vlink

Here, the color of a link already visited is defined. You can use RGB values and color values predefined for many browsers (see Appendix B).

Example:

```
<html>
  <head>
    <!—Here is information about the contents.-->
  </head>
  <body>
    Here are the contents.
  </body>
</html>
```

See also:

```
<head>, <html>, <frameset>
```

11.2.8

Tag/Attribute	*2.0*	*3.0*	*3.2*	*4.0*	*Internet Explorer*	*Netscape*
 	X	X	X	X	1.0	1.0
clear			X	X	1.0	1.0

With this tag, you can enforce a linewrap.

clear

This attribute was enhanced in order to deal with images that are moved to the left or right by the attribute `align` in `<img>`. You can now use it to deal with all objects that are relocated by `align`.

Value	Meaning
none	A completely normal linewrap is generated.
left	The line is wrapped and the next line is inserted far enough below for the left-hand margin to be free from images (or other objects).
right	The line is wrapped and the next line is inserted far enough below for the right-hand margin to be free from images (or other objects).
all	The line is wrapped and the next line is inserted far enough below for both margins to be free from images (or other objects).

Table 11.5 ***The values of clear in
***

Example:

```
This is the first line<br>
and this is the second.
```

See also:

`<nobr>, <wbr>`

11.2.9 <button>

Tag/Attribute	2.0	3.0	3.2	4.0	Internet Explorer	Netscape
<button>				X	4.0B1	
accesskey				X	4.0B1	
disabled				X	4.0B1	
name				X	4.0B1	
tabindex				X	4.0B1	
type				X	4.0B1	
value				X	4.0B1	

This tag can generate buttons in forms.

accesskey

With `accesskey`, you can define a keyboard shortcut by which you can access the button. Assign a unique letter to the attribute and it will be executed when you depress this key with the associated shortcut key, which depends on the browser and operating system.

disabled

This stand-alone attribute causes the button to be identified as inactive, and terminates the functionality of the button.

name

Specifies the designation of the button so that it can be identified on submission to scripts.

tabindex

Specifies the tab index of the button. Positive values stand for the position of the button in the list of objects that can be activated with [Tab]. Negative values mean that the button does not appear in the tab index.

type

Indicates what function the button is to have in the form.

Value	*Meaning*
button	Defines the button as multifunctional. (The button is given its own script.)
reset	The button resets the form.
submit	The button sends the form data.

Table 11.6 *The values of type in <button>*

value

Specifies the value of the button that is to be submitted to the script if it has been activated.

Example:

```
<button type="submit" name="send" tabindex=1>
  <img SRC="an_image.gif">
</button>
```

See also:

```
<fieldset>, <form>, <input>, <keygen>, <label>,  <legend>,
<optgroup>, <option>, <select>, <textarea>
```

11.3 C

11.3.1 <caption>

Tag/Attribute	*2.0*	*3.0*	*3.2*	*4.0*	*Internet Explorer*	*Netscape*
<caption>		X	X	X	2.0	1.1
align		X	X	X	2.0	1.1
valign					2.0	

This tag can be used only within `<table> ... </table>` and is located on the same level as `<tr>`. It generates a table header or caption over the entire table width.

align

Specifies the alignment within a table cell.

Value	*Meaning*
bottom	The contents are aligned downwards. (In Internet Explorer, undo with valign).
top	The contents are aligned upwards. (In Internet Explorer, undo with valign).
center	The contents are aligned centrally. (Only in Internet Explorer).
left	The contents are aligned to the left. (Only in Internet Explorer).
right	The contents are aligned to the right. (Only in Internet Explorer).

Table 11.7 ***The values of align in <caption>***

valign

Specifies the vertical alignment within the table cell.

Value	*Meaning*
bottom	The contents are aligned downwards.
top	The contents are aligned upwards.

Table 11.8 ***The values of valign in <caption>***

Example:

```
<table border=1>
  <caption>Browser statistic</caption>
  <tr><th>Browser</th><th>Market share</th></tr>
  <tr><td>Microsoft Internet Explorer</td><td>60.4 %</td>
  </tr>
  <tr><td>Netscape Communicator</td><td>38.5 %</td></tr>
  <tr><td>Others</td><td>1.1 %</td></tr>
</table>
```

See also:

`<col>, <colgroup>, <thead>, <tbody>, <tfoot>, <table>, <th>, <td>, <tr>`

11.3.2 <center>

Tag/Attribute	2.0	3.0	3.2	4.0	Internet Explorer	Netscape
<center>			X	X	1.0	1.0

Centers a text block with all other HTML elements.

Example:

```
This text is left aligned<br>
<center>and this is centered.</center>
```

See also:

```
<blockquote>, <code>, <h1>, <h2>, <h3>, <h4>, <h5>, <h6>,
<multicol>, <p>, <pre>
```

11.3.3 <code>

Tag/Attribute	2.0	3.0	3.2	4.0	Internet Explorer	Netscape
<code>	X	X	X	X	1.0	1.0

With this tag, you can format a source code. This is normally shown in a font type that prints each letter the same width.

Example:

```
<code>if(x==y) return;</code>
```

See also:

```
<blockquote>, <center>, <h1>, <h2>, <h3>, <h4>, <h5>, <h6>,
<multicol>, <p>, <pre>
```

11.3.4 <col>

Tag/Attribute	2.0	3.0	3.2	4.0	Internet Explorer	Netscape
<col>				X	3.0A1	
align				X	4.0B1	
bgcolor					4.0	
char				X		
charoff				X		
span				X	3.0A1	
valign				X	4.0B1	
width				X	3.0A1	

This tag represents an enhancement to the usual tables. Here, presets for the columns in the table are located. This tag is always within a `<colgroup> ... </colgroup>` configuration. No data is embedded here, only formatting operations are performed.

align

Specifies the horizontal alignment within the column.

Value	Meaning
center	The contents are aligned centrally.
left	The contents are aligned to the left.
right	The contents are aligned to the right.

Table 11.9 *The values of align in <col>*

bgcolor

Here, the background color of the column is defined. You can use RGB values and color values predefined for many browsers (see Appendix B).

char

Here, you can indicate the character against which the cell contents are aligned (for instance, the period for decimal numbers). The first appearance of this character will be counted as relevant.

charoff

Specifies the distance from the first-occurring alignment character defined in `char` in pixels.

span

Indicates how many columns in the normal table structure are spanned by the current column.

valign

Specifies the vertical alignment within the column.

Value	Meaning
bottom	The contents are aligned downwards.
top	The contents are aligned upwards.

Table 11.10 *The values of valign in <col>*

width

Specifies the overall width of the column in pixels or as a percentage of the browser window width.

Example:

```
<table border=1 cols=2>
  <colgroup>
    <col ALIGN="right">
  </colgroup>
  <colgroup>
    <col ALIGN="center">
    <col ALIGN="center">
  </colgroup>
  <caption>Browser statistic</caption>
  <tr><th>Browser</th><th>Market share</th></tr>
  <tr><td>Microsoft Internet Explorer</td><td>60.4 %</td>
  </tr>
  <tr><td>Netscape Communicator</td><td>38.5 %</td></tr>
  <tr><td>Others</td><td>1.1 %</td></tr>
</table>
```

See also:

`<caption>, <colgroup>, <thead>, <tbody>, <tfoot>, <table>, <th>, <td>, <tr>`

11.3.5 <colgroup>

Tag/Attribute	2.0	3.0	3.2	4.0	Internet Explorer	Netscape
<colgroup>				X	3.0A1	
align				X	4.0B1	
bgcolor					4.0	
char				X		
charoff				X		
span				X	3.0A1	
valign				X	4.0B1	
width				X	4.0B1	

This tag is used in `<table> … </table>` and contains only `<col>` tags. It is used to enable the columns to be formatted even before the table data capture.

align

Specifies the horizontal alignment within the column group.

Value	Meaning
center	The contents are aligned centrally.
left	The contents are left aligned.
right	The contents are right aligned.

Table 11.11 *The values of align in <colgroup>*

11 TAKE THAT!

bgcolor

Here, the background color of the color group is defined. You can use RGB values and color values predefined for many browsers (see Appendix B).

char

Here, you can identify the character against which the cell contents will be aligned (for instance, the period for decimal numbers). Only the first appearance of this character is counted as relevant.

charoff

Specifies the distance from the first-occurring alignment character defined in `char` in pixels.

span

Indicates how many columns are in the group without having to list them all with `<col>`.

valign

Specifies the vertical alignment within the group of rows.

Value	Meaning
bottom	The contents are aligned downwards.
top	The contents are aligned upwards.

Table 11.12 *The values of valign in <colgroup>*

width

Specifies the overall width of the column in pixels or as a percentage of the browser window width.

Example:

```
<table border=1 cols=2>
  <colgroup>
    <col ALIGN="right">
  </colgroup>
  <colgroup>
    <col ALIGN="center">
    <col ALIGN="center">
  </colgroup>
  <caption>Browser statistic</caption>
  <tr><th>Browser</th><th>Market share</th></tr>
  <tr><td>Microsoft Internet Explorer</td><td>60.4 %</td>
  </tr>
  <tr><td>Netscape Communicator</td><td>38.5 %</td></tr>
  <tr><td>Others</td><td>1.1 %</td></tr>
</table>
```

See also:

`<caption>, <col>, <thead>, <tbody>, <tfoot>, <table>, <th>, <td>, <tr>`

11.3.6 <comment>

Tag/Attribute	*2.0*	*3.0*	*3.2*	*4.0*	*Internet Explorer*	*Netscape*
<comment>					1.0	

Passages flanked by `<comment>` ... `</comment>` are commented on by the browser and ignored.

Example:

```
This text does <comment>not </comment>appear on the screen.
```

See also:

```
<!-- ... -->
```

11.4.1 <div>

Tag/Attribute	2.0	3.0	3.2	4.0	Internet Explorer	Netscape
<div>		X	X	X	3.0A1	2.0
align		X	X	X	3.0A1	2.0
clear		X				
nowrap					4.0	

This tag identifies a section of text that is to start with a linewrap and also end with a linewrap.

align

Specifies the horizontal alignment of the section.

Value	Meaning
center	The contents are aligned centrally.
justify	The contents are printed as a justified block.
left	The contents are left aligned.
right	The contents right aligned.

Table 11.13 *The values of align in <div>*

clear

This attribute was enhanced in order to deal with images that are moved to the left or right by the attribute `align` in `<img>`. You can now use it to deal with all objects that are relocated by `align`.

Value	Meaning
none	A completely normal linewrap is generated.
left	The line is wrapped and the next line is inserted far enough below for the left margin to be free of images (or other objects).
right	The line is wrapped and the next line is inserted far enough below for the right margin to be free of images (or other objects).
all	The line is wrapped and the next line is inserted far enough below for both margins to be free of images (or other objects).

Table 11.14 *The values of clear in <div>*

nowrap

Indicates whether the normal HTML conventions for linewrap apply or are ignored.

Value	*Meaning*
false	The normal conventions apply: text that reaches the end of a line is automatically wrapped.
true	Text that reaches the end of a line is not wrapped. Only explicitly specified formatting (, <p>, etc) is followed.

Table 11.15 ***The values of nowrap in <div>***

Example:

```
<div>This is a separate paragraph</div>
```


11.5 E

11.5.1 <embed>

Tag/Attribute	*2.0*	*3.0*	*3.2*	*4.0*	*Internet Explorer*	*Netscape*
<embed>					3.0B2	1.1
height					3.0B2	1.1
src					3.0B2	1.1
width					3.0B2	1.1

This tag is used to embed plug-in data in the browser. The above-mentioned attributes are interrogated directly by the browser and all others are submitted to the plug-in unprocessed.

height

Specifies the height of the plug-in in pixels or as a percentage of the height of the browser window.

src

Specifies the URL of the plug-in data to be displayed.

width

Specifies the width of the plug-in in pixels or as a percentage of the width of the browser window.

Example:

```
<embed src="a_song.mid" controls>
  <noembed>
    Your browser does not support the embedding of the
    <a HREF="a_song.mid">song</a>.
  </noembed>
</embed>
```

See also:

```
<applet>, <noembed>, <noscript>, <param>, <script>
```


11.6 F

11.6.1 <fieldset>

Tag/Attribute	*2.0*	*3.0*	*3.2*	*4.0*	*Internet Explorer*	*Netscape*
<fieldset>				X	4.0B2	
align					4.0	

Combines the input elements of forms in groups.

align

Specifies the horizontal alignment within the group.

Value	*Meaning*
center	The contents are aligned centrally.
left	The contents are left aligned.
right	The contents are right aligned.

Table 11.16 *The values of align in <fieldset>*

Example:

```
<form>
  <fieldset>
    <legend accesskey="b" tabindex=1>
      Order newsletter
    </legend>
```

```
    <label accesskey="y">
      <input type="radio" name=news value="yes">yes
    </label><br>
    <label accesskey="n">
      <input type="radio" name=news value="no">no
    </label><br>
  </fieldset>
</form>
```

See also:

<button>, <form>, <input>, <keygen>, <label>, <legend>, <optgroup>, <option>, <select>, <textarea>

11.6.2 <font>

Tag/Attribute	2.0	3.0	3.2	4.0	Internet Explorer	Netscape
<font>			X	X	1.0	1.0
color			X	X	1.0	2.0
face				X	1.0	3.0B5
point-size						4.0B5
size			X	X	1.0	1.0

This tag is probably the most useful means in HTML 4 for configuring text. The attributes affect the font type and size.

color

Here, the color of the text is defined. You can use RGB values and color values predefined for many browsers (see Appendix B).

face

Expects a list of font names, separated by commas. The first font type found (and installed on the user's system) is used as the output font type for the text enclosed by this tag.

point-size

Specifies the point size of the font type and is an alternative to `size`.

size

Represents the font size. Possible values are `1` to `7`. If you put a `+` or `-` in front of the value, the size will be calculated relative to the current font size.

Example:

```
<font face="arial" size=+2>
```

See also:

```
<b>, <big>, <i>, <q>, <s>, <small>, <strong>, <sub>, <sup>,
<tt>, <u>
```

11.6.3 <form>

Tag/Attribute	2.0	3.0	3.2	4.0	Internet Explorer	Netscape
<form>	X	X	X	X	1.0	1.0
accept				X		
accept-charset				X		
action	X	X	X	X	1.0	1.0
autocomplete					5.0	
enctype	X	X	X	X	1.0	1.0
method	X	X	X	X	1.0	1.0
name				X	3.0B1	2.0
target				X	3.0A1	2.0

Here, a form is set up. All form elements (for instance `<input>`) are enclosed by `<form>` ... `</form>`.

accept

Indicates which MIME formats the form is allowed to send in order that the script or server can react correctly to them. These formats are separated by commas.

accept-charset

Specifies the character sets the form is allowed to send. They are separated by commas.

action

Specifies the address of the script or server that is to evaluate the form data.

autocomplete

Switches the automatic complete function on (`on`) or off (`off`).

enctype

Specifies the MIME media type into which the data is to be encoded during the send process.

method

Indicates how the form is to send the data.

Value	*Meaning*
post	Here, the data is sent as a separate data stream directly to the script.
get	Here, the data is attached to the URL and they are then submitted together to the target script.

Table 11.17 ***The values of method in <form>***

name

Specifies the name of the form so that it can be addressed by scripts and changed if necessary.

target

Specifies the target frame in which the results data is to be displayed after the form data has been sent.

Example:

```
<form method="post" action="mailto:my@address.co.uk">
  <fieldset>
    <legend accesskey="b" tabindex=1>
    Order newsletter</legend>
    <label accesskey="y" name="yes">
      <input type="radio" name=news value="yes">yes
    </label><br>
    <label accesskey="n" name="no">
      <input type="radio" name=news value="no">no
    </label><br>
  </fieldset>
  <input type="submit" value="send form">
  <input type="reset" value="reset form">
</form>
```

See also:

```
<button>, <fieldset>, <input>, <keygen>, <label>,
<legend>, <optgroup>, <option>, <select>, <textarea>
```

11.6.4 <frame>

Tag/Attribute	2.0	3.0	3.2	4.0	Internet Explorer	Netscape
<frame>				X	3.0A1	2.0
application					5.0	
bordercolor					4.0B2	3.0B5
frameborder				X	3.0A1	3.0B5
longdesc				X		
marginheight				X	3.0A1	2.0
marginwidth				X	3.0A1	2.0
name				X	3.0A1	2.0
noresize				X	3.0A1	2.0
scrolling				X	3.0A1	2.0
src				X	3.0A1	2.0

With this tag, you generate a border within `<frameset> ... </frameset>`. The attributes of this tag affect the individual frames.

application

Indicates whether the frame contents are an HTA (HTML application) and therefore free from the Internet Explorer security requirements.

Value	Meaning
no	The security requirements remain unchanged.
yes	The contents of this border are reliable.

Table 11.18 *The values of application in <frame>*

bordercolor

Here, the color of the frame border is defined. You can use RGB values and color values predefined for many browsers (see Appendix B). Any values previously set with `<frameset>` are overwritten.

frameborder

Indicates whether a border is to be drawn round the frame. (This is only switched off, however, if all frames positioned on the border have switched it off.)

Value	Meaning
0	The border is switched off (Netscape).
1	The border is switched on (Netscape),
no	The border is switched off (Microsoft).
yes	The border is switched on (Microsoft).

Table 11.19 ***The values of the attribute frameborder in <frame>***

longdesc

Indicates an address that provides a longer description of the contents of the border.

marginheight

Specifies the top and bottom distance between the frame border and the text. The value must be greater than `0` and is indicated in pixels.

marginwidth

Specifies the left and right-hand distance between the frame border and the text. The value must be greater than `0` and is indicated in pixels.

name

Gives the frame a name with which other tags can address it with their `target` attribute.

noresize

This stand-alone attribute prevents any change in the frame size.

scrolling

Indicates whether scroll bars are to be displayed.

Value	Meaning
auto	Reveal scroll bars if required.
no	Never reveal scroll bars.
yes	Always reveal scroll bars.

Table 11.20 ***The values of scrolling in <frame>***

src

Specifies the URL of the page that is to be displayed in the frame.

Example:

```
<html>
  <head>
    <title>An example frame</title>
  </head>
  <frameset rows=20%,60%,20%>
    <frame src="a.htm" name="top">
    <frameset cols=50%,50%>
      <frame src="b.htm" name="center left">
      <frame src="c.htm" name="center right">
    </frameset>
    <frame src="d.htm" name="bottom">
  </frameset>
  <noframes>
    <head>
      <title>An example frame (unfortunately, your browser
is too
      old)</title>
    </head>
    <body>
      <center>
        WARNING!<P>
        YOU ARE USING A BROWSER THAT DOES NOT
        SUPPORT FRAMES. PLEASE CLICK
        <a href="a.htm">HERE</a> TO GO TO A VERSION WITHOUT
        FRAMES<p>
      </center>
    </body>
  </noframes>
</html>
```

See also:

<frameset>, <noframes>

11.6.5 <frameset>

Tag/Attribute	2.0	3.0	3.2	4.0	Internet Explorer	Netscape
<frameset>				X	3.0A1	2.0
border					4.0B1	3.0B5
bordercolor					4.0B2	3.0B5
cols				X	3.0A1	2.0
frameborder					3.0A1	3.0B5
framespacing					3.0A1	
rows				X	3.0A1	2.0

This tag specifies that the page is to generate borders. It replaces the `<body>` tag and contains `<frame>` tags and possibly further `<frameset>` instructions.

border

This attribute is defined in the outermost`<frameset>` tag and specifies the border thickness for all frames in pixels. If the value is `0`, a `frameborder=no` is enforced in all frames.

bordercolor

Here, the color of the frame border is defined. You can use RGB values and color values predefined for many browsers (see Appendix B).

cols

Specifies the widths of the individual columns, separated by commas.

Value	Meaning
Positive integers	Width in pixels.
Percentage value	Percentage width of current frame.
`*`, `2*`, ...	Proportions of available residual width.

Table 11.21 *The values of cols in <frameset>*

frameborder

Indicates whether a border is to be drawn round the frame. (This is only switched off, however, if all frames located on the border have switched it off.)

Value	Meaning
0	The border is switched off (Netscape).
1	The border is switched on (Netscape).
no	The border is switched off (Microsoft).
yes	The border is switched on (Microsoft).

Table 11.22 ***The values of the attribute frameborder in <frame>***

framespacing

Specifies the width of the gap between individual frames in pixels.

rows

Specifies the heights of the individual rows, separated by commas.

Values	Meaning
Positive whole numbers	Width in pixels.
Percentage value	Percentage width of current frame.
, 2, ...	Proportions of available residual width.

Table 11.23 ***The values of rows in <frameset>***

Example:

```
<html>
  <head>
    <title>An example frame</title>
  </head>
  <frameset rows=20%,60%,20%>
    <frame src="a.htm" name="top">
    <frameset cols=50%,50%>
      <frame src="b.htm" name="center left">
      <frame src="c.htm" name="center right">
    </frameset>
    <frame src="d.htm" name="bottom">
  </frameset>
  <noframes>
    <head>
      <title>An example frame (unfortunately, your browser
is too old)</title>
    </head>
    <body>
      <center>
```

```
            WARNING!<P>
            YOU ARE USING A BROWSER THAT DOES NOT
            SUPPORT FRAMES. PLEASE CLICK
            <a href="a.htm">HERE</a> TO GO TO A VERSION WITHOUT
            FRAMES<p>
          </center>
        </body>
    </noframes>
</html>
```

See also:

<body>, <head>, <html>, <frame>, <noframes>

11.7 H

11.7.1 <h1> ... <h6>

Tag/Attribute	2.0	3.0	3.2	4.0	Internet Explorer	Netscape
<h1> ... <h6>	X	X	X	X	1.0	1.0
align		X	X	X	1.0	1.0
clear		X				

Here, a header is generated <h1> gives a first-degree header and <h6> a sixth-degree one.

align

Specifies the horizontal alignment of the header.

Value	Meaning
center	The header is aligned centrally.
left	The header is aligned to the left.
right	The header is aligned to the right.

Table 11.24 *The values of align in <h1> ... <h6>*

clear

This attribute was enhanced in order to deal with images that are moved to the left or right by the attribute align in <img>. You can now use it to deal with all objects that are relocated by align.

Value	Meaning
none	A completely normal linewrap is generated.
left	The line is wrapped and the next line inserted far enough below for the left-hand margin to be free of images (or other objects).
right	The line is wrapped and the next line inserted far enough below for the right-hand margin to be free of images (or other objects).
all	The line is wrapped and the next line inserted far enough below for both margins to be free of images (or other objects).

Table 11.25 ***The values of clear in <h1> to <h6>***

Example:

```
<h1>1 Introduction</h1>
<h2>1.1 What is HTML?</h2>
<h2>1.2 Requirements</h2>
<h3>1.2.1 Text editor</h3>
<h3>1.2.2 Browser</h3>
<h2>1.3 HTML principles</h2>
<h3>1.3.1 Hello World! </h3>
<h3>1.3.2 Tags</h3>
<h3>1.3.3 Head and Body</h3>
<h3>1.3.4 Attributes</h3>
```

See also:

`<blockquote>, <center>, <code>, <multicol>, <p>, <pre>`

11.7.2 <head>

Tag/Attribute	2.0	3.0	3.2	4.0	Internet Explorer	Netscape
<head>	X	X	X	X	1.0	1.0
profile				X		

This tag identifies the head of an HTML line. The area between `<head> ... </head>` contains no actual document information, but only information about the contents of the document.

profile

Indicates a list of URLs for META data profiles, which are separated with spaces.

Example:

```
<html>
  <head>
    <!—Here is information about the contents.-->
  </head>
  <body>
    Here are the contents.
  </body>
</html>
```

See also:

```
<body>, <html>, <frameset>
```

11.7.3 <hr>

Tag/Attribute	2.0	3.0	3.2	4.0	Internet Explorer	Netscape
<hr>	X	X	X	X	1.0	1.0
align			X	X	1.0	1.0
color					3.0A1	
noshade			X	X	1.0	1.0
size			X	X	1.0	1.0
width			X	X	1.0	1.0

Represents a horizontal separating line on the screen.

align

Specifies the horizontal alignment of the line.

Value	Meaning
center	The line is aligned centrally.
left	The line is aligned to the left.
right	The line is aligned to the right.

Table 11.26 *The values of align in <hr>*

color

Here, the color of the line is defined. You can use RGB values and color values predefined for many browsers (see Appendix B).

noshade

This stand-alone attribute specifies that the line is to be in a single color and without a 3D effect.

size

Specifies the width of the line in pixels.

width

Specifies the width of the line in pixels or relative to the browser width.

Example:

```
<hr width=50%>
```


11.7.4 <html>

Tag/Attribute	2.0	3.0	3.2	4.0	Internet Explorer	Netscape
<html>	X	X	X	X	1.0	1.0

This tag has the highest level in the hierarchy. All other tags are located in `<html>` ... `</html>`. This tag therefore serves to identify the complete HTML code as such.

Example:

```
<html>
  <head>
    <!—Here is information about the contents.-->
  </head>
  <body>
    Here are the contents.
  </body>
</html>
```

See also:

```
<body>, <head>, <frameset>
```

11.8.1 <i>

Tag/Attribute	2.0	3.0	3.2	4.0	Internet Explorer	Netscape
<i>	X	X	X	X	1.0	1.0

With this tag, you can identify text that is to be shown in italics.

Example:

```
<i>This text is printed in italics,</i> but this is not.
```

See also:

```
<b>, <big>, <font>, <q>, <s>, <small>, <strong>, <sub>,
<sup>, <tt>, <u>
```

11.8.2 <img>

Tag/Attribute	2.0	3.0	3.2	4.0	Internet Explorer	Netscape
<img>	X	X	X	X	1.0	1.0
align	X	X	X	X	1.0	1.0
alt	X	X	X	X	1.0	1.0
border			X	X	1.0	1.0
controls					2.0	
dynsrc					2.0	
height		X	X	X	1.0	1.0
hspace			X	X	1.0	1.0
ismap	X	X	X	X	1.0	1.0
longdesc				X		
loop					2.0	
lowsrc					4.0B1	1.0
name				X	4.0	3.0
src	X	X	X	X	1.0	1.0
start					2.0	
suppress						4.0
usemap			X	X	1.0	2.0
vrml					2.0	
vspace			X	X	1.0	1.0
width		X	X	X	1.0	1.0

This tag is the standard variant for embedding images, graphics and videos in an HTML page.

align

Specifies the alignment of the text following the image.

Value	Meaning
middle	The text is aligned vertically in the middle.
left	The text is aligned to the left.
right	The text is aligned to the right.
top	The text is aligned upwards.
bottom	The text is aligned downwards.

Table 11.27 ***The values of align in <img>***

alt

The value of this attribute is output if the browser does not recognize `<img>`. This can sometimes apply in the case of old text browsers, for instance.

border

Specifies the width of the border that is to be displayed around an image if it serves as an anchor for a link. It contains the color that a normal textlink would have.

controls

This stand-alone attribute indicates whether the page user is to have control over the running of a video or some other data source defined via `dynsrc`.

dynsrc

This attribute specifies the address of a video that is to be played as a result of this tag.

height

Specifies the height of the image in pixels or as a percentage value of the height of the browser window.

hspace

Specifies the left and right-hand distance between the image and all other HTML components in pixels.

11

TAKE THAT!

ismap

This stand-alone attribute specifies that hot areas have been defined for this image and can be activated by clicking.

longdesc

Specifies the address that provides a longer description of the contents of the image.

loop

Indicates how often a video is to be repeated.

lowsrc

Specifies the URL of an image with lower quality that is loaded before the image is reloaded from `src` with high resolution.

name

Indicates a designation for the image so that it can be addressed later via script languages.

src

Specifies the URL of an image that is to be displayed here.

start

This attribute is used in connection with `dynsrc` and indicates when the video is to be started.

Value	Meaning
fileopen	The video is played as soon as it has been completely downloaded.
mouseover	The video is not played until it has been completely downloaded and the mouse has been moved over it.

Table 11.28 ***The values of start in <img>***

suppress

This attribute indicates whether the revealing of an icon, displayed when the image has not yet been completely loaded down, is to be suppressed.

Value	Meaning
false	The normal browser remains in force.
true	Suppresses the icon.

Table 11.29 ***The values of suppress in <img>***

usemap

Specifies the address of the client's own image map specification.

vrml

Indicates a URL for a VRML world and starts a VRML plugin if this is installed.

vspace

Specifies the top and bottom distances between the image and all other HTML components in pixels.

width

Specifies the width of the image in pixels or as a percentage value of the width of the browser window.

Example:

```
<img src="an_image.jpg" old="My portrait">
<img src="a_film.jpg" old="A film should run here." dyn-
src="a_film.avi">
```

See also:

```
<area>, <bgsound>, <map>, <object>
```

11.8.3 <input>

Tag/Attribute	2.0	3.0	3.2	4.0	Internet Explorer	Netscape
<input type="button">				X	3.0B1	1.0
accesskey				X	4.0B1	
disabled				X	4.0B1	
height						4.0B2
name				X	3.0B1	1.0
tabindex				X	4.0B1	
value				X	3.0B1	1.0
width						4.0B2

11 TAKE THAT!

This tag is used in forms that were generated with `<form> ... </form>`. With the value `button` it produces a button for attribute `type`.

accesskey

With `accesskey`, you can define a keyboard shortcut by which you can access the form element. Assign a letter to the attribute and it will be executed when you depress the appropriate key with the associated shortcut key, which depends on the browser and operating system.

disabled

This stand-alone attribute causes the form element to be identified as inactive, and suppresses the functionality of the element.

height

Specifies the height of the button in pixels.

name

Specifies the designation of the form element so that it can be identified by scripts. The value of the attribute is also indicated during evaluation of the form.

tabindex

Specifies the tab index of the form element. Positive values stand for the position of the element in the list of objects that can be activated with [Tab]. Negative values mean that the element does not appear in the tab index.

value

Specifies the return value to the script in the event that this form element has been activated.

width

Specifies the width of the button in pixels.

See also:

`<button>, <fieldset>, <form>, <keygen>, <label>, <legend>, <optgroup>, <option>, <select>, <textarea>`

Tag/Attribute	*2.0*	*3.0*	*3.2*	*4.0*	*Internet Explorer*	*Netscape*
<input type="checkbox">	X	X	X	X	1.0	1.0
accesskey				X	4.0B1	

Tag/Attribute	2.0	3.0	3.2	4.0	Internet Explorer	Netscape
checked	X	X	X	X	1.0	1.0
disabled		X		X	4.0B1	
name	X	X	X	X	1.0	1.0
tabindex				X	4.0B1	
value	X	X	X	X	1.0	1.0

This tag is used in forms generated with `<form>` ... `</form>`. With the value `checkbox` , it produces a checkbox for the attribute `type`.

accesskey

With `accesskey`, you can define a keyboard shortcut by which you can access the form element. Assign a letter to the attribute and it will be executed when you depress the appropriate key with the associated shortcut key, which depends on the browser and operating system.

checked

This stand-alone attribute specifies that the form element in the standard setting of the form is to be activated.

disabled

This stand-alone attribute causes the form element to be identified as inactive, and suppresses the functionality of the element.

name

Specifies the designation of the form element so that it can be identified by scripts. The value of the attribute is also indicated during evaluation of the form.

tabindex

Specifies the tab index of the form element. Positive values stand for the position of the element in the list of objects that can be activated with [Tab]. Negative values mean that the element does not appear in the tab index.

value

Specifies the return value to the script in the event that this form element has been activated.

See also:

`<button>`, `<fieldset>`, `<form>`, `<keygen>`, `<label>`, `<legend>`, `<optgroup>`, `<option>`, `<select>`, `<textarea>`

Tag/Attribute	*2.0*	*3.0*	*3.2*	*4.0*	*Internet Explorer*	*Netscape*
<input type="file">		X	X	X	4.0B2	2.0
accept				X		
accesskey				X	4.0B2	
disabled		X		X	4.0B2	
name		X	X	X	4.0B2	2.0
readonly					4.0B2	
tabindex				X		
value		X	X	X		

This tag is used in forms generated with `<form> ... </form>`. With the value `file` it produces a file selection field for the attribute `type`.

accept

Indicates which MIME formats the form is allowed to send in order that the script or server can react correctly to them. These formats are separated by commas.

accesskey

With `accesskey`, you can define a keyboard shortcut by which you can access the form element. Assign a letter to the attribute and it will be executed when you depress the appropriate key with the associated shortcut key, which depends on the browser and operating system.

disabled

This stand-alone attribute causes the form element to be identified as inactive, and suppresses the functionality of the element.

name

Specifies the designation of the form element so that it can be identified by scripts. The value of the attribute is also indicated during evaluation of the form.

readonly

This stand-alone attribute specifies that the contents of this form element cannot be amended by the reader of the page.

tabindex

Specifies the tab index of the form element. Positive values stand for the position of the element in the list of objects that can be activated with [Tab]. Negative values mean that the element does not appear in the tab index.

value

Specifies the return value to the script (i.e. the filename).

See also:

`<button>, <fieldset>, <form>, <keygen>, <label>, <legend>, <optgroup>, <option>, <select>, <textarea>`

Tag/Attribute	*2.0*	*3.0*	*3.2*	*4.0*	*Internet Explorer*	*Netscape*
<input type= "hidden">	X	X	X	X	1.0	1.0
name	X	X	X	X	1.0	1.0
value	X	X	X	X	1.0	1.0

This tag is used in forms generated with `<form>` ... `</form>`. With the value `hidden` it produces for the attribute `type` a hidden field on which the user of the page has no influence, but which can interact with the script.

name

Specifies the designation of the form element so that it can be identified by scripts. The value of the attribute is also indicated during evaluation of the form.

value

Specifies the return value to the script.

See also:

`<button>, <fieldset>, <form>, <keygen>, <label>, <legend>, <optgroup>, <option>, <select>, <textarea>`

Tag/Attribute	*2.0*	*3.0*	*3.2*	*4.0*	*Internet Explorer*	*Netscape*
<input type= "image">	X	X	X	X	1.0	1.0
accesskey				X	4.0B1	
align	X	X	X	X	1.0	1.0
alt				X	4.0B2	4.0
border						1.0
disabled		X		X	4.0B2	
height					4.0B1	1.1

Tag/Attribute	2.0	3.0	3.2	4.0	Internet Explorer	Netscape
ismap				X		
name	X	X	X	X	1.0	1.0
src	X	X	X	X	1.0	1.0
tabindex				X	4.0B1	
usemap				X		2.0
value	X	X	X	X		
width					4.0B1	1.1

This tag is used in forms generated with `<form> ... </form>`. With the value `image`, it generates for the attribute `type` an image on which you can click in order to send the form data. It operates like `type=submit`, but also sends the coordinates to the script on which you clicked in the image.

accesskey

With `accesskey`, you can define a keyboard shortcut by which you can access the form element. Assign a letter to the attribute and it will be executed when you depress the appropriate key with the associated shortcut key, which depends on the browser and operating system.

align

Specifies the alignment of the text following the image.

Value	Meaning
middle	The text is aligned vertically in the middle.
left	The text is aligned to the left.
right	The text is aligned to the right.
top	The text is aligned upwards.
bottom	The text is aligned downwards.

Table 11.30 *The values of align in <input type="image">*

alt

The value of this attribute is output if the browser cannot show any images. This sometimes applies in the case of old text browsers.

border

Specifies the width of the border that is to be displayed around an image. It contains the color that a normal text link would have.

disabled

This stand-alone attribute causes the form element to be identified as inactive, and suppresses the functionality of the element.

height

Specifies the height of the image in pixels.

ismap

This stand-alone attribute specifies that hot areas have been defined for this image, and can be activated by clicking on them.

name

Specifies the designation of the form element so that it can be identified by scripts. The value of the attribute is also indicated during evaluation of the form.

src

Specifies the URL of an image that is to be displayed here.

tabindex

Specifies the tab index of the form element. Positive values stand for the position of the element in the list of objects that can be activated with [Tab]. Negative values mean that the element does not appear in the tab index.

usemap

Specifies the address of the client's own image map specifications.

value

Specifies the return value to the script in the event that this form element has been activated.

width

Specifies the width of the image in pixels.

See also:

<button>, <fieldset>, <form>, <keygen>, <label>, <legend>, <optgroup>, <option>, <select>, <textarea>

Tag/Attribute	*2.0*	*3.0*	*3.2*	*4.0*	*Internet Explorer*	*Netscape*
<input type= "password">	X	X	X	X	1.0	1.0
accesskey				X	4.0B1	
autocomplete					5.0	
disabled		X		X	4.0B1	
name	X	X	X	X	1.0	1.0
readonly				X	4.0B1	
tabindex				X	4.0B1	
value	X	X	X	X	1.0	1.0
vcard_name					5.0	

This tag is used in forms generated with `<form>` ... `</form>`. With the value `password`, it produces a password input line for the attribute `type`.

accesskey

With `accesskey`, you can define a keyboard shortcut by which you can access the form element. Assign a letter to the attribute and it will be executed when you depress the appropriate key with the associated shortcut key, which depends on the browser and operating system.

autocomplete

Switches the automatic complete function on (`on`) or off (`off`).

disabled

This stand-alone attribute causes the form element to be identified as inactive, and suppresses the functionality of the element.

name

Specifies the designation of the form element so that it can be identified by scripts. The value of the attribute is also indicated during evaluation of the form.

readonly

This stand-alone attribute specifies that the contents of this form element cannot be amended by the reader of the page.

tabindex

Specifies the tab index of the form element. Positive values stand for the position of the element in the list of objects that can be activated with [Tab]. Negative values mean that the element does not appear in the tab index.

value

Specifies the return value to the script.

vcard_name

Indicates a field name of the personal Microsoft visiting card (`vcard`) whose value is to be preset here. The contents of this field are not passed on to the recipient of the form data until the form has been sent.

Value	*Meaning*
vCard.Business.City	Company's address: City
vCard.Business.Country	Company's address: Country
vCard.Business.Fax	Company's address: Fax number
vCard.Business.Phone	Company's address: Phone number
vCard.Business.State	Company's address: State
vCard.Business.StreetAddress	Company's address: Street and building number
vCard.Business.URL	Company's address: Homepage address
vCard.Business.Zipcode	Company's address: Zip code
vCard.Cellular	Cellphone number
vCard.Company	Company's name
vCard.Department	Department
vCard.DisplayName	Displayed name
vCard.Email	E-mail address
vCard.FirstName	First name
vCard.Gender	Gender
vCard.Home.City	Private address: City
vCard.Home.Country	Private address: Country
vCard.Home.Fax	Private address: Fax number
vCard.Home.Phone	Private address: Phone number
vCard.Home.State	Private address: State
vCard.Home.StreetAddress	Private address: Street and building number
vCard.Home.Zipcode	Private address: Zip code
vCard.Homepage	Homepage address
vCard.JobTitle	Job title
vCard.LastName	Last name
vCard.MiddleName	Middle name
vCard.Notes	Notes
vCard.Office	Office
vCard.Pager	Pager number

Table 11.31 ***Values for vcard_name in <input type="password">***

See also:

`<button>, <fieldset>, <form>, <keygen>, <label>, <legend>, <optgroup>, <option>, <select>, <textarea>`

Tag/Attribute	*2.0*	*3.0*	*3.2*	*4.0*	*Internet Explorer*	*Netscape*
<input type= "radio">	X	X	X	X	1.0	1.0
accesskey				X	4.0B1	
checked	X	X	X	X	1.0	1.0
disabled		X		X	4.0B1	
name	X	X	X	X	1.0	1.0
tabindex				X	4.0B1	
value	X	X	X	X	1.0	1.0

This tag is used in forms generated with `<form> ... </form>`. With the value `radio` it produces a radio button for the attribute `type`.

accesskey

With `accesskey`, you can define a keyboard shortcut by which you can access the form element. Assign a letter to the attribute and it will be executed when you depress the appropriate key with the associated shortcut key, which depends on the browser and operating system.

checked

This stand-alone attribute specifies that the form element is to be activated in the standard setting of the form.

disabled

This stand-alone attribute causes the form element to be identified as inactive, and suppresses the functionality of the element.

name

Specifies the designation of the form element so that it can be identified by scripts. The value of the attribute is also indicated during evaluation of the form.

tabindex

Specifies the tab index of the form element. Positive values stand for the position of the element in the list of objects that can be activated with [Tab]. Negative values mean that the element does not appear in the tab index.

value

Specifies the return value to the script in the event that this form element has been activated.

See also:

`<button>`, `<fieldset>`, `<form>`, `<keygen>`, `<label>`, `<legend>`, `<optgroup>`, `<option>`, `<select>`, `<textarea>`

Tag/Attribute	*2.0*	*3.0*	*3.2*	*4.0*	*Internet Explorer*	*Netscape*
<input type= "reset">	X	X	X	X	1.0	1.0
accesskey				X	4.0B1	
disabled		X		X	4.0B1	
height						4.0B2
tabindex				X	4.0B1	
value	X	X	X	X	1.0	1.0
width						4.0B2

This tag is used in forms generated with `<form>` ... `</form>`. With the value `reset` it provides for the attribute `type`, a button that can reset the form.

accesskey

With `accesskey`, you can define a keyboard shortcut by which you can access the form element. Assign a letter to the attribute and it will be executed when you depress the appropriate key with the associated shortcut key, which depends on the browser and operating system.

disabled

This stand-alone attribute causes the form element to be identified as inactive, and suppresses the functionality of the element.

height

Specifies the height of the button in pixels.

tabindex

Specifies the tab index of the form element. Positive values stand for the position of the element in the list of objects that can be activated with [Tab]. Negative values mean that the element does not appear in the tab index.

value

Specifies the return value to the script in the event that this form element has been activated.

width

Specifies the width of the button in pixels.

See also:

<button>, <fieldset>, <form>, <keygen>, <label>, <legend>, <optgroup>, <option>, <select>, <textarea>

Tag/Attribute	*2.0*	*3.0*	*3.2*	*4.0*	*Internet Explorer*	*Netscape*
<input type="submit">	X	X	X	X	1.0	1.0
accesskey				X	4.0B1	
disabled		X		X	4.0B1	
height						4.0B2
name	X	X	X	X	1.0	1.0
tabindex				X	4.0B1	
value	X	X	X	X	1.0	1.0
width						4.0B2

This tag is used in forms generated with `<form>` ... `</form>`. With the value `submit`, it produces for the attribute `type` a button that sends the form contents.

accesskey

With `accesskey`, you can define a keyboard shortcut by which you can access the form element. Assign a letter to the attribute and it will be executed when you depress the appropriate key with the associated shortcut key, which depends on the browser and operating system.

disabled

This stand-alone attribute causes the form element to be identified as inactive, and suppresses the functionality of the element.

height

Specifies the height of the button in pixels.

name

Specifies the designation of the form element so that it can be identified by scripts. The value of the attribute is also indicated during evaluation of the form.

tabindex

Specifies the tab index of the form element. Positive values stand for the position of the element in the list of objects that can be activated with [Tab]. Negative values mean that the element does not appear in the tab index.

value

Specifies the return value to the script in the event that this form element has been activated.

width

Specifies the width of the button in pixels.

See also:

`<button>, <fieldset>, <form>, <keygen>, <label>, <legend>, <optgroup>, <option>, <select>, <textarea>`

Tag/Attribute	2.0	3.0	3.2	4.0	Internet Explorer	Netscape
<input type= "text">	X	X	X	X	1.0	1.0
accesskey				X	4.0B1	
autocomplete					5.0	
disabled		X		X	4.0B1	
maxlength	X	X	X	X	1.0	1.0
name	X	X	X	X	1.0	1.0
readonly				X	4.0B1	
size	X	X	X	X	1.0	1.0
tabindex				X	4.0B1	
value	X	X	X	X	1.0	1.0
vcard_name					5.0	

This tag is used in forms generated with `<form>` ... `</form>`. With the value `text` it produces a text input field for the attribute `type`.

accesskey

With `accesskey`, you can define a keyboard shortcut by which you can access the form element. Assign a letter to the attribute and it will be executed when you depress the appropriate key with the associated shortcut key, which depends on the browser and operating system.

autocomplete

Switches the automatic complete function on or off.

disabled

This stand-alone attribute causes the form element to be identified as inactive, and suppresses the functionality of the element.

maxlength

Specifies the maximum character length for an input text.

name

Specifies the designation of the form element so that it can be identified by scripts. The value of the attribute is also indicated during evaluation of the form.

readonly

This stand-alone attribute specifies that the contents of the form element cannot be amended by the reader of the page.

size

Specifies the displayed character length for the input text.

tabindex

Specifies the tab index of the form element. Positive values stand for the position of the element in the list of objects that can be activated with [Tab]. Negative values mean that the element does not appear in the tab index.

value

Specifies the return value to the script.

vcard_name

Specifies the field name of the personal Microsoft visiting card (`vcard`) whose value is to be preset here. The contents of this field are not passed on to the recipient of the form data until the form has been sent.

Value	Meaning
vCard.Business.City	Company's address: City
vCard.Business.Country	Company's address: Country
vCard.Business.Fax	Company's address: Fax number
vCard.Business.Phone	Company's address: Phone number
vCard.Business.State	Company's address: State
vCard.Business.StreetAddress	Company's address: Street and building number
vCard.Business.URL	Company's address: Homepage address
vCard.Business.Zipcode	Company's Address: Zip code
vCard.Cellular	Cellphone number
vCard.Company	Company's name
vCard.Department	Department
vCard.DisplayName	Displayed name
vCard.Email	E-mail address
vCard.FirstName	First name
vCard.Gender	Gender
vCard.Home.City	Private address: City
vCard.Home.Country	Private address: Country
vCard.Home.Fax	Private address: Fax number
vCard.Home.Phone	Private address: Phone number
vCard.Home.State	Private address: State
vCard.Home.StreetAddress	Private address: Street and building number
vCard.Home.Zipcode	Private address: Zip code
vCard.Homepage	Homepage address
vCard.JobTitle	Job title
vCard.LastName	Last name
vCard.MiddleName	Middle name
vCard.Notes	Notes
vCard.Office	Office
vCard.Pager	Pager number

Table 11.32 ***Values for vcard_name in <input type="text">***

See also:

`<button>, <fieldset>, <form>, <keygen>, <label>, <legend>, <optgroup>, <option>, <select>, <textarea>`

11.8.4 <isindex>

Tag/Attribute	2.0	3.0	3.2	4.0	Internet Explorer	Netscape
<isindex>	X	X	X	X	1.0	1.0
action					1.0	1.0
prompt		X	X	X	1.0	1.0

This tag is needed to enable a special interactive search in your HTML document.

action

Specifies the address of a script that processes `<isindex>` data.

prompt

Indicates an alternative user prompt you are given if you want to do a search.

Example:

```
<isindex prompt="Your search inquiry:">
```

See also:

`<base>, <meta>, <scripts>, <style>, <title>`

11.9 K

11.9.1 <keygen>

Tag/Attribute	2.0	3.0	3.2	4.0	Internet Explorer	Netscape
<keygen>						3.0
challenge						3.0
name						3.0

This tag calculates an encryption code, which can be used in Netscape in forms to make the data transfer more secure.

challenge

Is taken as the basis of the randomly generated key.

name

Indicates a designation for this form element so that it can be addressed by scripts.

Example:

```
<form method="post" action="http://www.address.co.uk/
secret/a_script.cgi">
   <keygen name="Key" challenge="0815">
   <input type="text" name="Input">
</form>
```

See also:

```
<button>, <fieldset>, <form>, <input>, <label>, <legend>,
<optgroup>, <option>, <select>, <textarea>
```


11.10 L

11.10.1 <label>

Tag/Attribute	*2.0*	*3.0*	*3.2*	*4.0*	*Internet Explorer*	*Netscape*
<label>				X	4.0B2	
accesskey				X	4.0B2	
for				X	4.0B2	

This tag is used to add a description to form fields and thereby also simplify navigation within forms.

accesskey

With `accesskey`, you can define a keyboard shortcut by which you can access the marking. Assign a letter to the attribute and it will be executed when you depress the appropriate key with the associated shortcut key, which depends on the browser and operating system.

for

Indicates to which form field this marking is assigned.

Example:

```
<form>
  <fieldset>
    <legend accesskey="b" tabindex=1>
      Order newsletter
    </legend>
    <label accesskey="y">
      <input type="radio" name=news value="yes">yes
```

```
    </label><br>
    <label accesskey="n">
      <input type="radio" name=news value="no">no
    </label><br>
  </fieldset>
</form>
```

See also:

```
<button>, <fieldset>, <form>, <input>, <keygen>, <legend>,
<optgroup>, <option>, <select>, <textarea>
```


11.10.2 <legend>

Tag/Attribute	2.0	3.0	3.2	4.0	Internet Explorer	Netscape
<legend>				X	4.0B2	
accesskey				X	4.0	
align				X	4.0B2	

This tag specifies the designation for a <fieldset>.

accesskey

With accesskey, you can define a keyboard shortcut by which you can access the legend. Assign a letter to the attribute and it will be executed when you depress the appropriate key with the associated shortcut key, which depends on the browser and operating system.

align

Specifies the horizontal alignment within the legend.

Value	Meaning
center	The contents are aligned centrally.
left	The contents are aligned to the left.
right	The contents are aligned to the right.

Table 11.33 ***The values of align in <legend>***

Example:

```
<form>
  <fieldset>
    <legend accesskey="b" tabindex=1>
      Order newsletter
    </legend>
```

```
    <label accesskey="y">
      <input type="radio" name=news value="yes">yes
    </label><br>
    <label accesskey="n">
      <input type="radio" name=news value="no">no
    </label><br>
  </fieldset>
</form>
```

See also:

```
<button>, <fieldset>, <form>, <input>, <keygen>, <label>,
<optgroup>, <option>, <select>, <textarea>
```

11.10.3 <li>

Tag/Attribute	2.0	3.0	3.2	4.0	Internet Explorer	Netscape
<li>	X	X	X	X	1.0	1.0
clear		X				
type			X	X	1.0	1.0
value			X	X	1.0	1.0

This tag defines a list element. It is used in all the usual list types.

clear

This attribute was enhanced in order to deal with images that are moved to the left or right by the attribute `align` in `<img>`. You can now use it to deal with any object that is relocated with `align`.

Value	Meaning
none	A completely normal linewrap is generated.
left	The line is wrapped and the next line is inserted far enough below for the left-hand margin to be free of images (or other objects).
right	The line is wrapped and the next line is inserted far enough below for the right-hand margin to be free of images (or other objects).
all	The line is wrapped and the next line is inserted far enough below for both margins to be free of images (or other objects).

Table 11.34 ***The values of clear in <li>***

type

Indicates which list points are to be used.

Value	Meaning
A	A, B, C, D, etc
a	a, b, c, d, etc.
I	I, II, III, IV, etc
i	i, ii, iii, iv, etc
1	1, 2, 3, 4, etc
disc	Filled circle
square	Filled square
circle	Unfilled circles

Table 11.35 ***The values of type in <li>***

value

Indicates a different value for the listing than the current value following the last list element.

Example:

```
<ul>
  <li type="disc">Circle (filled)
  <li type="circle">Circle
  <li type="square">Square
</ul>
```

See also:

```
<menu>, <ol>, <ul>
```

11.10.4 <listing>

Tag/Attribute	2.0	3.0	3.2	4.0	Internet Explorer	Netscape
<listing>	X	X	X	X	1.0	1.0

Reproduces the source text up to the closing tag `</listing>` word for word.

Example:

```
<listing>
Here, you can actually type out tags (for instance <br>) and
they are output on the screen exactly as written but without
having any effect.
</listing>
```

11.11.1 <map>

Tag/Attribute	2.0	3.0	3.2	4.0	Internet Explorer	Netscape
`<map>`			X	X	1.0	2.0
name			X	X	1.0	2.0

This tag is needed for producing image maps. It contains the hot areas as `<area>` and the image in `<img>` with set `ismap` attribute.

name

Here, the designation for the image map (which then also operates as a read character) is entered, enabling you to jump directly to this point in the document.

Example:

```
<map name="An Image Map">
  <area shape="rectangle" coords="10,20,30,40"
  href="http://www.address.co.uk/a.htm">
  <area shape="circle" COORDS="60,50,20"
  href="http://www.address.co.uk/b.htm">
  <area shape="polygon" coords="5,100,10,110,0,110"
  href="http://www.address.co.uk/c.htm">
</map>
```

See also:

`<area>, <bgsound>, <img>, <object>`

11.11.2 <menu>

Tag/Attribute	2.0	3.0	3.2	4.0	Internet Explorer	Netscape
<menu>	X	X	X	X	1.0	1.0
compact	X	X	X	X		
type						4.0

This tag operates exactly the same as `<ul>`, but is intended especially for single-line list elements.

compact

This stand-alone attribute specifies that a space-saving representation is to be selected.

type

Indicates which list points are to be used.

Value	Meaning
A	A, B, C, D, etc.
a	a, b, c, d, etc.
I	I, II, III, IV, etc.
i	i, ii, iii, iv, etc.
1	1, 2, 3, 4, etc.
disc	Filled circles.
square	Filled squares.
circle	Unfilled circles.

Table 11.36 ***The values of type in <menu>***

Example:

```
<menu>
  <li type="disc">Circle (filled)
  <li type="circle">Circle
  <li type="square">Square
</menu>
```

See also:

`<li>, <ol>, <ul>`

11.11.3 <meta>

Tag/Attribute	2.0	3.0	3.2	4.0	Internet Explorer	Netscape
<meta>	X	X	X	X	2.0	1.1
content	X	X	X	X	2.0	1.1
http-equiv	X	X	X	X	2.0	1.1
name	X	X	X	X	2.0	1.1
scheme				X		

This tag represents a universal information mechanism providing information about the contents of the HTML page. Many search engines implement, for instance, lists of keywords using the tag `<meta>`.

content

Specifies the value that refers to `name` .

http-equiv

Indicates a text that is sent to the server, together with the http head, before the actual HTML text.

name

Indicates a designation for the information.

Tip Should this attribute not be set, `http-equiv` is necessary.

TAKE THAT! 11

scheme

Provides additional information about the format of `content` if several formats are to be supported.

Example:

```
<meta http-equiv="refresh" content="10; url=http://
www.address.co.uk/next.htm">
```

See also:

```
<base>, <isindex>, <scripts>, <style>, <title>
```

11.11.4 <multicol>

Tag/Attribute	2.0	3.0	3.2	4.0	Internet Explorer	Netscape
<multicol>						3.0B5
cols						3.0B5
gutter						3.0B5
width						3.0B5

This tag defines several columns of the same width into which the text flows and integrates.

cols

Specifies the number of columns to be used.

gutter

Specifies the spacing between the individual columns in pixels.

width

Specifies the width of the columns in pixels.

Example:

```
<multicol cols=2 gutter=20>
  This text is evenly distributed over two columns.
  Images and other HTML elements are also
  divided.
</multicol>
```

See also:

```
<blockquote>, <center>, <code>, <h1>, <h2>, <h3>, <h4>,
<h5>, <h6>, <p>, <pre>
```


11.12 N

11.12.1 <nobr>

Tag/Attribute	*2.0*	*3.0*	*3.2*	*4.0*	*Internet Explorer*	*Netscape*
<nobr>					1.0	1.0

Identifies a text passage that is not to contain any automatically generated line-wraps.

Example:

```
<nobr>
  This complete text is to stay in one line. This
  sentence also belongs in the first line. Only
  here<br>is there a manual return.
</nobr>
```

See also:

```
<br>, <wbr>
```

11.12.2 <noembed>

Tag/Attribute	2.0	3.0	3.2	4.0	Internet Explorer	Netscape
<noembed>					3.0B2	2.0

This tag is used within `<embed> ... </embed>`. It identifies a sourcecode that is to be executed only if the browser cannot process the tag `<embed>`.

Example:

```
<embed src="a_song.mid" controls>
  <noembed>
    Your browser does not support embedding of the
    <a HREF="a_song.mid">song</a>.
  </noembed>
</embed>
```

See also:

`<applet>, <embed>, <noscript>, <param>, <script>`

11.12.3 <noframes>

Tag/Attribute	2.0	3.0	3.2	4.0	Internet Explorer	Netscape
<noframes>				X	3.0A1	2.0

This tag identifies a sourcecode that is to be executed only if the browser cannot process the tag `<frameset>`.

Example:

```
<html>
  <head>
    <title>An example frame</title>
  </head>
  <frameset rows=20%,60%,20%>
    <frame src="a.htm" name="top">
    <frameset cols=50%,50%>
      <frame src="b.htm" name="center left">
      <frame src="c.htm" name="center right">
    </frameset>
    <frame src="d.htm" name="bottom">
  </frameset>
  <noframes>
    <head>
      <title>An example frame (unfortunately, your browser
```

```
is too
      old)</title>
    </head>
    <body>
      <center>
        WARNING<P>
        YOU ARE USING A BROWSER THAT DOES NOT
        SUPPORT FRAMES. PLEASE CLICK
        <a href="a.htm">HERE</a>TO GO TO A VERSION WITHOUT
        FRAMES!<p>
      </center>
    </body>
  </noframes>
</html>
```

See also:

<frame>, <frameset>

11.12.4 <noscript>

Tag/Attribute	2.0	3.0	3.2	4.0	Internet Explorer	Netscape
<noscript>				X	3.0	3.0B5

This tag identifies a sourcecode that is to be executed only if the browser cannot process the tag <noscript>.

Example:

```
<script language="JavaScript">
  <!-- document.write("This is a JavaScript.") -->
</script>
<noscript>
  Unfortunately, this is not a JavaScript.
</noscript>
```

See also:

<applet>, <embed>, <noembed>, <param>, <script>

11.13.1 <object>

Tag/Attribute	2.0	3.0	3.2	4.0	Internet Explorer	Netscape
`<object>`				X	3.0AI	
accesskey					4.0	
align				X	3.0AI	
border				X		
classid				X	3.0AI	
code					4.0	
codebase				X	3.0AI	
codetype				X	3.0AI	
data				X	3.0AI	
declare				X		
height				X	3.0AI	
hspace				X		
name				X	3.0AI	
standby				X		
tabindex				X		
type				X	3.0AI	
usemap				X		
vspace				X		
width				X	3.0AI	

This tag is a universal multimedia embedding tag.

accesskey

With `accesskey`, you can define a keyboard shortcut by which you can access the object. Assign a letter to the attribute and it will be executed when you depress the appropriate key with the associated shortcut key, which depends on the browser and operating system.

align

Specifies the horizontal alignment of the object.

Value	*Meaning*
center	The object is aligned centrally.
left	The object is aligned to the left.
right	The object is aligned to the right.

Table 11.37 ***The values of align in <object>***

border

Specifies the width of the border that is displayed around an image if it serves as the anchor for a link. It contains the color that a normal textlink would have.

classid

Specifies the address to the sourcecode of the object.

code

Refers to the class of the object. The URL is indicated either relative to `codebase` or absolute.

codebase

Specifies the directory in which the code is located and to which `code` is to refer.

codetype

Specifies the MIME format of the code.

data

Indicates an address for the object data (for instance, that of an image).

declare

This stand-alone attribute specifies that the object must not be loaded until it has been invoked by an HTML element or a script.

height

Specifies the height of the object in pixels.

hspace

Specifies the left and right-hand distance between the object and all other HTML components in pixels.

name

Specifies the designation of the form element so that it can be identified by scripts. The value of the attribute is also indicated during evaluation of the form.

standby

Indicates a text that is displayed provided this object is reloaded by the browser.

tabindex

Specifies the tab index of the object. Positive values stand for the position of the object in the list of objects that can be activated with [Tab]. Negative values mean that the object does not appear in the tab index.

type

Specifies the MIME type of the object.

usemap

Specifies the address of the client's own image map specifications.

vspace

Specifies the top and bottom distances between the object and all other HTML components in pixels.

width

Specifies the width of the object in pixels.

See also:

`<area>, <bgsound>, <img>, <map>`

11.13.2 <ol>

Tag/Attribute	2.0	3.0	3.2	4.0	Internet Explorer	Netscape
<ol>	X	X	X	X	1.0	1.0
clear		X				
compact	X	X	X	X		
start			X	X	1.0	1.0
type			X	X	1.0	1.0

This tag generates an ordered (consecutively numbered) list.

clear

This attribute has been enhanced in order to deal with images that are moved to the left or right by the attribute `align` in `<img>`. You can now use it to deal with any object relocated with `align`.

Value	Meaning
none	A completely normal linewrap is generated.
left	The line is wrapped and the next line is inserted far enough below for the left-hand margin to be free of images (or other objects).
right	The line is wrapped and the next line is inserted far enough below for the right-hand margin to be free of images (or other objects).
all	The line is wrapped and the next line is inserted far enough below for both margins to be free of images (or other objects).

Table 11.38 ***The values of clear in <ol>***

compact

This stand-alone attribute specifies that a place-saving representation is to be selected.

start

Specifies the starting value of the numbering.

type

Indicates which list points are to be used.

Value	Meaning
`A`	A, B, C, D, etc.
`a`	a, b, c, d, etc.
`I`	I, II, III, IV, etc.
`i`	i, ii, iii, iv, etc.
`1`	1, 2, 3, 4, etc.
`disc`	Filled circles.
`square`	Filled squares.
`circle`	Unfilled circles.

Table 11.39 ***The values of type in <ol>***

Example:

```
<ol>
  <li type="disc">Circle (filled)
  <li type="circle">Circle
  <li type="square">Square
</ol>
```

See also:

```
<li>, <menu>, <ul>
```


11.13.3 <optgroup>

Tag/Attribute	2.0	3.0	3.2	4.0	Internet Explorer	Netscape
<optgroup>				X		
disable				X		
label				X		

With this tag, you can bring together several `<option>` tags of a selection field and form them into a hierarchy.

disable

This stand-alone attribute specifies that this element has been temporarily deactivated.

label

Indicates a shortened name for the option group.

Example:

```
<form>
  <select name="Products">
    <option value="Mon">Monitor
    <option value="Pri">Printer
    <optgroup label="Computer">
      <option value="HDD">Hard disk
      <option value="Hou">Housing
      <option value="CPU">Processor
    </optgroup>
  </select>
</form>
```

See also:

<button>, <fieldset>, <form>, <input>, <keygen>, <label>, <legend>, <option>, <select>, <textarea>

11.13.4 <option>

Tag/Attribute	2.0	3.0	3.2	4.0	Internet Explorer	Netscape
<option>	X	X	X	X	1.0	1.0
disable		X		X		
label				X		
selected	X	X	X	X	1.0	1.0
value	X	X	X	X	1.0	1.0

Specifies the individual options for a selection field.

disable

This stand-alone attribute specifies that this element has been temporarily deactivated.

label

Indicates a shortened name for the option.

selected

This stand-alone attribute specifies that this option in the presets is to be selected.

value

Specifies the value for this element that is to be submitted in the form if it has been selected.

Example:

```
<form>
  <select name="Products">
    <option value="Mon">Monitor
    <option value="Pri">Printer
    <optgroup label="Computer">
      <option value="HDD">Hard disk
      <option value="Hou">Housing
      <option value="CPU">Processor
    </optgroup>
  </select>
```

```
</form>
```

See also:

<button>, <fieldset>, <form>, <input>, <keygen>, <label>, <legend>, <optgroup>, <select>, <textarea>

11.14 P

11.14.1 <p>

Tag/Attribute	2.0	3.0	3.2	4.0	Internet Explorer	Netscape
<p>	X	X	X	X	1.0	1.0
align		X	X	X	1.0	1.0
clear		X				

Generates a paragraph.

align

Specifies the horizontal alignment within the paragraph.

Value	Meaning
center	The contents are centrally aligned.
left	The contents are aligned to the left.
right	The contents are aligned to the right.

Table 11.40 ***The values of align in <p>***

clear

This attribute has been enhanced in order to deal with images moved to the left or right by the attribute `align` in `<img>`. You can use it to deal with any object relocated with `align`.

Value	Meaning
none	A completely normal linewrap is generated.
left	The line is wrapped and the next line is inserted far enough below for the left-hand margin to be free of images (or other objects).
right	The line is wrapped and the next line is inserted far enough below for the right-hand margin to be free of images (or other objects).
all	The line is wrapped and the next line is inserted far enough below for both margins to be free of images (or other objects).

Table 11.41 ***The values of clear in <p>***

Example:

```
This text serves as a demonstration.
<p>This is a separate paragraph.</p>
And here the text starts again.
```

See also:

`<blockquote>, <center>, <code>, <h1>, <h2>, <h3>, <h4>, <h5>, <h6>, <multicol>, <pre>`

11.14.2 <param>

Tag/Attribute	2.0	3.0	3.2	4.0	Internet Explorer	Netscape
<param>			X	X	3.0A1	2.0
name			X	X	3.0A1	2.0
type				X		
value			X	X	3.0A1	2.0
valuetype				X		

This tag is responsible for parameter submission to embedded objects (`<object>`, `<applet>`, etc).

name

This attribute specifies the name of the parameter.

type

Specifies the MIME types of the data sources defined in `value`, if `valuetype` has the value `ref`.

value

Specifies the value of the parameter `name`.

valuetype

Specifies the nature of the value `value` .

Value	Meaning
data	The value is passed on directly to the object.
ref	Here, `value` is identified as the URL.
object	Identifies `value` as an object-internal reference.

Table 11.42 ***The values of valuetype in <param>***

11 TAKE THAT!

Example:

```
<applet codebase="http://www.address.co.uk/java/"
code="an_applet.class" >
  <param name="Line1" value="Textline 1">
  <param name="Line2" value="Textline 2">
  <param name="Line2" value="Textline 2">
  You do not have a Java-compatible browser!<br>
</applet>
```

See also:

`<applet>, <embed>, <noembed>, <noscript>, <script>`

11.14.3 <plaintext>

Tag/Attribute	2.0	3.0	3.2	4.0	Internet Explorer	Netscape
<plaintext>	X	X	X	X	1.0	1.0

Here, the subsequent text is output on the screen word for word. Even a closing `</plaintext>` tag is ignored.

Example:

```
Here is normal HTML text.
<plaintext>
And from here onwards, everything appears on the screen 1:1.
```

11.15 Q

11.15.1 <q>

Tag/Attribute	2.0	3.0	3.2	4.0	Internet Explorer	Netscape
<q>				X	4.0	
cite				X		

This tag identifies short quotes. The quotation marks are set by the browser.

cite

Indicates a URL whose target identifies the source of the quote.

Example:

```
<q cite="http://www.spectrosoftware.de">...and life becomes
colorful</q>.
```

See also:

```
<b>, <big>, <font>, <i>, <s>, <small>, <strong>, <sub>,
<sup>, <tt>, <u>
```

11.16 S

11.16.1 <s>

Tag/Attribute	2.0	3.0	3.2	4.0	Internet Explorer	Netscape
<s>		X		X	1.0	3.0B5

Displays the enclosed text struck through.

Example:

```
<s>This text is struck through,</s> but this is not.
```

See also:

```
<b>, <big>, <font>, <i>, <q>, <small>, <strong>, <sub>,
<sup>, <tt>, <u>
```

11.16.2 <script>

Tag/Attribute	2.0	3.0	3.2	4.0	Internet Explorer	Netscape
<script>				X	3.0B1	2.0B3
charset				X		
defer				X	4.0	
event				X	4.0	
for				X	4.0	
language				X	3.0B1	2.0B3
src				X	3.02	3.0B5
type				X	4.0	

The tag `<script>` is used to identify script languages. JavaScript, for instance, is one of these script languages. You use `<script>` to distinguish JavaScript text from the HTML sourcecode.

charset

This attribute indicates which character set is to be used for the script. The standard setting is ISO-8859-1.

defer

This is a stand-alone attribute and therefore does not need any value allocation. If it is set, the browser is informed that the script will not generate any screen output whatever.

event

Specifies the event for which the script was written. More on this topic later.

for

Indicates which element is bound to this event script. Again, we will tell you more about this later.

language

This attribute indicates which language has been used for the script.

src

Here, an external data source can be addressed. This is useful when, for instance, many HTML files are using one and the same script.

type

This attribute specifies the MIME type of the script source code.

Example:

```
<script language="JavaScript">
  <!-- document.write("This is a  JavaScript.") -->
</script>
<noscript>
  Unfortunately, this is not a JavaScript.
</noscript>
```

See also:

`<base>, <isindex>, <meta>, <style>, <title>, <applet>, <embed>, <noembed>, <noscript>, <param>`

11.16.3 <select>

Tag/Attribute	*2.0*	*3.0*	*3.2*	*4.0*	*Internet Explorer*	*Netscape*
<select>	X	X	X	X	1.0	1.0
accesskey					4.0B1	
align					4.0	
disabled		X		X	4.0B1	
multiple	X	X	X	X	1.0	1.0
name	X	X	X	X	1.0	1.0
size	X		X	X	1.0	1.0
tabindex				X	4.0B1	

Indicates a selection list whose elements are defined with `<option>`.

accesskey

With `accesskey`, you can define a keyboard shortcut by which you can access the selection field. Assign a letter to the attribute and it will be executed when you depress the appropriate key with the associated shortcut key, which depends on the browser and operating system.

align

Specifies the horizontal alignment of the selection field.

Value	Meaning
center	The field is aligned centrally.
left	The field is aligned to the left.
right	The field is aligned to the right.

Table 11.43 *The values of align in <select>*

disabled

Specifies that the selection list has been temporarily deactivated.

multiple

Specifies that there are several options from which you can choose.

name

Specifies the designation of the form element so that it can be identified by scripts. The value of the attribute is also indicated during evaluation of the form.

size

Specifies the displayed character length of the options.

tabindex

Specifies the tab index of the selection field. Positive values stand for the position of the field in the list of objects that can be activated with [Tab]. Negative values mean that the selection field does not appear in the tab index.

Example:

```
<form>
  <select name="Products">
    <option value="Mon">Monitor
    <option value="Pri">Printer
    <optgroup label="Computer">
      <option value="HDD">Hard disk
      <option value="Hou">Housing
      <option value="CPU">Processor
    </optgroup>
  </select>
</form>
```

See also:

```
<button>, <fieldset>, <form>, <input>, <keygen>, <label>,
<legend>, <optgroup>, <option>, <textarea>
```

11.16.4 <small>

Tag/Attribute	2.0	3.0	3.2	4.0	Internet Explorer	Netscape
<small>		X	X	X	3.0A1	1.1

Means that the enclosed text is to be displayed in a smaller font type.

Example:

```
<small>This text is printed small,</small> but this is not.
```

See also:

```
<b>, <big>, <font>, <i>, <q>, <s>, <strong>, <sub>, <sup>,
<tt>, <u>
```

11.16.5 <span>

Tag/Attribute	2.0	3.0	3.2	4.0	Internet Explorer	Netscape
<span>				X	3.0B1	4.0B2

This tag is used in order to format stylesheets directly in the HTML source text. This is useful if you can assign a format via CSS that would not be solvable using HTML .

11.16.6 <strong>

Tag/Attribute	2.0	3.0	3.2	4.0	Internet Explorer	Netscape
<strong>	X	X	X	X	1.0	1.0

Emphasizes the enclosed text (usually by printing it in bold).

Example:

```
<strong>This text is emphasized,</strong> but this is not.
```

See also:

```
<b>, <big>, <font>, <i>, <q>, <s>, <small>, <sub>, <sup>,
<tt>, <u>
```

11.16.7 <style>

Tag/Attribute	*2.0*	*3.0*	*3.2*	*4.0*	*Internet Explorer*	*Netscape*
<style>		X	X	X	3.0B1	4.0B2
disabled					4.0	
media				X	4.0	
title				X		
type				X	3.0B1	4.0B2

This tag is invoked in the head of an HTML page, and offers one of several variants for inserting stylesheets in the HTML page.

disabled

This stand-alone attribute specifies that insertion of the stylesheet is to be ignored momentarily.

media

Specifies the type of output for which the assignment of the stylesheet is to be used. Several nominations are possible if you separate them with commas.

Value	*Meaning*
screen	The stylesheet is used when the HTML page is output on a computer screen.
print	The stylesheet is used when the HTML page is output on a printer.
projection	The stylesheet is used when the HTML page is output onto a projecting output device.
braille	The stylesheet is used when the HTML page is output onto a device for formatting text for the blind.
speech	The stylesheet is used when the HTML page is output via speech output.
all	The stylesheet is used when the HTML page is output on all the above-mentioned output media.

Table 11.44 *The values of media in <style>*

title

This attribute assigns to the stylesheet a designation that enables the CSS to be addressed specifically in order to switch it on, off or over.

type

Specifies the MIME type of the stylesheet.

See also:

```
<base>, <isindex>, <meta>, <scripts>, <title>
```

11.16.8 <sub>

Tag/Attribute	2.0	3.0	3.2	4.0	Internet Explorer	Netscape
<sub>		X	X	X	3.0B1	1.1

Reproduces the enclosed text lower down.

Example:

```
<sub>This text is printed lower,</sub> but this is not.
```

See also:

```
<b>, <big>, <font>, <i>, <q>, <s>, <small>, <strong>,
<sup>, <tt>, <u>
```

11.16.9 <sup>

Tag/Attribute	2.0	3.0	3.2	4.0	Internet Explorer	Netscape
<sup>		X	X	X	3.0B1	1.1

Reproduces the enclosed higher up.

Example:

```
<sup>This text is printed higher,</sup> but this is not.
```

See also:

```
<b>, <big>, <font>, <i>, <q>, <s>, <small>, <strong>,
<sub>, <tt>, <u>
```

11.17.1 <table>

Tag/Attribute	2.0	3.0	3.2	4.0	Internet Explorer	Netscape
<table>		X	X	X	2.0	1.1
align		X	X	X	2.0	2.0
background					2.0	4.0B3
bgcolor				X	2.0	3.0B1
border		X	X	X	2.0	1.1
bordercolor					2.0	4.0
borderdark					2.0	
borderlight					2.0	
cellpadding			X	X	2.0	1.1
cellspacing			X	X	2.0	1.1
cols					3.0A1	4.0B2
datapagesize				X	4.0	
frame				X	3.0A1	
height					2.0	1.1
rules				X	3.0A1	
summary				X		
width		X	X	X	2.0	1.1

This tag defines a table.

align

Specifies the horizontal alignment of the table within the browser window.

Value	Meaning
center	The table is aligned centrally.
left	The table is aligned to the left.
right	The table is aligned to the right.

Table 11.45 ***The values of align in <table>***

background

Specifies the address of a background image for the table.

bgcolor

Here, the background color of the table is defined. You can use RGB values and color values predefined for many browsers (see Appendix B).

border

Specifies the width of the table border.

bordercolor

Here, the main color of the table border is defined. You can use RGB values and color values predefined for many browsers (see Appendix B).

bordercolordark

Here, the dark color of the table border is defined with a 3D effect. You can use RGB values and color values predefined for many browsers (see Appendix B).

bordercolorlight

Here, the light color of the table border is defined with a 3D effect. You can use RGB values and color values predefined for many browsers (see Appendix B).

cellpadding

Specifies the distance between the cell contents and the cell frame.

cellspacing

Specifies the distance of the cells from each other.

cols

Specifies the number of columns in the table.

datapagesize

Specifies the size of a datapage in the case of endless tables.

frame

Indicates where the external border of the table is to be drawn.

Value	Meaning
void	No borders are displayed.
above	A border is revealed only at the top edge.
below	A border is revealed only at the bottom edge.
hsides	A border is revealed at the top and bottom edges.
vsides	A border is revealed at the left and right-hand edges.
lhs	A border is revealed only on the left-hand side.
rhs	A border is revealed only on the right-hand side.
box	A border is displayed on all four sides.
border	A border is displayed on all four sides.

Table 11.46 *The values of frame in <table>*

height

Specifies the height of the table in pixels or as a percentage of the height of the browser window.

rules

Defines the internal separating lines of the table.

Value	Meaning
none	No separating lines are displayed.
groups	Separating lines that separate the groups set up with `<thead>`, `<tbody>`, `<tfoot>` and `<colgroup>` are displayed.
rows	Horizontal separating lines are displayed.
cols	Vertical separating lines are displayed.
all	All separating lines between the cells are displayed.

Table 11.47 *The values of rules in <table>*

summary

Reproduces a summary of the table contents (important for browsers with speech output).

width

Specifies the width of the table in pixels or as a percentage of the width of the browser window.

Example:

```
<table border=1>
  <caption>Browser statistic</caption>
  <tr><th>Browser</th><th>Market share</th></tr>
  <tr><td>Microsoft Internet Explorer</td><td>60.4 %</td>
  </tr>
  <tr><td>Netscape Communicator</td><td>38.5 %</td></tr>
  <tr><td>Others</td><td>1.1 %</td></tr>
</table>
```

See also:

`<caption>, <col>, <colgroup>, <thead>, <tbody>, <tfoot>, <th>, <td>, <tr>`

11.17.2 <tbody>

Tag/Attribute	*2.0*	*3.0*	*3.2*	*4.0*	*Internet Explorer*	*Netscape*
<tbody>				X	3.0AI	
align				X	4.0BI	
bgcolor					4.0BI	
char				X		
charoff				X		
valign				X	4.0BI	

Defines the table body of a table.

align

Specifies the horizontal alignment within the cell.

Value	*Meaning*
center	The contents are aligned centrally.
left	The contents are aligned to the left.
right	The contents are aligned to the right.

Table 11.48 *The values of align in <tbody>*

bgcolor

Here, the background color of the cell is defined. You can use RGB values and color values predefined for many browsers (see Appendix B).

char

Here, you can specify the character against which the cell contents are aligned (for instance, the period for decimal numbers). The first occurrence of this character is counted as relevant.

charoff

Specifies the distance from the first-occurring alignment character defined in `char` in pixels.

valign

Specifies the vertical alignment within the cell.

Value	Meaning
bottom	The contents are aligned downwards.
top	The contents are aligned upwards.

Table 11.49 ***The values of valign in <tbody>***

Example:

```
<table border=1>
  <thead>
    <tr><th colspan=2>Browser statistic</th></td>
  </thead>
  <tbody>
    <tr><th>Browser</th><th>Market share</th></tr>
    <tr><td>Microsoft Internet Explorer</td>
        <td>60.4 %</td>
    </tr>
    <tr><td>Netscape Communicator</td><td>38.5 %</td></tr>
    <tr><td>Others</td><td>1.1 %</td></tr>
  </tbody>
  <tfoot>
    <tr><td colspan=2>As at: Mid- 2000</td></td>
  </tfoot>
</table>
```

See also:

`<caption>, <col>, <colgroup>, <table>, <tfoot>, <th>, <thead>, <td>, <tr>`

11.17.3 <td>

Tag/Attribute	2.0	3.0	3.2	4.0	Internet Explorer	Netscape
<td>		X	X	X	2.0	1.1
align		X	X	X	2.0	1.1
background					3.0A1	4.0B3
bgcolor				X	2.0	3.0B1
bordercolor					2.0	
bordercolordark					2.0	
bordercolorlight					2.0	
char				X		
charoff				X		
colspan		X	X	X	2.0	1.1
headers				X		
height			X	X	2.0	1.1
nowrap		X	X	X	2.0	1.1
rowspan		X	X	X	2.0	1.1
scope				X		
valign		X	X	X	2.0	1.1
width			X	X	2.0	1.1

Defines a datacell of a table.

align

Specifies the horizontal alignment within the cell.

Value	Meaning
center	The contents are aligned centrally.
left	The contents are aligned to the left.
right	The contents are aligned to the right.

Table 11.50 *The values of align in <td>*

background

Specifies the address of a background image for the cell.

bgcolor

Here, the background color of the cell is defined. You can use RGB values and color values predefined for many browsers (see Appendix B).

bordercolor

Here, the main color of the cell border is defined. You can use RGB values and color values predefined for many browsers (see Appendix B).

bordercolordark

Here, the dark color of the cell border is defined with a 3D effect. You can use RGB values and color values predefined for many browsers (see Appendix B).

bordercolorlight

Here, the light color of the cell border is defined with a 3D effect. You can use RGB values and color values predefined for many browsers (see Appendix B).

char

Here, you can specify the character against which the cell contents are aligned (for instance, the period for decimal numbers). The first occurrence of this character is counted as relevant.

charoff

Specifies the distance from the first-occurring alignment character defined in `char` in pixels.

colspan

Indicates over how many columns the cell is to extend.

headers

Again indicates to which cell headers the cell belongs. This can be advantageous with speech output. The list elements are separated with spaces.

height

Specifies the height of the cell in pixels or as a percentage of the height of the browser window.

11

TAKE THAT!

nowrap

Indicates whether the normal HTML conventions for linewrap apply or are ignored.

Value	*Meaning*
false	The normal conventions apply: Text reaching the end of a line is automatically wrapped.
true	Text reaching the end of a line is not wrapped. Only explicitly specified formatting (` `, `<p>`, etc) will be followed.

Table 11.51 ***The values of nowrap in <td>***

rowspan

Indicates over how many rows the cell extends.

valign

Specifies the vertical alignment within the cell.

Value	*Meaning*
bottom	The contents are aligned downwards.
top	The contents are aligned upwards.

Table 11.52 ***The values of valign in <td> and <th>***

width

Specifies the width of the cell in pixels or as a percentage of the width of the browser window.

Example:

```
<table border=1>
  <caption>Browser statistic</caption>
  <tr><th>Browser</th><th>Market share</th></tr>
  <tr><td>Microsoft Internet Explorer</td><td>60.4 %</td>
  </tr>
  <tr><td>Netscape Communicator</td><td>38.5 %</td></tr>
  <tr><td>Others</td><td>1.1 %</td></tr>
</table>
```

See also:

```
<caption>, <col>, <colgroup>, <thead>, <tbody>, <tfoot>,
<table>,  <th>, <tr>
```

11.17.4 <textarea>

Tag/Attribute	2.0	3.0	3.2	4.0	Internet Explorer	Netscape
<textarea>	X	X	X	X	1.0	1.0
accesskey				X	4.0B1	
cols	X	X	X	X	1.0	1.0
disabled		X		X	4.0B1	
name	X	X	X	X	1.0	1.0
readonly				X	4.0B1	
rows	X	X	X	X	1.0	1.0
tabindex				X	4.0B1	
wrap				X	4.0	2.0

Defines a text field in a form.

accesskey

With `accesskey`, you can define a keyboard shortcut by which you can access the text field. Assign a letter to the attribute and it will be executed when you depress the appropriate key with the associated shortcut key, which depends on the browser and operating system.

cols

Specifies the text columns of the text field.

disabled

This stand-alone attribute specifies that this form element has been temporarily deactivated.

name

Specifies the designation of the form element so that it can be identified by scripts. The value of the attribute is also indicated during evaluation the form.

readonly

This stand-alone attribute specifies that the contents of this form element cannot be amended by the reader of the page.

rows

Specifies the text rows of the text field.

tabindex

Specifies the tab index of the text field. Positive values stand for the position of the element in the list of objects that can be activated with [Tab]. Negative values mean that the text field does not appear in the tab index.

wrap

Indicates how the lines are to be wrapped.

Value	*Meaning*
off	The lines are wrapped exactly as entered. If no (ø) has been depressed, no wrap takes place.
soft	The lines are wrapped in the display, but sent in the way in which they were input.
hard	The lines are wrapped in the display and also sent to the script in the same way.

Table 11.53 ***The values of wrap in <textarea>***

See also:

`<button>`, `<fieldset>`, `<form>`, `<input>`, `<keygen>`, `<label>`, `<legend>`, `<optgroup>`, `<option>`, `<select>`

11.17.5 <tfoot>

Tag/Attribute	*2.0*	*3.0*	*3.2*	*4.0*	*Internet Explorer*	*Netscape*
<tfoot>				X	3.0A1	
align				X	4.0B1	
bgcolor					4.0B1	
char				X		
charoff				X		
valign				X	4.0B1	

Defines the table foot of a table.

align

Specifies the horizontal alignment within the cell.

Value	*Meaning*
center	The contents are aligned centrally.
left	The contents are aligned to the left.
right	The contents are aligned to the right.

Table 11.54 *The values of align in <tfoot>*

bgcolor

Here, the background color of the cell is defined. You can use RGB values and color values predefined for many browsers (see Appendix B).

char

Here, you can specify the character against which the cell contents are aligned (for instance, the period for decimal numbers). The first occurrence of this character is counted as relevant.

charoff

Specifies the distance to the first-occurring alignment character defined in `char` in pixels.

valign

Specifies the vertical alignment within the cell.

Value	*Meaning*
bottom	The contents are aligned downwards.
top	The contents are aligned upwards.

Table 11.55 *The values of valign in <tfoot>*

Example:

```
<table border=1>
  <thead>
    <tr><th colspan=2>Browser statistics</th></td>
  </thead>
  <tbody>
    <tr><th>Browser</th><th>Market share</th></tr>
    <tr><td>Microsoft Internet Explorer</td>
        <td>60.4 %</td>
    </tr>
    <tr><td>Netscape Communicator</td><td>38.5 %</td></tr>
```

```
    <tr><td>Others</td><td>1.1 %</td></tr>
  </tbody>
  <tfoot>
    <tr><td colspan=2>As at: Mid- 2000</td></td>
  </tfoot>
</table>
```

See also:

<caption>, <col>, <colgroup>, <table>, <tbody>, <th>, <thead>, <td>, <tr>

11.17.6 <th>

Tag/Attribute	2.0	3.0	3.2	4.0	Internet Explorer	Netscape
<th>		X	X	X	2.0	1.1
abbr				X		
align		X	X	X	2.0	1.1
axis		X		X		
background					3.0A1	4.0B3
bgcolor				X	2.0	3.0B1
bordercolor					2.0	
bordercolordark					2.0	
bordercolor-light					2.0	
char				X		
charoff				X		
colspan		X	X	X	2.0	1.1
height			X	X	2.0	1.1
nowrap		X	X	X	2.0	1.1
rowspan		X	X	X	2.0	1.1
scope				X		
valign		X	X	X	2.0	1.1
width			X	X	2.0	1.1

Defines the header cell of a table.

abbr

Defines an abbreviation for a `<th>` cell.

align

Specifies the horizontal alignment within the cell.

Value	Meaning
center	The contents are aligned centrally.
left	The contents are aligned to the left.
right	The contents are aligned to the right.

Table 11.56 ***The values of align in <th>***

axis

Defines an abbreviation for a `<th>` cell.

background

Specifies the address of a background image for the cell.

bgcolor

Here, the background color of the cell is defined. You can use RGB values and color values predefined for many browsers (see Appendix B).

bordercolor

Here, the main color of the cell border is defined. You can use RGB values and color values predefined for many browsers (see Appendix B).

bordercolordark

Here, the dark color of the cell border is defined with a 3D effect. You can use RGB values and color values predefined for many browsers (see Appendix B).

bordercolorlight

Here, the light color of the cell border is defined with a 3D effect. You can use RGB values and color values predefined for many browsers (see Appendix B).

char

Here, you can specify the character against which the cell contents are to be aligned (for instance, the period for decimal numbers). The first occurrence of this character is counted as relevant.

charoff

Specifies the distance to the first-occurring alignment character defined in `char` in pixels.

colspan

Indicates over how many columns the cell extends.

height

Specifies the height of the cell in pixels or as a percentage of the height of the browser window.

nowrap

Indicates whether the normal HTML conventions for linewrap apply or whether they are ignored.

Value	*Meaning*
false	The normal conventions apply: text reaching the end of a line is automatically wrapped.
true	Text reaching the end of a line is not wrapped. Only explicitly specified formatting (` `, `<p>`, etc) is followed.

Table 11.57 ***The values of nowrap in <th>***

rowspan

Indicates over how many rows the cell extends.

scope

Indicates for which datacells this header cell supplies the header.

Values	*Meaning*
col	This cell is the header for all other cells in the column.
colgroup	This cell is the header for all other cells in the column group.
row	This cell is the header for all other cells in the row.
rowgroup	This cell is the header for all other cells in the group of rows.

Table 11.58 ***The values of scope in <th>***

valign

Specifies the vertical alignment within the cell.

Value	Meaning
bottom	The contents are aligned downwards.
top	The contents are aligned upwards.

Table 11.59 *The values of valign in <th>*

11

TAKE THAT!

width

Specifies the width of the cell in pixels or as a percentage of the width of the browser window.

Example:

```
<table border=1>
  <caption>Browser statistic</caption>
  <tr><th>Browser</th><th>Market share</th></tr>
  <tr><td>Microsoft Internet Explorer</td><td>60.4 %</td>
  </tr>
  <tr><td>Netscape Communicator</td><td>38.5 %</td></tr>
  <tr><td>Others</td><td>1.1 %</td></tr>
</table>
```

See also:

```
<caption>, <col>, <colgroup>, <thead>, <tbody>, <tfoot>,
<table>, <tr>
```

11.17.7 <thead>

Tag/Attribute	2.0	3.0	3.2	4.0	Internet Explorer	Netscape
<thead>				X	3.0A1	
align				X	4.0B1	
bgcolor					4.0B1	
char				X		
charoff				X		
valign				X	4.0B1	

Defines the table head of a table.

align

Specifies the horizontal alignment within the cell.

Value	Meaning
center	The contents are aligned centrally.
left	The contents are aligned to the left.
right	The contents are aligned to the right.

Table 11.60 ***The values of align in <thead>***

bgcolor

Here, the background color of the cell is defined. You can use RGB values and color values predefined for many browsers (see Appendix B).

char

Here, you can specify the character against which the cell contents are aligned (for instance, the period for decimal numbers). The first occurrence of this character is counted as relevant.

charoff

Specifies the distance to the first-occurring alignment character defined in `char` in pixels.

valign

Specifies the vertical alignment within the cell.

Value	Meaning
bottom	The contents are aligned downwards.
top	The contents are aligned upwards.

Table 11.61 ***The values of valign in <thead>***

Example:

```
<table border=1>
  <thead>
    <tr><th colspan=2>Browser statistic</th></td>
  </thead>
  <tbody>
    <tr><th>Browser</th><th>Market share</th></tr>
    <tr><td>Microsoft Internet Explorer</td>
        <td>60.4 %</td>
    </tr>
    <tr><td>Netscape Communicator</td><td>38.5 %</td></tr>
    <tr><td>Others</td><td>1.1 %</td></tr>
  </tbody>
```

```
  <tfoot>
    <tr><td colspan=2>As at: Mid-2000</td></td>
  </tfoot>
</table>
```

See also:

`<caption>, <col>, <colgroup>, <table>, <tbody>, <tfoot>, <th>, <td>, <tr>`

11.17.8 <title>

Tag/Attribute	2.0	3.0	3.2	4.0	Internet Explorer	Netscape
<title>	X	X	X	X	1.0	1.0

Indicates in the HTML head the title of the HTML page.

See also:

`<base>, <isindex>, <meta>, <scripts>, <style>`

11.17.9 <tr>

Tag/Attribute	2.0	3.0	3.2	4.0	Internet Explorer	Netscape
<tr>		X	X	X	2.0	1.1
align		X	X	X	2.0	1.1
bgcolor				X	2.0	3.0B1
bordercolor					2.0	
bordercolordark					2.0	
bordercolorlight					2.0	
char				X		
charoff				X		
valign		X	X	X	2.0	1.1

Defines a table row.

align

Specifies the horizontal alignment within the row.

Value	*Meaning*
center	The contents are aligned centrally.
left	The contents are aligned to the left.
right	The contents are aligned to the right.

Table 11.62 ***The values of align in <col>***

bgcolor

Here, the background color of the row is defined. You can use RGB values and color values predefined for many browsers (see Appendix B).

bordercolor

Here, the main color of the row border is defined. You can use RGB values and color values predefined for many browsers (see Appendix B).

bordercolordark

Here, the dark color of the row border is defined with a 3D effect. You can use RGB values and color values predefined for many browsers (see Appendix B).

bordercolorlight

Here, the light color of the row border is defined with a 3D effect. You can use RGB values and color values predefined for many browsers (see Appendix B).

char

Here, you can specify the character against which the cell contents are aligned (for instance, the period for decimal numbers). The first occurrence of this character is counted as relevant.

charoff

Specifies the distance to the first-occurring alignment character defined in `char` in pixels.

valign

Specifies the vertical alignment within the row.

Value	Meaning
bottom	The contents are aligned downwards.
top	The contents are aligned upwards.

Table 11.63 *The values of valign in <tr>*

Example:

```
<table border=1>
  <caption>Browser statistic</caption>
  <tr><th>Browser</th><th>Market share</th></tr>
  <tr><td>Microsoft Internet Explorer</td><td>60.4 %</td>
  </tr>
  <tr><td>Netscape Communicator</td><td>38.5 %</td></tr>
  <tr><td>Others</td><td>1.1 %</td></tr>
</table>
```

See also:

`<caption>, <col>, <colgroup>, <thead>, <tbody>, <tfoot>, <table>, <th>, <td>`

11.17.10 <tt>

Tag/Attribute	2.0	3.0	3.2	4.0	Internet Explorer	Netscape
<tt>	X	X	X	X	1.0	1.0

Outputs the enclosed text in font type Courier.

See also:

`<b>, <big>, <font>, <i>, <q>, <s>, <small>, <strong>, <sub>, <sup>, <u>`

11.18 U

11.18.1 <u>

Tag/Attribute	2.0	3.0	3.2	4.0	Internet Explorer	Netscape
<u>	X	X	X	X	1.0	3.0B5

Underlines the enclosed text.

Example:

```
<u>This text is underlined</u> but this is not.
```

See also:

```
<b>, <big>, <font>, <i>, <q>, <s>, <small>, <strong>,
<sub>, <sup>, <tt>
```

11

TAKE THAT!

11.18.2 <ul>

Tag/Attribute	2.0	3.0	3.2	4.0	Internet Explorer	Netscape
<ul>	X	X	X	X	1.0	1.0
clear		X				
compact	X	X	X	X		
type			X	X	4.0	1.0

Defines an unordered list (enumeration list).

clear

This attribute has been enhanced in order to deal with images moved to the left or right by the attribute `align` in `<img>` . You can now use it to deal with all objects relocated with `align` .

Value	Meaning
none	A completely normal linewrap is generated.
left	The line is wrapped and the next line inserted far enough below it for the left-hand margin to be free of images (or other objects).
right	The line is wrapped and the next line inserted far enough below it for the right-hand margin to be free of images (or other objects).
all	The line is wrapped and the next line inserted far enough below it for both margins to be free of images (or other objects).

Table 11.64 ***The values of clear in <ul>***

compact

This stand-alone attribute specifies that a space-saving representation is to be selected.

type

Indicates which list points are to be used.

Value	Meaning
A	A, B, C, D, etc.
a	a, b, c, d, etc.
I	I, II, III, IV, etc.
i	i, ii, iii, iv, etc.
1	1, 2, 3, 4, etc.
disc	Filled circles.
square	Filled squares.
circle	Unfilled circles.

Table 11.65 ***The values of type in <ul>***

Example:

```
<ul>
  <li type="disc">Circle (filled)
  <li type="circle">Circle
  <li type="square">Square
</ul>
```

See also:

<li>, <menu>, <ol>

11.19 W

11.19.1 <wbr>

Tag/Attribute	2.0	3.0	3.2	4.0	Internet Explorer	Netscape
<wbr>					1.0	1.0

Indicates to the browser where a word can be split, although this does not necessarily mean that it will be split there.

Example:

```
A food<wbr>store has burned down.
```

See also:

, <nobr>

11.20 X

11.20.1 <xml>

Tag/Attribute	2.0	3.0	3.2	4.0	Internet Explorer	Netscape
<xml>					5.0	
src					5.0	

This tag is used to incorporate XML text in an HTML document.

src

This attribute specifies the address of the XML document.

11.20.2 <xmp>

Tag/Attribute	2.0	3.0	3.2	4.0	Internet Explorer	Netscape
<xmp>	X	X	X	X	1.0	1.0

Here, the subsequent text is output on the screen word for word. The closing `</xmp>` tag disables this mode.

11.21 !

11.21.1 <!– … –>

Tag/Attribute	2.0	3.0	3.2	4.0	Internet Explorer	Netscape
<!-- ... -->	X	X	X	X	1.0	1.0

Passages flanked by `<!-- ... -->` are commented on by the browser and ignored.

Example:

```
This text does <!-- not --> appear on the screen.
```

See also:

`<comment>`

Part III

Go ahead!

Tips and tricks

12

In this chapter, we want to introduce you to yet another application area of XML.

12.1 WAP

Internet pages for mobile phones, known as WAP pages, can also be created using XML. The language you use for this is WML (`Wireless Markup Language`) , which is an XML application. The following paragraphs give you a brief introduction to the configuration of WAP pages.

12.2 Structure of a WML

As WML is part of XML, every WML document also begins with an XML declaration and a DTD.

```
<?xml version="1.0"?>
<!DOCTYPE wml
  PUBLIC "-//WAPFORUM//DTD WML 1.1//EN"
  "http://www.wapforum.org/DTD/wml_1.1.xml">
```

The XML declaration and the document type declaration with this public DTD are necessary for producing a functioning WAP page . The root element is also predefined, and must be specified as `<wml>`.

Owing to the lack of space on a mobile phone display, a WAP page is structured to contain several cards. A whole page is called a deck. You can use links to jump back and forth between the individual cards.

An example:

```
<?xml version="1.0"?>
<!DOCTYPE wml
  PUBLIC "-//WAPFORUM//DTD WML 1.1//EN"
  "http://www.wapforum.org/DTD/wml_1.1.xml">
<wml>
  <card id="card1" title="HelloWorld!">
    Hello World!
  </card>
</wml>
```


This WML file contains only one card, with the `title` `HelloWorld!` and the `ID` `card1`. With most mobile phones, the title appears in a separate line at the top of the display. You address the card using its ID, the unambiguous designation of the card.

To view your WAP page, you need a WAP browser. We use the WAP browser WinWAP, which you can download from http://www.winwap.org.

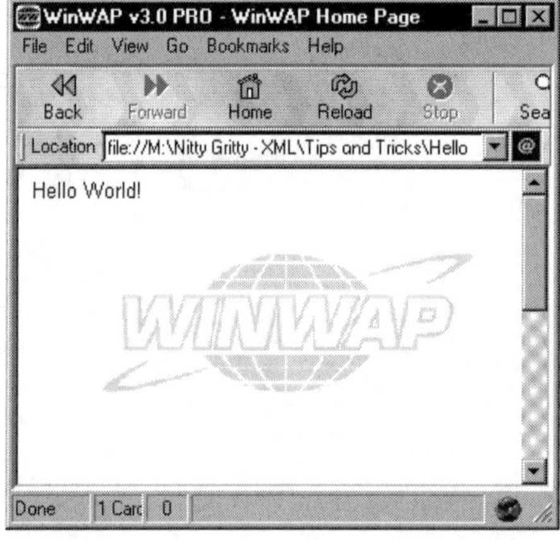

Figure 12.1 ***View of the WAP page in WinWAP***

12.3 Text alignment and formatting

Even with the limited space available on a mobile phone, you still have some text formatting capability.

Another example:

```
<?xml version="1.0"?>
<!DOCTYPE wml
  PUBLIC "-//WAPFORUM//DTD WML 1.1//EN"
```

```
  "http://www.wapforum.org/DTD/wml_1.1.xml">
<wml>
  <card id="card1" title="Text formatting">
    <p align="left">
      <i>This paragraph is<br/>in italics and left-justified</i>
    </p>
    <p align="center">
      <b>This paragraph is <br/>bold and centered</b>
    </p>
    <p align="right">
      <small>
        This paragraph is <br/>regular and right-justified
      </small>
    </p>
  </card>
</wml>
```


As you can see, the syntax is very simple. With the element `<p>`, you define a paragraph that changes to a new paragraph at its end. You can also align paragraphs. The blank element `<br/>` enforces a linewrap and the other elements are self-explanatory. `<b>` stands for bold, `<i>` stands for italic and `<small>` designates smaller text.

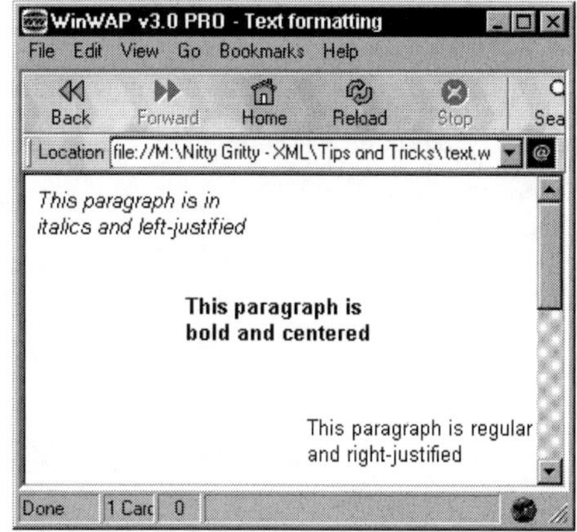

Figure 12.2 ***Text alignment with WM***

12.4 WML links

For there to be any point in setting up cards, we also need to link them with one another. To make a link, we use the element <a>. You will already be familiar with the attribute href from the stylesheets. It specifies the location, which is that of the second card in this case. The card address comprises the ID of the card and a preceding #symbol.

```
<?xml version="1.0"?>
<!DOCTYPE wml
  PUBLIC "-//WAPFORUM//DTD WML 1.1//EN"
  "http://www.wapforum.org/DTD/wml_1.1.xml">
<wml>
  <card id="card1" title="first card">
    <br/><br/>
    <p align="center"><b>This is the first card</b></p>
    <br/>
    <p align="center">
    <a href="#card2">To the second card</a>
    </p>
  </card>
  <card id="card2" title="second card">
    <br/><br/>
    <p align="center"><b>This is the second card</b></p>
    <br/>
    <p align="center">
    <a href="#card1">To the first card</a>
    </p>
  </card>
</wml>
```

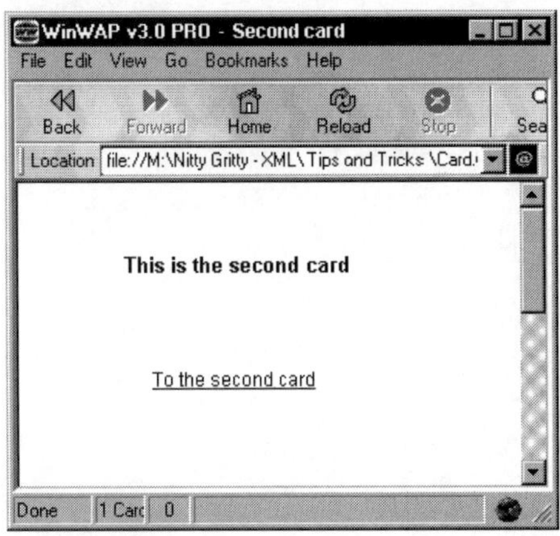

Figure 12.3 ***Navigating in the document***

In the same way, you can link not just cards, but also external files, for example:

```
<a href="HelloWorld.wml">A link to the HelloWorld file</a>
```

or two WAP pages:

```
<a href="http://www.mydomain.co.uk/index.wml">
  My WAP page
</a>
```

12.5 Selection menu

In addition to simple links, you can also make further selections in WML by other means. The selection menu gives you the opportunity of creating a selection list of any length.

The elements we need for this are `<select>` and `<option>`. The element `<select>` is the actual selection menu. The element `<option>` extends the list and defines, with the attribute `onpick`, what is to happen when a point is selected.

```
<?xml version="1.0"?>
<!DOCTYPE wml
  PUBLIC "-//WAPFORUM//DTD WML 1.1//EN"
  "http://www.wapforum.org/DTD/wml_1.1.xml">
<wml>
  <card id="card1" title="first card">
    <br/><br/>
    <p align="center"><b>Select page:</b></p>
    <br/>
```

```
    <p align="center">
      <select name="variable">
        <option onpick="HelloWorld.wml">
          HelloWorld!
        </option>
        <option onpick="Text.wml">
          Text formatting
        </option>
        <option onpick="card.wml">
          Changing cards
        </option>
      </select>
    </p>
  </card>
</wml>
```

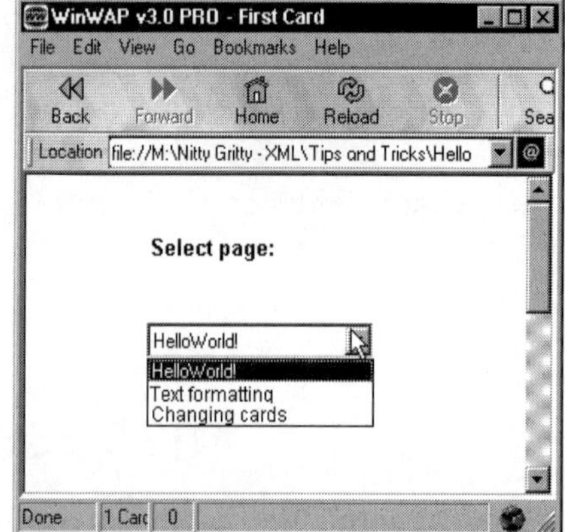

Figure 12.4 ***Navigating with menu***

12.6 WML reference

Below, you will find a reference for the WML elements for creating Wap pages.

12.6.1 <?xml version="1.0">

A WML document is also a proper XML document and therefore, here again, the first line in the document is the XML declaration.

12.6.2 <!– comment –>

This element enables comments to be written in the WML document.

12.6.3 <!DOCTYPE ..>

With the document-type declaration, the DTD for a WML document is incorporated.

```
<!DOCTYPE wml
  PUBLIC "-//WAPFORUM//DTD WML 1.1//EN"
  "http://www.wapforum.org/DTD/wml_1.1.xml"
>
```

This declaration must follow directly after the XML declaration.

12.6.4 <a>

With `<a></a>`, links are defined in a WML document. Between the start and closing tags is the name of the link; the value of the attribute `href` defines the target. Links can invoke a local `card` in a WML document.

```
<a href="#card4">XML</a>
```

an external file:

```
<a href="HelloWorld.wml">Example 1</a>
```

or a different WAP page:

```
<a href="http://www.mydomain.co.uk/index.wml">
  My WAP page
</a>
```

12.6.5 <b>

The text within this element is shown in bold.

```
<b>This text is formatted in bold</b>
```

12.6.6 <big>

The text within this element is shown slightly larger than normal.

```
<big>This text is shown larger than normal</big>
```

12.6.7

This blank element causes a linefeed at the current location.

```
<br/>
```

12 GO AHEAD!

12.6.8 <card>

This element differentiates the individual cards of a WAP page. With the attribute `id`, you define the ID of the page. You can use the element `<a>` to jump back to this again. With the attribute `title`, you define the name of the element.

```
<card id="card-id" title="name">
... contents ...
</card>
```

12.6.9 <do>

With this element, you define a menu in WML.

```
<do type="value" label="value" name="value">
...
</do>
```

The element has the following attributes:

Attribute	Value
type	This attribute indicates which action is to be undertaken. It serves to inform the device and does not have to be selected by it. The possible values are: accept: Serves to confirm prompts. prev: Reference to the previous page. help: Stands for a link to a help option. reset: For resetting a page. options: For invoking options. delete: Enables deleting.
name	Unambiguous name of the tag.
label	Defines what is to appear as the link name in the display.

Table 12.1 ***Possible attributes of the element <do>***

Within the <do> element is the action that will be undertaken when the key is depressed. There are four different types:

Action	Description
<go href="value"/>	Links to another card or WAP page.
<prev/>	Jumps back to the previous page.
<refresh/>	Reloads the current card.
<noop/>	No action. For example, to delete a <do> element at card level.

Table 12.2 ***Possible actions of the element <do>***

An example:

```
<do type="accept" label="further">
<go href="#card2"/>
</do>
```

12.6.10 <i>

The text within this element is shown in italics.

```
<i>This text is formatted in italics!</i>
```

12.6.11 <img/>

This element incorporates an image. The image must be stored in the special WBMP format.

```
<img src="image.wbmp" alt="imagename"/>
```

The element has the following attributes:

Attribute	Value
src	Defines the address for the image.
alt	Indicates the alternative text.

Table 12.3 ***Possible attributes of the element <img/>***

12 GO AHEAD!

12.6.12 <input>

With this element, you can define an input field.

```
<input name="value" value="value" type="value"></input>
```

The element has the following attributes:

Attribute	Value
name	Defines the name of the event variables.
value	The value of the input field to be displayed when invoked.
type	The type of input field (`text` or `password`).

Table 12.4 ***Possible attributes of the element <input>***

12.6.13 <meta>

In a similar way to HTML, it defines the metadata to be evaluated by search engines.

12.6.14 <onevent>

Defines what happens with particular events.

```
<onevent type="value"></onevent>
```

Possible values for the attribute `type`:

Action	Description
onpick	Reacts to the selection of an element from a selection list.
onenterforward	Reacts to a link or to input.
onenterbackward	Reacts to a characteristic function (back).
ontimer	Reaction to a `timer` event.

Table 12.5 ***Possible values of the attribute type***

12.6.15 <option>

This element enables various option fields that the user can select. With the attribute `value`, you determine the value of the selection field.

```
<option value="value"></option>
```

12.6.16 <p>

This element defines a text paragraph with which you can also define the text alignment `(align="center|left|right)`.

```
<p align="value"></p>
```

12.6.17 <select>

This element generates a selection list on the screen. Its values can be defined with `<option>`.

```
<select>
...
<option> ... </option>
...
</select>
```

The element <select> has the following attributes:

Attribute	Value
multiple	Indicates whether a multiple selection is allowed.
name	Indicates the event variable in which the event is stored.
iname	Indicates the variable in which the index position of the selection is stored (only in the case of multiple selection).
ivalue	Indicates the variable in which the index value of the selection is stored (only in the case of multiple selection).

Table 12.6 ***Possible attributes of the element <select>***

12 GO AHEAD!

12.6.18 <small>

The text within this element is shown slightly smaller than normal.

```
<small>
  This text is shown smaller than normal
</small>
```

12.6.19 <strong>

The text within this element is shown slightly larger and bolder than normal.

```
<strong>
This text is shown larger and bolder than normal
</strong>
```

12.6.20 <table>

This element defines a table. You must define the attribute columns, which defines the number of columns. The attribute title defines the table header.

```
<table title="Table1" columns="3">
...
</table>
```

12.6.21 <td>

This element defines a datacell of a table.

```
<td></td>
```

12.6.22 <timer></timer>

This element sets a timeframe which can then initiate the event.

```
<timer value="500"/>
```

With the attribute `value`, you define the timeframe in milliseconds.

12.6.23 <tr>

This element defines a table row.

```
<tr></tr>
```

12.6.24 <u>

The text within this element is shown underlined.

```
<u>This text is underlined</u>
```

12.6.25 <wml>

This element is the root element of a WML document.

```
<wml>
  ...
  contents
  ...
</wml>
```

Glossary

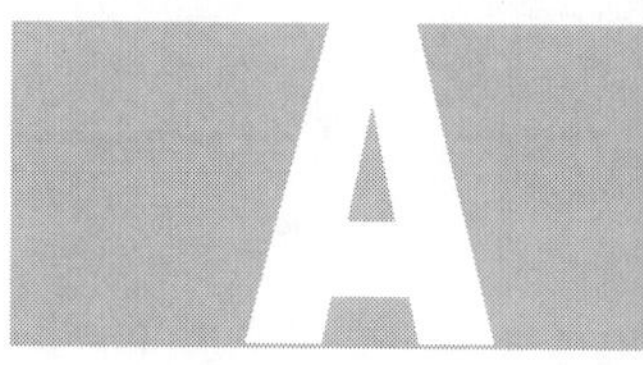

This section brings together all the terms used in the book that could perhaps do with further explanation.

Address

Every Internet service is contacted through its address. This can take one of many formats. An e-mail address might look something like this: name@provider.co.uk. On the other hand you could visit a homepage at an address that looks like this: http://www.provider.co.uk

Anchor

An anchor means a picture or text which you have to click on in order to access the page to which the linked object refers.

Attribute

An attribute can be assigned to a tag in HTML so as to describe more precisely the properties of the element that the tag will create. For instance if you use `<hr>` to create a horizontal line, you can use the attribute `size` to define how thick you want the line to be.

```
<hr size=4>
```

This command will create a considerably heavier line than `<hr>` on its own.

Body

The body of an HTML file contains all the data, pictures and other elements intended to be displayed in the window of your browser. The alignment and layout of all these elements are also defined in this part of the file.

Browser

A browser is a program that converts HTML language into displayable screen contents and interprets your inputs so that you can surf the Internet. Netscape Navigator and Microsoft Internet Explorer are the most popular browsers.

CGI

CGI (Common Gateway Interface) is a standard that defines a particular type of interface between computers. It is used to define such matters as the interchange of CGI scripts, for example.

CSS

See Stylesheet.

Dedicated line

A permanent, hard-wired link between two computers is known as a dedicated line.

Document Type Definition

See DTD.

Download

Transferring a file from another computer to your own is known as downloading.

DTD

DTD stands for Document Type Definition. It specifies the syntax to be used for a specific document type.

Dynamic HTML

Dynamic HTML is an extended form of HTML which you can use to program animation and many other elements.

Editor

See Text editor.

E-mail

You can send letters over the Internet just as if you were using an ordinary postal system. Just quote the address of the person you are writing to, type in your message and send off your letter. In a few minutes (or sometimes just a few seconds) the file reaches the addressee. This option is much faster than ordinary post and only costs you the online charges, which is how letters of this kind came to be known as e-mail.

FTP

In the context of the Internet, FTP stands for "File Transfer Protocol". Computers communicate with one another in different languages known as protocols. The FTP protocol provides an efficient method for navigating through the directories on a remote machine and for downloading and uploading files.

A

Guest access

Many service providers make software available to their subscribing members. To keep this benefit for members only, the provider asks for your user ID and password when you log in. But much of this data is often available to users of the Internet who are not subscribers to the provider concerned. Such people can log in under the name "anonymous" or "guest". In most instances a password is not needed. However, sometimes a provider will expect anonymous users to quote their e-mail address. You will be given adequate advance notice where this is the case.

Hard disk

A computer stores its operating system and its other programs on a hard disk. This piece of hardware is similar to a floppy disk, but is much faster and has much greater capacity.

Hardware

Computer hardware relates to the physical aspects of your computer, including, the monitor, keyboard, mouse, printer and any other devices connected to it.

Head

The head of an HTML file contains among other things the title of the page concerned.

Homepage

A homepage usually consists of several files which any Internet user can view. A homepage is usually written in HTML and you can display it by using your browser. Homepages give you information about people, companies, universities and other institutions.

HTML

HTML (Hypertext Markup Language) was developed to make it as easy as possible to create a website. HTML defines how text should be formatted and also enables you to define links to other documents, tables, input forms and lists.

HTTP

A

Hypertext Transfer Protocol (HTTP) is used for transferring HTML-based files. Homepages are chiefly sent using this protocol.

Internet

The Internet is a worldwide network of computers. It was originally developed by the military to make sure it would still have a functioning communications network even if one computer failed. Since then the Internet has assumed ever-increasing importance both for business and for leisure.

ISDN

Most major telecoms companies provide not only the usual analog telephone lines but also digital ISDN lines. In this option the voice is digitally sampled at the transmitting end and converted back into an acoustic signal at the receiving end. Because programs and files are stored and transmitted digitally, ISDN represents a very fast method of transmitting data.

Java

Programs written in JavaScript are transmitted over the Internet and run on your computer. This programming language was developed specially for the Internet.

Link

A link is a means of moving between two Internet pages. If you click on a link on the page you are currently displaying, you are taken to the linked page.

Modem

To transmit data over an ordinary telephone line you have to have a modem. This piece of kit converts data into acoustic signals (modulation). There is also a modem at the other end to convert the signals back into data (demodulation). Hence the term modem.

Network

A network is a group of computers that exchange data between one another. The Internet is therefore a massive network.

Operating system

Every computer has to have a basic program which it can call on startup. This program tells it how to react to inputs and how to deal with the hardware. This program is known as the operating system. MS-DOS, OS/2, Windows 95/98/NT/2000, MacOS and Unix are the commonest versions.

Pixel

A pixel (short for 'picture element') is the smallest item your screen can display. A screen resolution of 800x600 pixels lets you display 480,000 pixels in total.

Protocol

Data transmission protocols define how two machines should talk to each other and exchange information. They include information about how each machine introduces itself and how to terminate the connection cleanly.

Server

A computer that stores data and makes it available to other computers in a network is known as a server.

Service provider

A service provider is an organization which sets up a link between you and the Internet. You use a modem or ISDN line to dial in to your service provider, who then transmits the data you request to your computer.

SGML

SGML stands for Standard Generalized Markup Language and is a standard that defines how to describe the structure and contents of electronic documents.

Software

All the programs and data that you can save and store are known collectively as software.

Source text

The text which describes an HTML file is called the source text.

Special characters

A special character is any character that is not one of the letters from A to Z or one of the numbers from 0 to 9.

Storage capacity

You need to have enough storage capacity to keep your data safe. The expression covers all forms of memory and storage media, and is therefore used in connection with the amount of RAM or disk space available.

Stylesheet

A stylesheet is a type of formatting template that can be called into a number of HTML pages. This saves you a lot of effort, because you only have to change one file if you want to make general amendments.

Surfing

Surfing refers to the action of moving between Internet pages.

Tag

An HTML file consists of ordinary text. If you want to display other kinds of things, you need to show that they are not the same as ordinary text. You do this by using tags inside angled brackets.

Telnet

Telnet is a protocol that lets you run or control programs on other computers. It is text based.

Text editor

You would use a text editor to create or amend text files. A typical program of this kind is the Windows "Notepad" application.

Upload

The opposite of downloading. When you transfer a file from your own computer to another, this is called uploading.

URL

See Address.

VRML

VRML stands for Virtual Reality Modeling Language. As the name implies, you can use this language to represent virtual realities.

World Wide Web (WWW)

The world wide web is probably the most interesting of all the Internet services because this is where you find all the homepages.

XHTML

XHTML is actually nothing more than a variant of HTML 4 that conforms to XML standards. The layout of a document written in XHTML needs to be carefully validated.

XLINKS

XLINKS are comparable to normal hyperlinks except that they can also point to multiple targets.

XML

XML stands for Extensible Markup Language and is a shortened version of SGML. XML is another standard that defines how to describe the structure and contents of electronic documents.

XSL

XSL stands for Extensible Style Language and is used to create templates. Although you can format XML documents with the aid of stylesheets (see glossary) XSL is intended to offer options over and above those provided by CSS. XSL is divided into two parts. One is the transformation part (XSLT) and the other is the formatting part. The expression XSL usually means the formatting part. This uses formatting objects and is intended to do more than simply format XML documents for the web. This part has not yet been fully adopted by W3C.

XSLT

XSLT stands for Extensible Style Language Transformation and is the second part of XSL. XSLT can transform XML documents into HTML, WML or other formats. In contrast to XSL, XSLT 1.0 has already been declared a standard by W3C and work has already started on a draft of XSLT version 1.1.

Some interesting websites

XML is developing all the time. Here are a few useful links that could help to keep you on the ball.

B.1 References and information

The following websites are among the best for keeping up to date.

B.1.1 World Wide Web Consortium

The homepage of the World Wide Web Consortium (W3C) is certainly the most important website for anyone who writes documents for and via the Internet. It tells you all you need to know about the Internet at first hand.

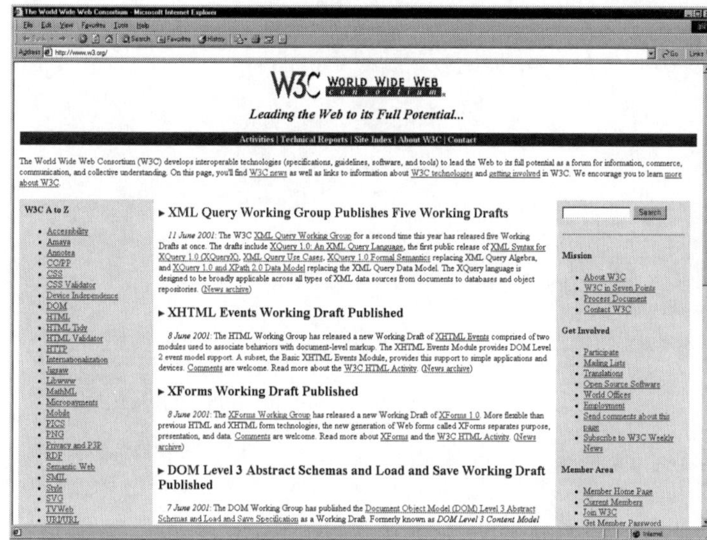

Figure 2.1 ***http://www.w3.org/***

B.1.2 *Practical XML*

Practical XML, by professionals for professionals. This Internet site developed by Stefan Mintert provides extracts and examples from the book of the same name written by Henning Behme and Stefan Mintert together with additional information. You will also find a link to the XML specifications issued by W3C.

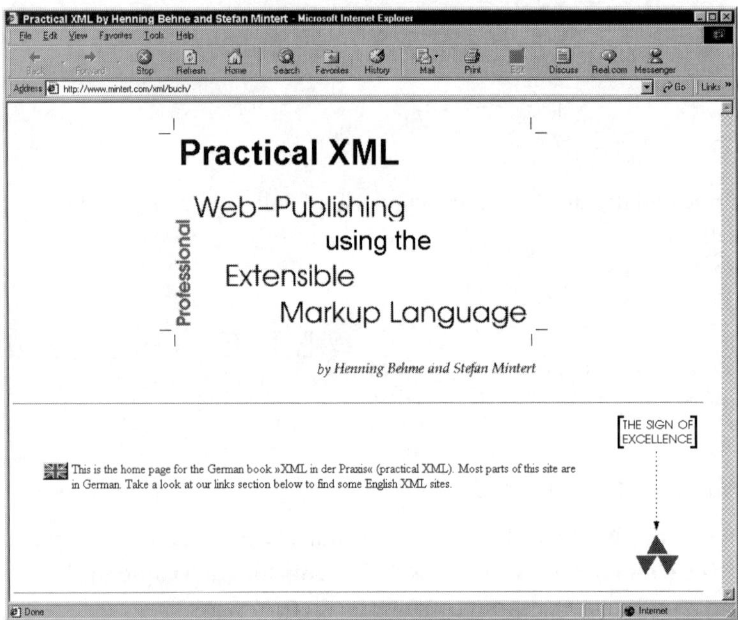

Figure 2.2 ***http://www.mintert.com/xml/buch/***

B.1.3 XHTML™ 1.0

This link takes you to a site concerning the XHTML specifications.

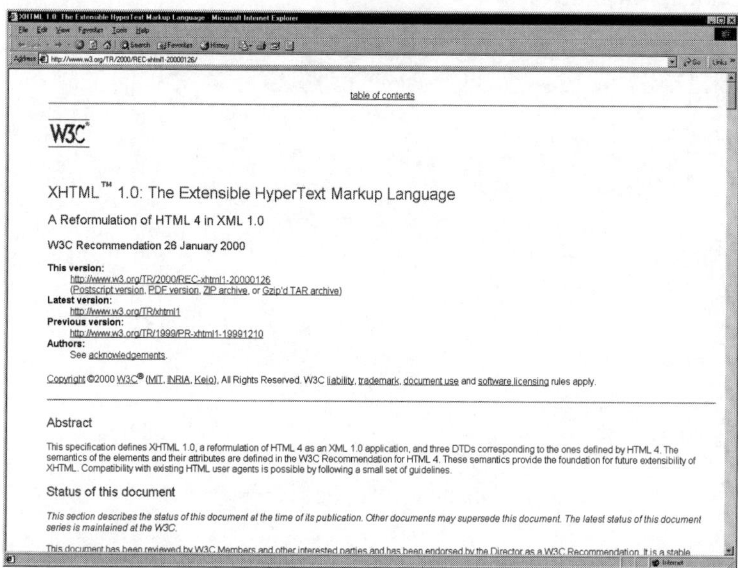

Figure 2.3 ***http://www.w3.org/TR/2000/REC-xhtml1-20000126/***

B.1.4 *Automating the web with the aid of XML*

This reference work on XML is entirely in German, but is quite comprehensive and also suitable for beginners.

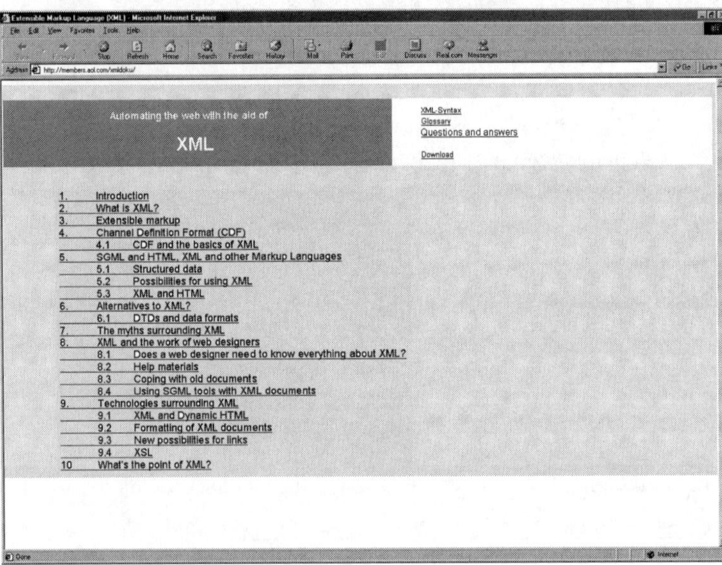

Figure 2.4 ***http://members.aol.com/xmldoku/***

B.1.5 SelfHTML

This tried and trusted reference on HTML also provides among other things extensive information on CSS, JavaScript, DHTML, CGI/Perl, etc.

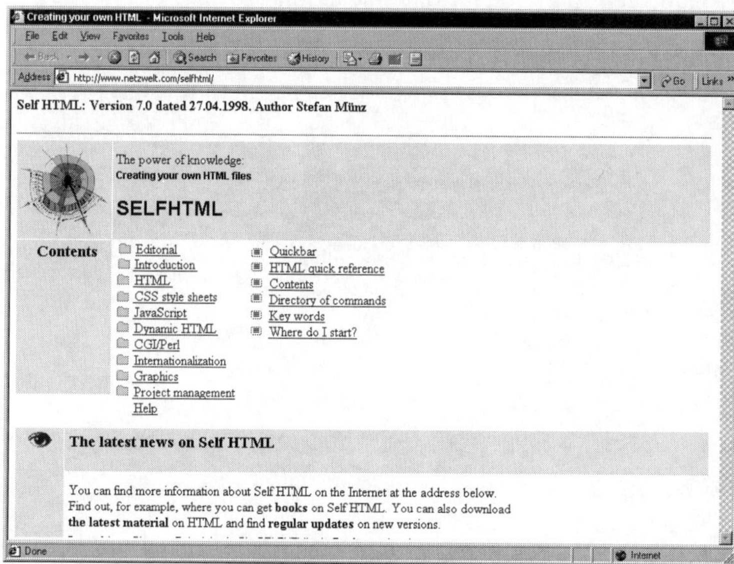

Figure 2.5 ***http://www.netzwelt.com/selfhtml/***

B.1.6 SelfXML

This page is under construction and will be ready quite soon. Since we expect it to be every bit as comprehensive and useful as its close relative SelfHTML, we recommend you to keep an eye on it from time to time.

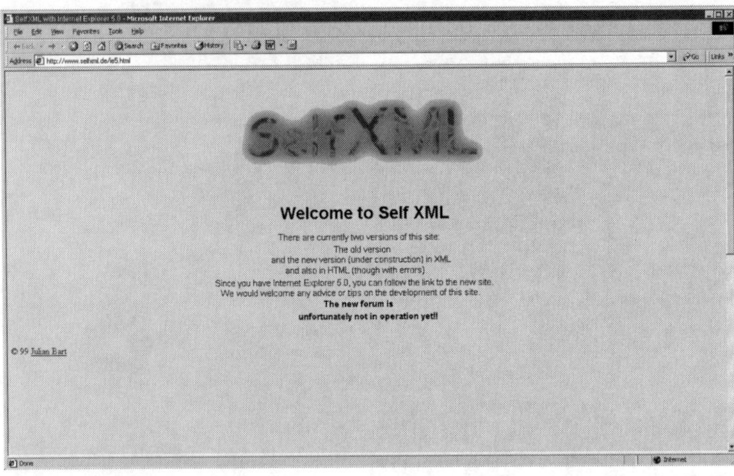

Figure 2.6 ***http://www.selfxml.de/ie5.html***

B.2 Further links

Since the number of Internet sites on the topic of XML is growing and changing all the time, we recommend that you simply use your search engine now and then or take a look at the sites mentioned below.

B.2.1 XMLtoday

XMLtoday is a site which offers not only the latest information on the subject but also a number of onward links.

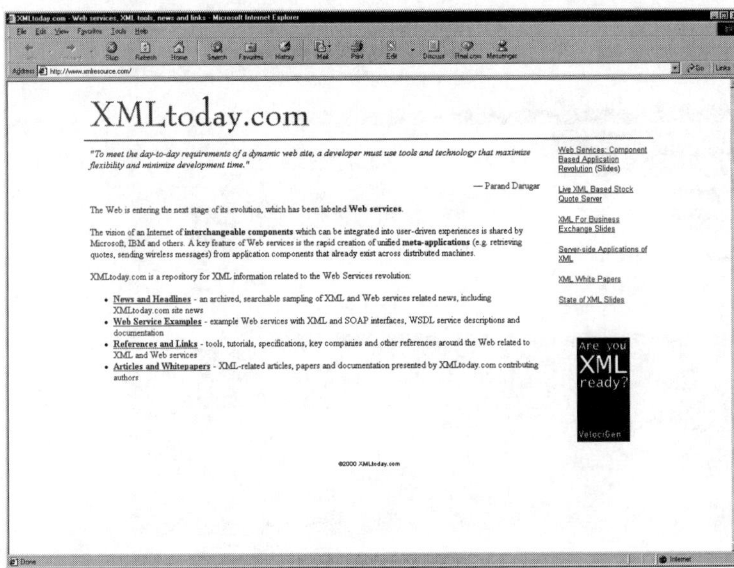

Figure 2.7 ***http://www.xmlresource.com/***

B.2.2 XML.com

XML.com is similar to XMLtoday but has considerably more information to offer.

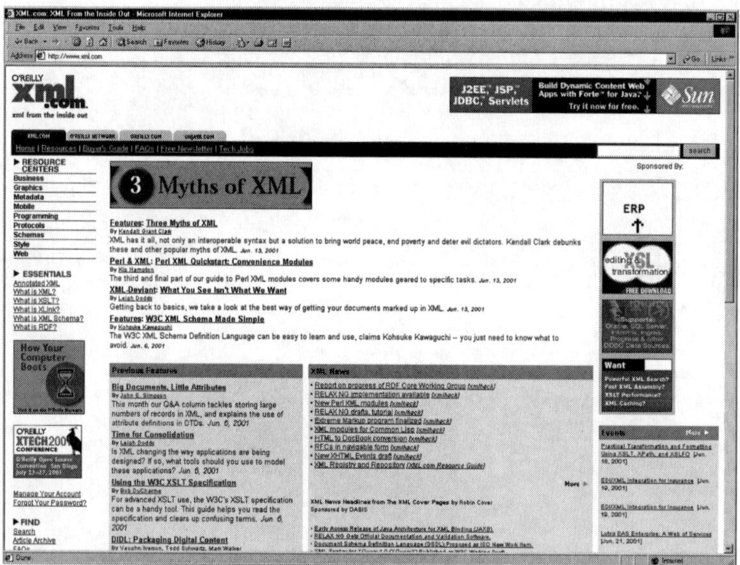

Figure 2.8 *http://www.xml.com*

B.2.3 *Startkabel XML*

Startkabel XML is an English language site based in the Netherlands with a link for almost every conceivable question on the subject of XML.

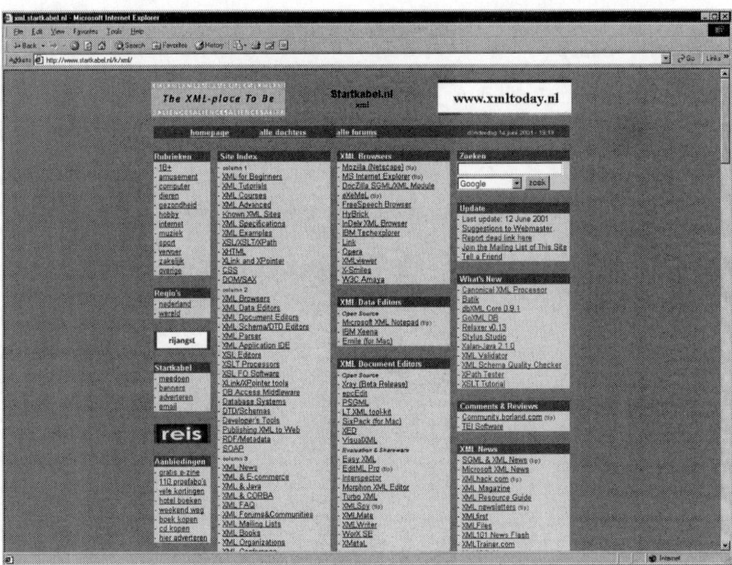

Figure 2.9 ***http://xml.startkabel.nl/k/xml/***

B.3 About the book

Finally here are a couple of interesting links involving this book and the Nitty-Gritty series.

B.3.1 Addison-Wesley

The Nitty-Gritty series is published by Addison-Wesley, who of course have their own website. You can search here for other technical books written by experts in their subject.

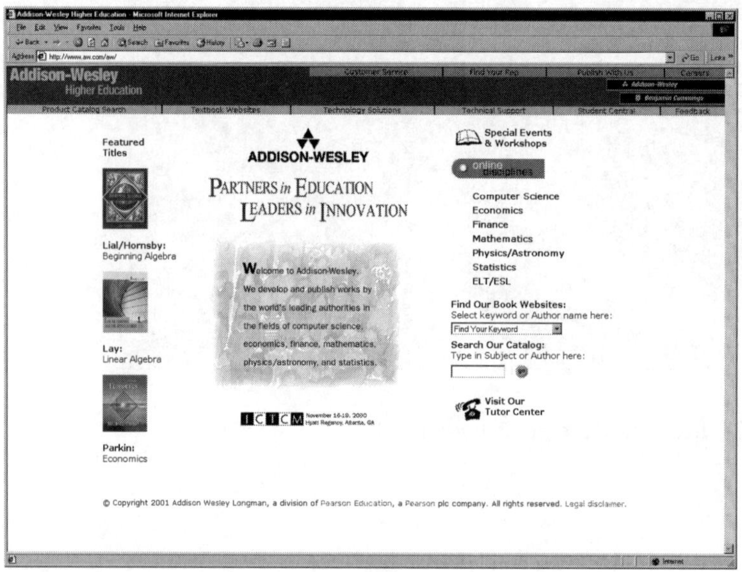

Figure 2.10 ***http://www.aw.com/cseng***

B.3.2 SPECTROauthors

This book was created by the team of writers at SPECTROsoftware GmbH. If you ever need more information about us and our books, you can find it here, although this site is in German. As you would expect, this site also gives the authors' e-mail addresses.

Figure 2.11 ***http://www.SPECTROauthors.de/***

B

Index

A

B

C

D

U

V

W

X

Y

Z